The economic theory of agricultural land tenure

The economic theory of agricultural land tenure

J. M. CURRIE

Lecturer in Economics, University of Manchester

CAMBRIDGE UNIVERSITY PRESS
Cambridge
London   New York   New Rochelle
Melbourne   Sydney

CAMBRIDGE UNIVERSITY PRESS
Cambridge, New York, Melbourne, Madrid, Cape Town, Singapore,
São Paulo, Delhi, Dubai, Tokyo

Cambridge University Press
The Edinburgh Building, Cambridge CB2 8RU, UK

Published in the United States of America by Cambridge University Press, New York

www.cambridge.org
Information on this title: www.cambridge.org/9780521126328

First published 1981
This digitally printed version 2009

A catalogue record for this publication is available from the British Library

ISBN 978-0-521-23634-8 Hardback
ISBN 978-0-521-12632-8 Paperback

Contents

Preface

In contrast to the Classical economists, Neo-classical economists have devoted relatively little theoretical attention to land and its tenure, at least until the recent extensive literature on share tenancy. Yet the tenure of agricultural land is of crucial importance for many developing countries.

The purpose of this book is to examine the various economic aspects of agricultural land tenure, in particular the impact of the nature of property rights on the behaviour of owner-operators, landowners and tenant farmers. Although the analytical tools required of the reader are modest – so that the book should be easily accessible to anyone with a background in intermediate microeconomic theory – the issues involved are relatively complicated. The reader should not expect a simple answer as to the respective merits of alternative institutional arrangements. The book is intended primarily for agricultural economists and for development economists.

This book developed from a PhD thesis in agricultural economics for the University of California, Berkeley. I would like to acknowledge my gratitude to my supervisors, the late Professor S. S. Hoos and Professor A. Schmitz. Much of the work for the thesis was completed during the period of a Hallsworth Fellowship at the University of Manchester.

I have benefited from helpful discussions with various students and members of staff, particularly John Salter, at the University of Manchester and from the careful typing of Sheila Dawson.

I am particularly indebted to two anonymous referees of a first draft; to Ian Steedman and Charles Mueller for valuable comments on selected chapters; and, above all, to Tony Rayner for extensive and penetrating comments on the entire manuscript. They are not, of course, responsible for any remaining errors.

Finally I would like to acknowledge the constant encouragement and assistance of Wat Thomas, without whom this book would certainly have never been written.

1

Introduction

When the 'sacredness of property' is talked of, it should always be remembered, that any sacredness does not belong in the same degree to landed property. No man made the land. It is the original inheritance of the whole species. Its appropriation is wholly a question of general expediency. When private property in land is not expedient, it is unjust. John Stuart Mill (p. 142).

I Forms of land tenure

Institutional arrangements with respect to the ownership and cultivation of agricultural land vary considerably both between and within countries. Land may be under individual private ownership, under some form of collective ownership or under social ownership. Land may be cultivated by individual families, by co-operatives or on a state basis. Individualistic farming may be associated with individual ownership or with some form of communal ownership. Collective farming may be associated with individual ownership, with collective ownership or with social ownership.

Even under systems which involve both individual private ownership and individual cultivation, institutional arrangements differ widely. The precise rights conferred by 'ownership' vary from being more or less absolute to being quite severely curtailed.[1] Moreover, land may be cultivated by owners; or by tenant farmers under leasehold arrangements. There are particularly wide disparities between tenancy arrangements, depending on the precise rights and obligations of landlords and tenants. Under a system of freedom of contract, the respective rights and obligations are determined by landlords and tenants, the basic role of the legal system being to enforce compliance with contractual obligations. Alternatively, rights and obligations may be stipulated in detail by the legal system.

This diversity in land tenure forms raises certain important issues. One issue of obvious significance is whether it is possible to derive meaningful propositions about the respective merits of different forms of tenure. Is it possible to demonstrate that one institutional arrangement is 'better', in terms of specified criteria, than some other, or even that one form is

1

'best'? Comparisons of land tenure institutions date back a long time in terms of the history of economic thought. This issue continues to attract attention, and rightly so. Agriculture is still the dominant activity in very many countries. Moreover, many countries have discovered that one of the main impediments to achieving economic development is the difficulty of transforming the agricultural sector. Attempts at land reform have not been distinguished by their unqualified success.

A related issue is whether it is possible to identify the sorts of considerations which determine, or at least influence, land tenure forms. Why, for example, where they have the freedom to choose, do landlord and tenant elect for one particular type of arrangement rather than another? While this type of question was not ignored completely by eighteenth- and nineteenth-century economists, it has been given much greater prominence in recent years. This line of inquiry has led to greater insights, although, somewhat paradoxically, it also carries with it an attendant danger of superficiality.

Different conclusions about the respective merits of tenure arrangements have been reached. Certain economists have argued that the form of land tenure 'does not matter', at least from the point of view of the allocation of resources. Others have criticized particular types of tenancy arrangements, notably share tenancies. Others seem to see little merit in any form of land tenure other than a system whereby farmers own the land they cultivate. Others seem to imply that whatever system exists must at least be 'efficient', for otherwise it would not have been 'chosen'.[2]

This lack of consensus undoubtedly results in part from ideological differences. But it also reflects the complexity of the issues involved. Yet there does seem to be a reluctance amongst certain theorists even to acknowledge these complexities, let alone to inquire into their significance. With certain exceptions, there are relatively few who have considered the implications of the form of land tenure in the context of different institutional arrangements with respect to financial capital and the hiring of labour. Still fewer have really confronted the problems posed by the spatial dimension of land. This is perhaps one reason why those who are concerned with the practicalities of land tenure often seem disdainful of 'Neo-classical economics'.

II The scope and nature of the inquiry

This book is written in the belief that the Neo-classical approach can offer insights into important questions, if only into the complexities of the issues involved.[3] It should be regarded as a method of approach. It should not be expected that *a priori* theorizing can demonstrate conclusively that one particular institutional arrangement is necessarily superior to any other, whatever the particular features of the country concerned and whatever its stage of development. Indeed, any proposition that one type of arrangement *is* 'optimal' – or any proposition that two or more types of arrangements are 'equivalent' – should be regarded with caution.

Although the analysis will be predominantly theoretical, we will refer quite extensively to land tenure developments in England.[4] We will draw on the experiences of several centuries involving different tenure forms and different stages of development. In particular, the English legislation relating to agricultural tenancies is of relevance to both developing and developed countries.

The subsequent analysis will concentrate on systems involving both private ownership of agricultural land and individualist, as opposed to co-operative, cultivation. As we have indicated, this still encompasses a wide variety of arrangements. We will be concerned not only with whether land is cultivated by owners or by tenant farmers but also with whether or not farmers employ hired workers. Although this is not a book about land reform as such, we will investigate briefly some of the implications of the analysis for public policy. We will take it for granted that any system is liable to be modified or completely reformed, if this is believed to be in the interest of society. As John Stuart Mill observed, there is nothing 'sacred' about private property in land.

2

Political economists and land

Suppose a man could with his own hands plant a certain scope of Land with Corn, that is, could Digg, or Plough, Harrow, Weed, Reap, Carry home, Thresh and Winnow so much as the Husbandry of this Land requires; and had withal Seed wherewith to sowe the same. I say, that when this man hath subducted his seed out of the proceed of his Harvest, and also, what himself hath both eaten and given to others in exchange for Clothes, and other natural necessaries; that the remainder of Corn is the natural and true Rent of the Land for that year; and the *medium* of seven years, or rather so many years as makes up the Cycle, within which Dearths and Plenties make their revolution, doth give the ordinary Rent of the Land in Corn. Sir William Petty (1662).[1]

1 Introduction

The objective of this chapter is to provide a brief historical review of some of the more important writings of economists on the subject of land. The review is designed to serve as a background to our subsequent considerations of various specific aspects of land tenure. The treatment is necessarily highly selective with respect to both authors and topics.

The next section briefly considers some of the views of the Physiocrats, a group of French economists whose major publications came in a twenty-year period from about 1756. An examination of their views is worthwhile partly because they are of interest in themselves, partly because they unwittingly provided much ammunition for subsequent attacks on private property rights in land and partly because they undoubtedly influenced the Classical economists, particularly Adam Smith.

The following section examines the relevant writings of the Classical economists. Adam Smith's *Wealth of Nations*, published in 1776, David Ricardo's *On the Principles of Political Economy and Taxation*, published in 1817, and John Stuart Mill's *Principles of Political Economy*, published in 1848, have had a particularly profound influence over subsequent generations of economists.

Land and rent occupied a focal position in Classical economics. However, with the development of Neo-classical economics land lost its particular significance. The final section describes the difference in emphasis of Neo-classical economics. Particular attention is given to the relevant writings of Wicksteed and Wicksell.

II The Physiocrats

The views of the Physiocrats must be considered in terms of the prevailing condition of the French economy. At that time French agriculture was backward and stagnant. In the northern provinces there were some large farms employing modern techniques. However, most of French agriculture was semi-feudalistic. Share cropping was widespread. The *métayers*, owning little or no capital themselves, relied on capital advances by the landowners. All farmers faced burdensome and unpredictable taxes. Furthermore, agriculture suffered from a variety of complex restrictions on both internal and external trade.

The essential achievement of the Physiocrats was to develop the first explicit model of an economic system. However, it was not a model of the conditions actually prevailing in France at the time. It was a reaction against them. Their model was an idealization. It was a model of the 'natural order', that is, the order which would evolve naturally in the absence of the sort of human distortions and interventions characteristic of contemporary France. The Physiocrats' objective was to instruct the nation, particularly statesmen, 'in the general laws of the natural order'. Once these laws were understood, their adoption would be seen as self-evident. Once they were adopted, human behaviour would be harmonized with the laws of nature.

The Physiocratic system

The Physiocratic system consisted of two economic sectors – agriculture and industry – and three socio-economic classes – a productive class, a proprietary class and a sterile class. The productive class was comprised solely of cultivators, who rented their land from the proprietary class. The sterile class was composed of artisans and craftsmen.

Quesnay's famous *Tableau Économique* was a general equilibrium model designed to demonstrate how produce and money circulated between the three classes. Briefly, the productive class employed food and raw materials, retained out of its own production, together with manufactures purchased from the sterile class, as inputs to produce more food and raw materials. The productive class paid money rents to the proprietary class. These rental incomes were used to purchase food from the productive class and manufactures from the sterile class. The sterile class used food and raw materials purchased from the productive class to produce manufactures. These manufactured goods were sold, in turn, to the productive and proprietary classes.

The Physiocrats accorded a crucial role to capital in agriculture. They regarded capital as a series of advances. Their *avances foncières* comprised drainage, fencing and other permanent improvements to the land. Their *avances primitives* comprised capital in the form of livestock and implements. Finally their *avances annuelles* comprised seeds, feed for livestock, the subsistence requirements of the cultivators and their workers and other recurring annual costs.

Net product of agriculture

The characteristic feature of the Physiocrats' system was its emphasis on the importance of agriculture. The Physiocrats believed that agriculture was unique in that the new wealth created by agricultural production exceeded the wealth destroyed in the process of production. Agriculture generated a *produit net*. This surplus was tangible: a given bundle of commodities was transformed through the productive process into a *larger* bundle of substantially similar commodities. The ability of agriculture to generate this surplus was ascribed to the contribution of land and thus to the abundance of nature: 'Land owes its fertility to the might of the Creator, and out of His blessing flow its inexhaustible riches. This power is already there, and man simply makes use of it.'[2]

Non-agricultural pursuits, though not necessarily undesirable, were thought to be unproductive or sterile in the sense that they were allegedly incapable of yielding such a surplus. Rather the industrial sector transformed the raw materials provided by the agricultural sector into *different* types of commodities. The remuneration of the artisans – the market value of the goods they produced – was just sufficient to cover the costs of their raw materials and of the food necessary to sustain them. There was no tangible surplus. According to Baudeau:

Raw material is transformed into beautiful and useful objects through the diligence of the artisan, but before his task begins it is necessary that others should supply the raw material and provide the necessary sustenance. When their part is completed others should recompense them and pay them for their trouble. The cultivators, on the other hand, produce their own raw material, whether for use or for consumption, as well as everything that is consumed by others. This is just where the difference between a productive and sterile class comes in.[3]

The net product of agriculture accrued to the proprietary class in the form of rents paid by the cultivators. The cultivators, themselves, were left with just enough to cover their necessary expenditures. They retained just enough food and raw materials out of their own production and received just enough manufactures from the sterile class to replace their own *avances annuelles* and to make good the depreciation in their *avances primitives*. The tenant farmers did *not* receive net profits.[4]

Importance of property rights

The Physiocrats were the defenders *par excellence* of private property rights in land. One of Quesnay's maxims asserted:

That the ownership of landed property and movable wealth should be guaranteed to those who are their lawful possessors; for security of ownership is the essential foundation of the economic order of society. In the absence of surety of ownership the territory would remain uncultivated. It would have neither proprietors nor farmers to make the expenditure necessary to improve and cultivate it, if protection of funds and products were not guaranteed to those who make the advances of this expenditure.[5]

The argument that security of ownership is indispensable did not itself establish the desirability of having a distinct proprietary class, especially one which received the entire net product of agriculture in the form of rents. However, the Physiocrats were in no doubt that the proprietary class was entitled to this remuneration. The proprietary class was part of the natural order: it was entrusted with the sacred task of providing the land which generated the net product. Moreover, the Physiocrats did not believe that the fertility of the land was derived *solely* from the 'might of the Creator'. They recognized – indeed, they emphasized – that the characteristics of the virgin land had been altered as a result of previous investment activities by the landed proprietors or their ancestors. According to Baudeau:

Before you can set up a farm where agriculture may be steadily practised year in and year out, what must be done? A block of buildings and a farmhouse must be built, roads made and plantations set, the soil prepared, the stones cleared, trees cut down and roots removed; drains must also be cut and shelters prepared. These are the *avances foncières*, the work that is incumbent on proprietors and the true basis of their claim to the privileges of proprietorship.[6]

This second justification for the rental payments to landlords was the more satisfactory and the more enduring. And yet it could not be entirely sufficient by itself. Even if one could determine the remuneration that landlords were entitled to on the basis of their past endeavours, it would never be possible to demonstrate that in all circumstances the actual remuneration of landowners would correspond precisely with this. Subsequent defenders of landlords have been understandably reluctant to resort to the notion that the right of property is a divine institution and that landlords are entitled to the surplus as the stewards of the Almighty.

Taxation of rent

One might expect that the Physiocrats, as staunch defenders of the landed class, would have opposed taxation of rent. In fact, they recommended that *all* the fiscal needs of the government should be met out of a tax on rents – their famous *l'impôt unique*. This seeming paradox was the inevitable implication of their model of the economy.

At best, any attempt to place the burden of taxation on cultivators or artisans would be self-defeating. To the extent that the remunerations of cultivators and artisans were necessary payments, such taxes would be passed on. They would fall on rents anyway. The Physiocrats concluded that it would be better to tax rent directly. At worst, such an attempt would impede the process of growth and perhaps bring about a decline. Thus another of Quesnay's maxims affirmed:

That taxes should not be destructive or disproportionate to the mass of the nation's revenue; and that they should be laid directly on the net product of landed property, and not on men's wages, or on produce where they would increase the costs of collection, operate to the detriment of trade, and destroy every year a portion of the nation's wealth. That they should also not be taken from the wealth of the farmers of landed property; for the *advances of a Kingdom's agriculture ought to be regarded as if they were fixed property requiring to be preserved with great care in order to ensure the production of taxes, revenue and subsistence for all classes of citizens.* Otherwise taxation degenerates into spoliation, and brings about a state of decline which very soon ruins the state.

La grande culture

Under the natural order, the tenant farmers would provide capital advances. There is some disagreement, however, as to whether the Physiocratic system involved the tenant farmers themselves performing the labour or whether this would be provided by a separate class of hired workers. Gide and Rist have advanced the former view on the grounds that hired workers were relatively uncommon in France at the time of the Physiocrats. However, bearing in mind that their system was not a description of contemporary conditions, the latter view is more persuasive. The Physiocrats undoubtedly wished to emulate the agricultural revolution taking place in England. They wanted to see a spread in the capitalist system of farming and the more widespread adoption of new techniques. They wanted to promote the amalgamation of farms. Another of Quesnay's maxims affirmed: '*That the land employed in the cultivation of corn* should be brought together, as far as possible, into large farms worked by rich husbandmen; for in large agricultural enterprises there is less expenditure required for the upkeep and repair of buildings, and proportionately much less cost and much more net product, than in small ones.' This vision of large farms could only be achieved through many hitherto tenants becoming hired workers.

As Meek has observed, there was an internal contradiction in the Physiocratic writings. The Physiocrats clearly believed that farmers would play a central role in the process of capital accumulation. Yet, according to their model, farmers received only that recompense necessary to replace their *avances annuelles* and to compensate for the depreciation in their *avances primitives*. Since the farmers did not share in the net product, they would be unable to accumulate capital.

This contradiction resulted from a failure to identify profit as a specific distributional category and as a component of the net product in the natural order. The failure to do so – a failure which may have been related to the lack of an explicit differentiation between tenant farmers and hired workers within agriculture – had even wider repercussions. It meant that they could not appreciate the possibility that industrial activity could generate a surplus. This, in turn, meant that they could not recognize the scope for the capitalist mode of production in industry.

Despite its defects, the Physiocratic system inevitably had a profound impact on the subsequent development of economic thought, notably on the ideas of Smith, Ricardo and Marx. Somewhat ironically, the Physiocrats provided ammunition for many subsequent attacks on the landlord class. They drew attention to the possibility of a surplus over and above the payments appropriate to recompense landowners for past endeavours. Their proposal for a single tax on the rent of land was subsequently taken up and popularized by Henry George. Moreover, they even introduced the argument that a tax on rent was not really paid by anyone, a notion which received great emphasis by later economists who subsequently advocated that the State should become a 'co-proprietor' of the soil.[7]

The impact of the Physiocrats on the French economy was considerably less significant. Their desire for agrarian reform in France was not achieved. In the event land-tenure reforms following upon the French Revolution had the opposite effect of extending peasant proprietorships, thus leading to further fragmentation of farms.[8]

III The Classical economists

The Classical system

The economic system envisaged by the Classical economists was based on three socio-economic groups – landowners, capitalist tenant farmers and landless labourers. The tripartite division of society into these 'three great orders' was alluded to in Smith's *Wealth of Nations*. With the publication of Ricardo's *Principles*, it became the foundation of Classical economics. Ricardo described both the Classical framework and 'the principal problem in Political Economy' in the opening paragraphs of his book:

> The produce of the earth – all that is derived from its surface by the united application of labour, machinery and capital, is divided among three classes of the community; namely, the proprietor of the land, the owner of the stock or capital necessary for its cultivation, and the labourers by whose industry it is cultivated.
>
> But in different stages of society, the proportions of the whole produce of the earth which will be alloted to each of these classes, under the names of rent, profits and wages, will be essentially different; depending on the actual fertility of the soil, on the accumulation of capital and population and on the skill, ingenuity and instruments employed in agriculture. To determine the laws which regulate this distribution is the principal problem in Political Economy (p. 5).

Thus, in contrast to the Physiocratic system, the Classical system involved a sharp distinction between the supply of farm labour and the provision of capital advances. Landless labourers provided the farm work. The tenant farmers advanced the capital employed in the production process. Whereas in the Physiocratic system the entire surplus accrued to the proprietary class, in the Classical system only part of the surplus was paid to landowners as rents. The remainder was retained by farmers as their profits. Profit constituted a return on capital. This tripartite division accorded largely with the agricultural situation in England in the latter part of the eighteenth century. An exact identification of the income categories of rent, profit and wages with mutually exclusive classes of people was, of course, impossible. A small owner-operator might receive an income payment which was in the nature of a rent for his land, a profit on his capital and wage for his labour. Nevertheless the class division was sufficiently well established to justify its use as the basis of a model of the economic system.

Notwithstanding the differences between the Physiocratic and Classical systems, there were similarities. Thus the Classical economists adopted the notion of capital as a series of advances. They distinguished between 'circulating capital' and 'fixed capital'. The former, which corresponded to *avances annuelles*, was capital which was used up in the process of production: 'it fulfils the whole of its office in the production in which it is engaged, by a single use'.[9] Fixed capital, which encompassed both *avances foncières* and *avances primitives*, was durable capital which could be used for several acts of production.[10]

Like the Physiocrats, the Classical economists accorded a critical role to the agricultural sector, as, indeed, the circumstances of the time demanded. Moreover, whereas they did reject the notion that *only* agriculture is productive, they never abandoned the distinction between productive and unproductive pursuits. Smith, in particular, regarded agriculture as especially productive. He could hardly contain his amazement that agriculture generated enough output not only to recompense the capitalists and the labourers but also to furnish rent payments to the owners of land. Smith attributed this to a bountiful nature, a notion that inevitably commanded the eloquent support of Reverend Malthus. However, as we shall see, Ricardo attributed this very same phenomenon to the niggardliness of nature.

The nature of rent

Smith described rent as 'the produce of those powers of nature, the use of which the landlord lends to the farmer'. Land, 'in almost any situation', yielded a surplus of food over and above that needed to ensure its continued cultivation – that is, over and above that needed, first, to replace the capital advances, including the wage payments to the workers, and, second, to provide the tenant farmers with the normal rate of profit on that capital. Landlords appropriated the surplus by means of monopoly power.

Rent, considered as the price paid for the use of land, is naturally the highest which the tenant can afford to pay in the actual circumstances of the land. In adjusting the terms of the lease, the landlord endeavours to leave him no greater share of the produce than what is sufficient to keep up the stock from which he furnishes the seed, pays the labour, and purchases and maintains the cattle and other instruments of husbandry, together with the ordinary profits of farming stock in the neighbourhood (p.247).

Thus Smith's basic theory of rent was that the 'natural' or 'normal' rent level was such as to leave the farmer with the 'natural' or 'normal' profit on capital advances.[11] Without an explanation of the determination of the normal rate of profit, this did not constitute a complete explanation of the decomposition of the surplus into rent and profit. To complete the explanation we need to invoke Smith's proposition that the normal rate of profit was determined in the economy at large by the forces of supply and demand, the main emphasis being placed on the latter, that is, on the scope for profitable investments.

As O'Brien has observed, Smith provided most of the basic building blocks for the Classical theory of rent.[12] The rest – notably the notion of the margin and the hypothesis of diminishing returns – were provided by James Anderson, in the year after the publication of the first edition of the *Wealth of Nations*. The basic concepts were developed by Malthus and Ricardo into a celebrated theory of rent – a theory later described by John Stuart Mill as the *pons asinorum* of economics. Although this theory might be more appropriately attributed to Malthus, it has almost universally been referred to as the Ricardian theory of rent.

The fundamental differences between the theory *initially* propounded by Ricardo and the theory of Smith was that Ricardo envisaged the profit rate as being determined *within* the agricultural sector. He believed that, with appropriate adjustments for riskiness, the rates of profit in manufacturing and commerce depended on the rate of profit in agriculture. In addition, he saw in the phenomenon of differential rents and in the shifting margin of cultivation a convenient way of explaining the determination of profits and the source of rents.

Ricardo advanced his theory of rent in 1815 in 'An Essay on the Influence of a Low Price of Corn on the Profit of Stock'. Briefly the theory was developed as follows: In the first settling of a country with sufficient fertile land for the initial population, the entire surplus of output over the outgoings necessary for cultivation would accrue to the owners of capital as profits. Thus if the individual employed capital to the value of 200 quarters of wheat and if, after replacing the capital, the value of the remaining produce – the surplus – was 100 quarters of wheat, the rate of profit to the capitalist would be 50 per cent. At first increased food requirements consequent upon population growth might be met by bringing into cultivation land equally fertile and equally well situated. However, with yet further increases in population, it might be necessary to resort to land less fertile or less advantageously situated. On such land more capital would have to be employed in order to obtain the same output. Thus the equivalent of 210 quarters of wheat might be required to obtain a total output of 300 and a surplus of 90. The rate of profit would therefore be 43 per cent. Now the rate of profit on this grade of land would constitute the 'normal' rate of profit. Competition would ensure that the same rate of profit of 43 per cent would be earned on the most fertile land. The remaining 7 per cent would accrue to the owners of that land in the form of rent. If the growth of population required the cultivation of land even less fertile or even less advantageously situated then the profit rate would be determined by the surplus on that land. The profit on the first and second grades of land would fall accordingly. The rent of the most fertile land would rise. Rent would also be paid for the land of the second grade. The convenient feature of this hypothesis of the emergence of differential rents was that the rate of profit earned on the marginal no-rent land defined the normal rate of profit. On intra-marginal land anything in excess of the normal rate of profit would be appropriated by landlords in the form of rent. This exposition in terms of marginal no-rent land permitted a remarkably simple explanation of a very complicated phenomenon.

If the rent theory of Smith and that of Ricardo differed significantly with respect to the determination of the rate of profit, other differences were more apparent than real. One such difference concerned the role of nature. Whereas Smith had sought to attribute rent to a bountiful nature, Ricardo (p. 76)[13] argued that the true explanation of rent lay in the niggardliness of nature: 'The labour of Nature is paid, not because she does much, but because she does little. In proportion as she becomes niggardly in her gifts she exacts a greater price for her work.' The statements that 'nature is bountiful' and that 'nature is niggardly' are what Joan Robinson ([a], p. 8) would presumably describe as metaphysical propositions. 'The hallmark of a metaphysical proposition is that it is not capable of being tested. We cannot say in what respect the world would be different if it were not true. The world would be just the same except that we would be making different noises about it.' The difference between Smith and Ricardo was one of perspective. Smith's noises were designed to draw attention to the fact that agriculture was capable of producing more food than was necessary for continued cultivation. The purpose of Ricardo's noises was to emphasize the importance of scarcity. *Both* conditions were necessary for the existence of rent payments from tenants to landowners. If agriculture was not capable of yielding a surplus of food over and above that needed to ensure continued cultivation, tenants, by definition, would not have been *able* to pay rents to landowners. If land of the best quality had not been scarce, farmers would not have *needed* to pay rents in order to obtain land.[14] In regard to the latter point, Ricardo (p. 70) wrote:

If all land had the same properties, if it were unlimited in quantity, and uniform in quality, no charge could be made for its use, unless where it possessed peculiar advantages of situation. It is only, then, because land is not unlimited in quantity and uniform in quality and because in the progress of population, land of an inferior quality, or less advantageously situated, is called into cultivation, that rent is ever paid for the use of it.

Malthus agreed with this analysis. Indeed, Ricardo attributed it to him. However, Malthus was evidently distressed that his friend took such an ungrateful view of the gifts of Providence. Had not the benevolent Creator recognized that if the necessaries of life could be obtained and distributed without limit, population would increase without limit?

The Ricardian Corn Model[15]

Ricardo's analysis of distribution, or at least the modern interpretation of it, can be explained somewhat more formally in terms of the so-called Ricardian Corn Model. Assume that there is a given total amount of unimproved land available for use in the production of a single commodity, corn. We do not require that all the land necessarily be cultivated. Assume that the only other input is hired labour. To keep the exposition as simple as possible, we will even ignore corn used as seed. A basic feature of the model is that production takes time. The capitalist farmers support the workers during the production process by advancing them wages in the form of corn from a 'wages fund', that is, from a stock of corn carried forward out of the production of the previous period. Regarding the agricultural sector as one large farm, *APL*, in Figure 2.1, represents the average product of labour and *MPL* represents the corresponding marginal product of labour. The average product of labour, the marginal product of labour, rents, profits and wages are all defined in terms of corn. The analysis is entirely in real terms. No problem of valuation arises.

The critical feature of the Corn Model is the phenomenon of diminishing .returns in the use of additional labour on the available supply of land. The Law of Diminishing Returns, first propounded by Anderson in 1777, was re-discovered, apparently independently, by Ricardo, Malthus, West and Torrens around 1815. This law was subsequently described by John Stuart Mill as 'the most important proposition in political economy'. According to Ricardo two factors explained the phenomenon of diminishing returns. Additional labour could be assimilated into agriculture by using the existing land under cultivation more intensively and/or by bringing additional land into cultivation. In the former case – the 'intensive margin' – it was taken as self-evident that the average product of labour, and thus the marginal product of labour, would decline. In the

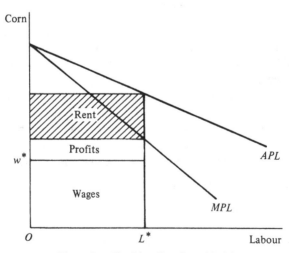

Figure 2.1. The Ricardian Corn Model

latter case – the 'extensive margin' – the average product of labour, and thus the marginal product of labour, would decline because the additional land would be of an inferior quality. It should be emphasized that the Classical economists visualized this Law as a dynamic phenomenon. They used it to predict the effects of actual changes in population over time.

One variant of the Corn Model – usually designated as applying to the 'short run' – assumes that, at any point in time, the wages fund is predetermined as a result of past developments and, further, that the total labour force is predetermined by the population level. As a result of competition for and among hired workers the market wage rate is given by the total wages fund divided by the inelastic supply of labour. The market wage rate is shown as w^* in Figure 2.1. The labour force, L^* in Figure 2.1, determines the marginal product of labour. Profit is then obtained as a residual: profit per worker is the difference between the marginal product of labour and the wage rate. Rent is also determined as a residual: it is the surplus on intra-marginal units of labour. The decomposition of total output into factor shares is illustrated in Figure 2.1.

The critical proposition that profit per worker is the difference between the marginal product of labour and the wage rate can be explained in terms of either the extensive margin or the intensive margin. Consider the extensive margin. Suppose that the cultivator of the least fertile land in use pays no rent. The difference between his output and the corn he has advanced to labour represents his profit. His rate of profit defines the normal rate of profit. Consider the cultivator of land of superior quality. His total output exceeds that necessary to replace his wage advances to labour and to provide him with normal profits. This surplus will be appropriated by the landowner in the form of rent. Thus lands of superior quality earn 'differential rents'. Consider the intensive margin. For each cultivator, the marginal product of labour is just sufficient to enable him to replace the corn advanced to that labour and provide him with the normal rate of profit. The surplus yield by intra-marginal units will be appropriated by his landlord.

One of the clearest expositions of the Ricardian rent theory was provided by James Mill (p. 224):

In applying capital, either to land of various degrees of fertility, or, in successive doses, to the same land, some portions of the capital so employed are attended with a greater produce, some with a less. That which yields the least yields all that is necessary for re-imbursing and rewarding the capitalist. The capitalist will receive no more than this remuneration for any portion of the capital which he employs, because the competition of others will prevent him. All that is yielded above this remuneration, the landlord will be able to appropriate. Rent, therefore, is the difference between the return made to the more productive portions, and that which is made to the least productive portion of capital employed upon the land.

Another variant of the Corn Model – usually designated as applying to the 'medium-run' or 'long-run' – also assumes that the total wages fund is predetermined by any point in time. However, this variant incorporates the Malthusian assumption that the supply of labour is perfectly elastic at a given wage rate. The level of hired labour is then determined as the number of workers who can be supported at that wage rate by the predetermined total wages fund. The decomposition of the total corn output into wages, profits and rent is the same as in the first variant.

A fundamental feature of the Corn Model is the intimate connection between distribution and growth. The key growth factor is capital accumulation in the form of an increase in the wages fund. As the wages fund increases, the demand for labour will rise and population will increase accordingly. Less fertile land will be brought into cultivation and land already under cultivation will be farmed more intensively. Total corn output will rise. Total corn rent will rise.

One of the most famous propositions attributed to Ricardo is that corn rents would necessarily rise not only absolutely, as Smith had maintained, but also as a proportion of total output. This proposition is not correct: corn rents as a proportion of total corn output might rise, remain constant or fall, depending on the rate at which returns diminish.[16] This popular misconception may derive from an initial mistake on Ricardo's part or from misleading exposition in his earlier writings. In any event, as Dobb (p. 86) has pointed out, it is clear from Ricardo's correspondence with Malthus and from revisions to the third edition of his book that he subsequently recognized that this proposition is not correct. Nevertheless a succession of economists have dismissed Ricardo's entire theory on the basis of the empirical assertion that rents have become relatively less significant as a distributive share.

A proposition which, as we have seen, was a critical feature of Ricardo's analysis was that the rate of profit would fall as a result of accumulation. Ricardo believed that there was some minimum rate of profit acceptable to capitalists. Once the rate of profit was driven down to that level, capital accumulation would cease. Growth would cease. The economy would reach a stationary state. The stationary state might be delayed by technological developments. But it could not be averted. Sooner or later a stationary state would be reached.

Rents and agricultural prices

An important implication of the Corn Model was that the price of corn determines the level of rent and not *vice versa*. As Ricardo (p. 74) observed: 'Corn is not high because a rent is paid, but a rent is paid because corn is high; and it has been justly observed, that no reduction would take place in the price of corn, although landlords should forego the whole of their rent.' Specifically the price of corn is regulated by the costs of production on marginal no-rent land. Rent is a price-determined surplus in the aggregate. On this basis, Ricardo and Malthus vigorously disputed the belief – widespread at the time – that the high level of food prices was the result of the high level of rents.

It has frequently been supposed that Ricardo's thesis depended on the existence of marginal no-rent land. This is incorrect. Ricardo took it as an empirical fact that 'as yet in every country, from the rudest to the most refined, there is land of such a quality that it cannot yield a produce more than sufficiently valuable to replace the stock employed upon it, together with the profits ordinary and usual in that country' (p. 328). However, in order to emphasize the general validity of his proposition, he was prepared to suppose that all lands in England did earn rent. The price of corn would be regulated by the costs of production at the *intensive margin*. It would still not depend on the level of rent.

James Mill (p. 228) reiterated the same points:

It may be safely affirmed, that there is no country, of any considerable extent, in which there is not land incapable of yielding rent: that is, incapable of yielding to human labour more than would be necessary for the maintenance of that labour ... The conclusion, however, may be established, by the clearest evidence without regard to the question, whether all land pays or does not pay rent. On land which pays the highest rent, we have seen that capital applied in successive doses, is not attended with equal results. The first dose yields more, possibly much more than the return for the capital. The second also may yield more, and so on. The rent, if accurately calculated, will be equal to all that is rendered by those several doses, over and above the profits of stock ... I therefore conclude, with assurance, that in the natural state of things, in every agricultural country, one portion of the capital employed upon the land pays no rent; that rent, therefore, consists wholly of that produce which is yielded by the more productive portions of capital, over and above a quantity equal to that which constitutes the return to the least productive portion, and which must be received, to afford his requisite profits, by the farmer.

Adam Smith (p. 249) had reached the same conclusion that agricultural rent is a price-determined surplus: 'Rent, it is to be observed, therefore, enters into the composition of the price of commodities in a different way from wages and profit. High and low wages and profit are the causes of high or low price; high or low rent is the effect of it.'

However, elsewhere in the *Wealth of Nations*, Smith appeared to contradict himself by treating rent as price-determining. Thus he referred to rent as a necessary cost of production and as a component part of price: 'the price of any instrument of husbandry, such as a labouring horse, is itself made up of the same three parts: the rent of the land on which he is reared, the labour of tending and rearing him, and the profits of the farmer who advances both the rent of this land and the wages of this labour' (p. 152). Similar apparently inconsistent statements could be found for some of the others, notably John Stuart Mill. Indeed, such was the confusion over the matter that Gide and Rist (p. 81) wrote, some 130 years after the publication of the *Wealth of Nations*: 'The celebrated controversy as to whether rent enters into prices is not a thing of yesterday. Its origin dates from the birth of political economy itself, and will probably only die with it.' Eventually, in a classic article published in 1929, Buchanan clarified the issues involved. When the Classical economists were concerned with distribution, they assumed that agricultural land has no alternative use other than non-paying idleness. Rents are not necessary payments. They constitute a surplus determined by the levels of commodity prices. This was surely what Smith had in mind when he claimed that high prices are the cause of high rents and not *vice versa*. This was certainly what Ricardo had in mind throughout virtually all his *Principles*.

When, however, the Classical economists were seeking to explain the 'natural' relative prices of individual food items, the alternative to using land in the production of some particular commodity may be to use the land in the production of some other commodity, rather than to withdraw the land entirely from cultivation. Rent may, therefore, be a necessary payment in order for land to be competed away from its alternative uses. Thus rent may enter as a necessary component of the price of a commodity, on the same basis as wages and profits. This is undoubtedly what Smith had in mind when he claimed that the three component elements in the prices of commodities are rents, profits and wages. The problem was not one of inconsistency. Rather it was a failure on the part of the Classical economists to delineate carefully between the two types of inquiry.

The status of agricultural landowners

It might be thought that Smith would have been hostile to landowners. After all, although he did acknowledge that the rent received by a landlord might be higher as a result of the owner's past expenditures on permanent improvements, he emphasized that the existence of rent could not be explained wholly or even mainly in terms of such improvements. Landlords demanded rents even for unimproved lands. Landlords even 'commonly' demanded increases in rents in consequence of improvements financed by the tenants. His celebrated assertion that landlords 'reap where they never sowed' would surely seem to suggest that Smith opposed the landowning class. And yet Smith was not basically hostile to landowners. The reason for this was that he believed that, because landlords benefit from economic growth in the form of increased rents, the interest of the landlord class 'is strictly and inseparably connected with the general interest of the society. Whatever promotes or obstructs the one, necessarily promotes or obstructs the other' (p. 356). This view was endorsed by Malthus (p. 194):

If under any natural resources in land, the main causes which conduce to the interests of the landholder are increase of capital, increase of population, improvements in agriculture, and an increasing demand for raw produce occasioned by the prosperity of commerce, it seems scarcely possible to consider the interests of the landlord as separated from the general interests of the society.

It might be thought that Ricardo would have been sympathetic to the owners of land. After all he was himself a landowner. More to the point, his theory concerning the connection between rents and prices would seem to absolve landowners from any responsibility for the very high corn prices. In his 1815 *Essay*, he observed:

The general profits of stock depend wholly on the profits of the last portion of capital employed on the land; if, therefore, landlords were to relinquish the whole of their rents, they would neither raise the general profits of stock, nor lower the price of corn to the consumer. It would have no other effect, as Mr. Malthus has observed, than to enable those farmers, whose lands now pay a rent, to live like gentlemen, and they would have to expend that portion of the general revenue which now falls to the share of the landlord (p. 21).

In fact, Ricardo's theory constituted a severe indictment of the landowning class. Ricardo conceded that landlords would benefit from economic growth. However, he recognized that it did not necessarily follow that the interest of the landlord class would be 'strictly and inseparably connected with the general interest of the society'. His point was that landowners, unlike the rest of society, had a vested interest in high corn prices. Now, he acknowledged that high rents and corn prices could not be achieved by the exploitation of monopoly power by landowners. However, high corn prices and rents could be achieved by measures which forced a resort to less fertile lands. High prices and rents could be brought about by impediments to trade. While the general interest of society would have been furthered by a policy of free trade, landowners benefited from restrictions on trade. They benefited from the Corn Laws.

The dealings between the landlord and the public are not like dealings in trade, whereby both the seller and the buyer may equally be said to gain, but the loss is wholly on the one side, and the gain wholly on the other; and if the corn could by importation be procured cheaper, the loss in consequence of not importing it is far greater on the one side, than the gain is on the other (p. 336).

Ricardo acknowledged that the immediate adoption of free trade might cause excessive hardship to farmers, especially those with poorer lands, because of existing contractual arrangements with landowners. His policy prescription in the 1815 *Essay* was a phased return to free trade. 'Although the nation would sacrifice much more than the farmers would save even by a temporary high price of corn, it might be just to lay restrictive duties on importation for three or four years, and to declare that, after that period, the trade in corn should be free' (p. 33). One of the main reasons Ricardo objected to protection was that the associated recourse to inferior lands would lead to a fall in the rate of profit. The economy would be that much nearer the minimum rate of profit at which capital accumulation and growth would cease. While there is some disagreement about how imminent Ricardo thought the stationary state to be, there is little doubt that he did not relish the prospect. He was certainly pessimistic about the nation's future under protection.

The Ricardian theory has been indirectly hostile to the landowning class in another way. Ricardo recognized that part of the payment from tenant to landowner might be in the nature of a return on past fixed investment undertaken at the landlord's expense. Accordingly he *defined* rent in a narrow and specialized way as 'that portion of the produce of the earth, which is paid to the landlord for the use of the original and indestructible powers of the soil' (p. 67). He emphatically distinguished between this definition of rent – now frequently described as 'pure rent' – and the usual description of rent as the annual payment from tenant to landowner. He wrote: 'This is a distinction of great importance, in an enquiry concerning rent and profits; for it is found that the laws which regulate the progress of rent, are widely different from those which regulate the progress of profits and seldom operate in the same direction' (p. 68). In some ways this was an unfortunate distinction. Certainly Ricardo admitted – somewhat uneasily – that once permanent improvements to land had actually been undertaken the return to those improvements followed the economic laws relating to rent.

Whatever the analytical merits of this distinction, it proved to be of critical importance for one particular reason: it focused attention on something which was unequivocally an unearned surplus. By definition such payments could not be justified in terms of past capital expenditures on improvements to the land.

Taxation of rent

Whereas Smith evidently regarded taxation of rent as a particularly appropriate way of raising money, he never went to the extreme of advocating the Physiocrats' *l'impôt unique*. In the light of his famous maxims on taxation this is hardly surprising. However, one might expect that Ricardo would have been a fervent advocate of taxation of rent. In fact he was apparently not a supporter of very heavy taxation of rent. It has been suggested that this was partly because he considered public expenditure to be inherently wasteful and partly because he did not devote much attention to the possibility of using taxation for redistributive purposes. To the extent that money had to be raised he did recommend that the best revenue base was a tax on rent combined with a tax on wage goods and a tax on income from government securities. However, he was evidently uneasy about taxing rent.

There are certain fundamental difficulties with respect to taxation of rent. An immediate difficulty centres around the distinction between pure rent and the usual description of rent as the annual payment from tenant to landowner. As Ricardo emphasized, a tax on the latter would fall not only on pure rent but also on that part of the payment which was in the nature of a profit on the landlord's capital. Such a tax would act as a disincentive to *future* investments. The solution would seem to be a tax exclusively on pure rent. But the practical difficulty, as Ricardo emphasized, would be actually to identify the pure rent component. Moreover, even if one could identify the pure rent component it would not necessarily be 'fair' to deprive the landowner of part or all of it by taxation. It is true that the landowner could not justify his right to pure rent by an appeal to past improvements to the land undertaken at his own expense. However, he might have purchased the land with capital accumulated as a result of his own labour. His purchase price would presumably reflect the expectation that he would receive pure rent payments. Thus the pure rent payments might already have been indirectly appropriated by the previous owner in the form of a high sale price for the land. To tax the present owner might unjustly deprive him of the fruits of his labour.

Of the Classical economists, the most famous advocate of taxation of rent was John Stuart Mill (p. 492):

The ordinary progress of a society which increases in wealth, is at all times tending to augment the incomes of landlords; to give them both a greater amount and a greater proportion of the wealth of the community, independently of any trouble or outlay incurred by themselves. They grow richer as it were in their sleep, without working, risking or economizing. What claim have they, on the general principle of social justice, to this accession of riches?

Developing the ideas of his father, he devised a brilliant scheme to circumvent the difficulties involved in the taxation of rent. The essence of his proposal was to tax 'unearned increments'. In order to meet the difficulty that landowners might have purchased land in the expectation of receiving current rent levels, he proposed to exempt current rents from taxation and to tax only increases in rent from some base year. Anticipating the further objection that purchase prices might have been based on the expectation of future increases in rents, he proposed to secure to landlords the current market price of their land. He recognized the difficulty of distinguishing in individual cases between an increase in rent owing to 'the general circumstances of society' and one which was due to the landlord's own expenditure. However, he believed a workable scheme was possible:

The only admissable mode of proceeding would be by a general measure. The first step should be a valuation of all land in the country. The present value of all land should be exempt from the tax; but after an interval had elapsed, during which society had increased in population, and capital, a rough estimate might be made of the spontaneous increase which had accrued to rent since the valuation was made. Of this the average price of produce would be some criterion ... On this and other data, an approximate estimate might be made, how much value had been added to the land of the country by natural causes; and in laying on a general land-tax, which for fear of miscalculation should be considerably within the amount thus indicated, there would be an assurance of not touching any increase of income which might be the result of capital expended or industry exerted by the proprietor (p. 493).

In this context it is worth mentioning briefly one of the 'offshoots' of Classical economics, namely, the popular movement associated with Henry George. In *Progress and Poverty*, first published in 1879, George launched a vehement attack on private property in land, blaming such rights for virtually all the maladies afflicting society. His remedy was the appropriation by the state of ground rent through taxation. Whereas the Mills had proposed the taxation of increases in land values due to the future progress of society, George advocated the appropriation of any present values attributable to the *past* progress of society. Like the Mills, he did not wish to tax improvements to the land; he advocated taxing pure ground rent only. However, he dismissed the objection that it would be difficult to distinguish between the return received for the original and indestructible powers of the soil and the returns attributable to improvements; indeed, he claimed that the distinction could always readily be made.

George maintained that a single tax on land would be sufficient to finance all government expenditure, so that it would be possible to abolish all other taxes – taxes which acted as disincentives and checks on the creation of wealth. Inevitably, his proposal for a single tax on land has been likened to the Physiocrats' *l'impôt unique* – George, himself, did so, somewhat cautiously confessing to an inadequate familiarity with their doctrines. Needless to say, whatever the similarities between their proposals, they arrived at them by very different routes.

Critics of the Ricardian theory of rent

Ricardo's theory was criticized for a variety of reasons. Many of these criticisms, as Wicksell observed many years later, 'scarcely deserve notice'. A number of the criticisms resulted from simple misunderstandings, notably, from the common belief that the theory either depended on or implied the existence of no-rent land. Other criticisms stemmed from taking Ricardo's story about the emergence of rent quite literally. Thus the American economist, Carey, asserted that, in contrast to Ricardo's story, cultivation typically proceeds from less fertile land to more fertile land. Whewell even sought to demolish the theory on the grounds that, when assessing what rent they should charge for their farms, landowners or their agents did not perform an intricate calculation involving a comparison of their own land with land on the margin of cultivation!

One of the most comprehensive attacks was launched by the Reverend Richard Jones in *An Essay on the Distribution of Wealth and the Sources of Taxation – Part I – Rent*, published in 1831. In contrast to others, the criticisms of Jones scarcely attracted the attention they deserved. His most fundamental challenge related to the use of deduction and *a priori* reasoning rather than observation and induction.

It wants no great deal of logical acuteness to perceive, that in political economy, maxims which profess to be universal, can only be founded on the most comprehensive views of society. The principles which determine the position and progress, and govern the conduct, of large bodies of the human race, placed under different circumstances, can be learnt only by an appeal to experience. He must, indeed, be a shallow reasoner, who by mere efforts of consciousness, by consulting his own views, feelings and motives, and the narrow sphere of his personal observations, and reasoning *a priori*, from them expects that he shall be able to anticipate the conduct, progress and fortunes of large bodies of men, differing from himself in moral or physical temperament, and influenced by differences, varying in extent and variously combined, in climate, soil, religion, education and government (p. xv).

Jones was particularly severe on Ricardo. 'Mr. Ricardo was a man of talent, and he produced a system very ingeniously combined, of purely hypothetical truths; which, however, a single comprehensive glance at the world as it actually exists, is sufficient to shew to be utterly inconsistent with the past and present condition of mankind' (p vii).

Jones drew a basic distinction between peasant rents and farmers' rents. Peasant rents encompassed labour rents, *métayage* rents, ryot rents and cottier rents. In each case the cultivators relied on their own labour; they extracted their own wages from the earth. In contrast, farmers' rents were paid by capitalists who cultivated using the labour of others. Jones dismissed Ricardo's explanation of the origin of rent as 'conjectural history'. His own explanation was that

in the actual progress of human society, rent has usually originated in the appropriation of the soil, at a time when the bulk of the people must cultivate it on such terms as they can obtain, or starve; and when their scanty capital of implements, seed, etc., being utterly insufficient to secure their maintenance in any other occupation than that of agriculture, is chained with themselves to the land by an overpowering necessity. The necessity then, which compels them to pay a rent, it need hardly be observed, is wholly independent of any difference in the quality of the ground they occupy, and would not be removed were the soils all equalized (p. 11).[17]

The subsequent displacement of peasant rents by farmers' rents requires the formation of a class of capitalists, separate from the labourers and the landowners. According to Jones, the capitalistic mode of production generally begins in the manufacturing sector and only later extends to agriculture. Moreover, this only happens once the ownership and occupation of land have ceased to be dominant.

When a race of capitalists have made their appearance, to take charge of a varied industry of a population, and advance from their own funds the wages of its labor, property in land, and the forms of tenancy it may give birth to, no longer influence in the first degree, either the springs of government, or the constituent elements of society (p. 185).

Jones took particular exception to Ricardo on the grounds that Ricardo implied that his theory was of universal validity, whereas the theory related solely to farmers' rents which, on an extravagant allowance, 'occupy one-hundredth part of the cultivated surface of the habitable globe' (p. 14).

Jones also challenged the proposition that over time agriculture would necessarily encounter diminishing returns.

That there is a certain point, beyond which human labour cannot be employed upon a limited spot of ground, without a diminished return to its exertions, must be admitted at once. But in the progress of those improvements in the art of cultivation, by which its most profitable amount of produce is approached, it may be very possible, that every successive portion of the capital and labor concentrated on the land, may be more economically and efficiently applied than the last. Such a law would be at least as probable *a priori* as that which supposes that heavier crops, and less productive cultivation, are inseparable (pp. 199–200).

Alternative forms of land tenure

The claim that Ricardo had concentrated solely on one particular type of system was valid. However, the same criticism could not be directed at Smith. In one chapter, Smith had sought to trace the evolution of land tenure in Europe. According to his narrative, large estates using slaves or serfs were followed by the system of *métayage*, which was succeeded in turn by 'farmers properly so-called, who cultivated the land with their own stock, paying a rent certain to the landlord' (p. 491). John Stuart Mill also considered various forms of tenure. In doing so, he appears to have drawn heavily on the study of Jones, although he ignored his criticisms of the Ricardian theory of rent and of the law of diminishing returns in particular. McCulloch and Fawcett also evaluated alternative forms of land tenure.

There was general agreement that large estates, relying on the labour of serfs or slaves, were detrimental to agricultural progress. The owners of large estates seldom had the time, inclination or ability to attend to the cultivation or improvement of their land. Slaves or serfs had little or no incentive to work hard.

The system of *métayage* was regarded as an improvement over labour rents, at least by Smith, Jones and Mill. Under share tenancy, the landowner would generally provide not only the land but also the capital necessary for cultivation. In return, the peasant would pay rent in the form of a share of the produce. The status of a share tenant was considerably greater than that of a slave or serf. At least he could acquire property and he was not subject to the same degree of supervision. However, there was a widespread view that this form of tenure was still extremely inefficient. In particular, it was maintained that a share tenant had little or no incentive to invest in improvements to his property since the landowner would receive one half of the increased produce. According to Smith, given that the tithe hindered improvement, a tax amounting to one half 'must have been an effectual bar to it' (p. 491). According to Jones: 'The divided interest which exists in the produce of cultivation, mars almost every attempt at improvement' (p. 102). Moreover, McCulloch (p. 177) noted that this system also provides an incentive for the tenant to attempt to defraud the landlord. Mill, however, was considerably more cautious. He acknowledged that the farmer's incentive was impaired by not receiving the entire benefit from his efforts. However, he argued that English observers had taken an extremely narrow view of the system, basing their conclusions almost solely on observations on performance in France. Evidently impressed by

Sismondi's praises of the operation of the system in Italy, he concluded: 'The metayer tenure is not one which we should be anxious to introduce where the exigencies of society had not naturally given birth to it; but neither ought we to be eager to abolish it on a mere *a priori* view of its disadvantages' (p. 192).

The Classical economists typically considered that the best form of tenancy was one involving rents which were fixed independently of output. Moreover, they were also generally well-disposed to owner-occupancy. Smith claimed that small proprietors were the most enthusiastic improvers. Arthur Young asserted that 'the magic of *property* turns sand into gold'. John Stuart Mill concluded that

> no other existing state of agricultural economy has so beneficial an effect on the industry, the intelligence, the frugality, the prudence of the population, nor tends on the whole so much to discourage an improvident increase of their numbers; and that no existing state, therefore, is on the whole so favourable, both to their moral and their physical welfare. Compared with the English system of cultivation by hired labour, it must be regarded as eminently beneficial to the labouring class (p. 182).

IV   Neoclassical economists and land

Under Neo-classical economics, land has lost the special significance it enjoyed in the theories of the Physiocrats and of the Classical economists. Land has become just another commodity. Thus according to Scitovsky (p. 227) 'There is no logical reason for treating land as a separate factor because, from the economist's point of view, it is similar in all essentials to produced factors.' This break with the Classical approach has sometimes been portrayed as an abrupt one, resulting from the 'marginal revolution' of the 1870s. However, this is not strictly true. Thus, for example, in his *Primer of Political Economy* – published in 1878, some seven years after the first edition of his *Theory of Political Economy* – Jevons himself related faithfully and lucidly the Ricardian story of the origin of rent and of the relationship between rent and the price of corn.

> That land will pay no rent at all which only gives produce enough to pay the wages of the labourers who work upon it, together with the interest of any capital which they require. The rent of better land will then consist of the surplus of its produce over that of the poorest cultivated land, after allowance has been made for the greater or less amount of labour and capital expended on it. Or we may look at the matter in this way: The price of corn is decided by the cost of producing it on land which just pays the expenses of cultivation, because when more corn is needed, it is from such land we must procure it, the better land

having been long since occupied. But corn of the same quality sells at the same price whatever be its cost of production; hence the rent of more fertile land will be the excess of the price of its produce over that of land which only just pays the cultivator and leaves no rent.

It was not until the preface to the second edition of his *Theory of Political Economy* that Jevons repudiated this analysis and launched into his famous attack on the influence of Ricardo on the development of economic science. The recantation of Jevons notwithstanding, the Ricardian theory continued to be considered by Gide in his *Principles of Political Economy*, by Marshall in his *Principles of Economics*, by Nicholson in his *Elements of Political Economy*, by Taussig in his *Principles of Economics* and by many others. Marshall, in particular, was concerned that there was an overreaction against the Classical treatment of land, resulting in part from misunderstandings of what Ricardo had said.

To trace in detail the complex process whereby land ceased to play a focal role in economic theory is beyond the scope of this work. We will simply reiterate certain familiar explanations. A major consideration is that land and its ownership had declined considerably in political, social and economic significance in developed economies. Land no longer merited such a prominent role. Even prior to the emergence of Neoclassical economics, Marx had abandoned the tri-partite division of society and had grouped the owners of land and capital together. Marx afforded much less prominence to agriculture, to diminishing returns and to the rent of land. He looked elsewhere for an explanation of a declining rate of profit.

A further consideration is that, in stark contrast to Marx, the development of Neoclassical economics involved a fundamental, if gradual, shift of emphasis away from the issues of distribution and growth towards a concern with exchange and with the allocation of resources between competing uses. With regard to land in particular, it was increasingly taken for granted that land had alternative uses. Thus, in his eventual repudiation of the Classical theory of rent, Jevons asserted that the case of competing uses, far from being exceptional, as John Stuart Mill had implied, was the rule:

Now Mill allows that when land capable of yielding rent in agriculture is applied to some other purpose, the rent which would have been produced in agriculture is an element in the cost of production of other commodities. But wherefore this distinction between agriculture and other branches of industry? Why does not the same principle apply between two different modes of agricultural employment? If land which has been yielding £2 per acre rent as pasture be ploughed up and used for raising wheat, must not the £2 per acre be debited against the expenses of the production of wheat? Suppose that somebody introduced the beetroot culture into England with a view to making sugar; this new branch of industry could not be said to pay unless it yielded, besides all other expenses, the full rents of the lands turned from other kinds of culture. But if this be conceded, the same principle must apply generally; a potato field should pay as well as a clover field, and a clover field as a turnip field; and so on. The market prices of the produce must adjust themselves so that this shall in the long run be possible (p. 70).

In the context of this shift of emphasis, as Skouras (p. 12) has observed, a key factor was the subsequent attention devoted to the static general equilibrium model of Walras.[18] In a framework of analysis which assumes that the economy has given initial stocks of productive resources it does not matter whether these are the free gifts of Nature or the result of past production. To return to Scitovsky:

From the point of view of an individual firm or person, all land has to be bought; and its purchase price may be regarded as its initial cost. As to society's point of view, we usually assume the existence of a large stock of capital goods inherited from the past; and none of our arguments or results hinges on whether these capital goods were produced at some distant past date or whether some of them have existed from time immemorial. From every point of view, therefore, land may be regarded as a capital good and the rent of land as similar in every respect to the gross earnings of a produced factor (p. 228).

In a framework of analysis, in which past history does not matter and in which prevailing property rights are taken for granted, it is easy to understand how the original rationale for the distinction between capital and the 'original and indestructible powers of the soil' might be overlooked. It is easy to understand how the real difficulties of actually drawing such a distinction, where capital is embodied in land, might be exaggerated. According to Wicksteed in *The Common Sense of Political Economy* (Book II, p. 574):

we have seen over and over again that it is impossible to draw the line either between land as a primitive gift of nature and land as embodying capital or the results of human effort, or between a change in the value of a piece of land caused by something that has been done to it and that caused by changes that have taken place elsewhere.

Wicksteed concluded that the attempt to draw an accurate distinction was not only hopeless but also unnecessary. Before we consider precisely why Wicksteed came to the conclusion that such a distinction was unnecessary, it is worth indicating briefly why, in one sense, this was incorrect. To do so it is sufficient to recall Ricardo's proposition that a tax on the actual payment from a farmer to a landowner – as opposed to a tax solely on pure rent – would have a disincentive effect on *future* investments in land improvement. This proposition was overlooked. It was overlooked perhaps because the new approach not only did not inquire into the past; it did not look to the future in any fundamental sense either!

Marginal productivity theory

The reason Wicksteed concluded that the distinction was unnecessary was the realization that the marginal productivity theory of factor reward could be extended to *all* factors, including land. As we have seen, the essence of the Ricardian model was a marginal productivity theory of profit-cum-wages; the rent of land was then determined as a residual. Wicksteed devoted his famous Chapter VI of *The Common Sense of Political Economy* to demonstrating that this treatment of rent as a residuum had led to 'many errors in nomenclature and in thought'. He argued that, rather than treating land as constant and labour as variable, it would be equally legitimate to treat labour as the constant and land as the variable. The reward for land would be determined by its 'marginal efficiency'. By means of a laborious example, he sought to demonstrate that it did not matter which approach was used. Both factors would be remunerated in accordance with their marginal efficiency. Total product would be exhausted. Wicksteed (p. 570) even went so far as to claim that the Ricardian theory of rent did not constitute a theory of rent at all:

For if rent is simply what is left when the other factors have been satisfied, we have not established a law of rent, but have assumed that we know how to determine the shares of everything except land, and then simply stated that what is not anything else is rent ... Instead of elaborating a theory of rent the current exposition tacitly assumes a (correct) theory with reference to everything except land, and then claims that no theory at all is necessary for land.

While Wicksteed was correct, on his own terms, to argue that the marginal productivity theory could be applied to land, this inference that a residual theory is no theory at all is invalid. As Blaug (p. 496) has observed, there is no justification for the belief that a residual-claimant explanation of the remuneration of a factor is inherently unsatisfactory.

Wicksteed's attempt to demonstrate that the remuneration of factors of production in accordance with their marginal productivities results in the total product being exhausted was unsatisfactory. It was soon recognized that a sufficient condition for this is that the production function exhibit constant returns to scale. Wicksteed regarded constant returns to scale as more or less self-evident and his example in the chapter on rent assumed this property. However, if the production function does not exhibit constant returns to scale throughout – and for others it was by no means self-evident why it should – it is no longer clear that total product will be exhausted.

The way out of this dilemma was provided by Walras and Wicksell. In his *Lectures on Political Economy*, Wicksell provided a particularly lucid explanation. Briefly the argument was that under perfect competition long-run equilibrium involves each firm operating at the 'optimal' scale of operation defined by minimum long-run average cost. At this point there are *local* constant returns to scale. According to Wicksell (p. 129): 'This scale of operations is under the given circumstances, the "optimum" towards which the firm must always, economically speaking, gravitate; and as it lies at the point of transition from "increasing" to "diminishing returns" (relatively to the scale of production) the firm will here conform to the law of *constant* returns.' The remuneration of each factor will be determined by the law of marginal productivity. Total product will be exhausted. In this way Wicksell completed the demonstration that there is nothing special about land that requires a distinct theory regarding its remuneration.

In regard to marginal productivity theory, two brief observations are worth making. Firstly, it is a theory of the demand for factors of production. A complete explanation of factor prices necessarily involves consideration of the nature of supply. This was emphasized by Marshall. He did attach significance to the 'fixity' of land. In the context of the short run, he noted that other factors might similarly be fixed and might therefore earn 'quasi-rents'. In the context of the long run, he noted that, whereas the quantities of other factors could be varied, from the point of view of society as a whole, the supply of land was limited. Secondly, it is worth noting that both Wicksteed and Wicksell emphasized that distribution in accordance with marginal productivity is not necessarily 'fair'. According to Wicksteed (p. 573): 'It is open to any one to examine or to dispute the ethical or social claim of any factor of production to a share, in accordance with its marginal significance, or to argue that there is no industrial necessity to allow such a claim.' In this regard, they contrasted sharply with the views of another famous contributor to the development of marginal productivity theory, John Bates Clark. He believed that a fair distribution *is* one where rewards are determined by marginal productivity. It is also worth noting that for both Wicksteed and Wicksell, on the one hand, and for Clark on the other, past history did not matter. It did not matter for Wicksteed and Wicksell because they were concerned with explaining distributive shares rather than with considerations of equity. It did not matter for Clark because he regarded distribution in accordance with marginal productivity as necessarily equitable. However, for those who are concerned with equity and who reject the value judgment of Clark, whether rental payments are attributable to the original and indestructible powers of the soil or whether they are due to past improvements to land may well be of relevance.

Alternative forms of land tenure

Wicksell went significantly beyond simply demonstrating the proposition which Wicksteed had advanced but failed to demonstrate satisfactorily. Wicksell's analysis, initially in terms of two inputs land and labour, suggested that it is immaterial whether the owners of labour rent land or whether the owners of land hire labour or whether some third party employs both labour and land. In each case land and labour would be remunerated in accordance with their marginal productivities; competitive forces would ensure that profit would tend to zero. A major purpose of this book is to evaluate the proposition that the particular institutional arrangement does not matter. For the moment, it is worth noting that, whereas Wicksell was careful to emphasize the restrictive assumptions involved in his analysis, his *caveats* have often been overlooked.

Until the late 1960s, there was a peculiar dichotomy regarding the question as to whether the form of tenure does matter. On the one hand, owner-occupancy and fixed-rent tenancy were regarded as equivalent. Either arrangement would lead to 'efficiency' in the use of resources: the value of the marginal product of each factor would be equated to its price. On the other hand, share-rent tenancy was regarded as 'inefficient'. This belief was based on the argument, formalized by Marshall, that an arrangement whereby the tenant pays the landowner a share of output would act as a disincentive: the tenant would only employ a factor up to the point where *his* share of the value of the marginal product was equated to its price. Recently the view that share-tenancy is necessarily an inefficient arrangement has been challenged, notably, by Cheung and Stiglitz. The result has been a renewed debate as to whether the form of land tenure does matter. We will consider the various arguments in some detail in the following chapters.

3

The analytical framework

It is easy enough to make models on stated assumptions. The difficulty is to find the assumptions that are relevant to reality. The art is to set up a scheme that simplifies the problem so as to make it manageable without eliminating the essential character of the actual situation on which it is intended to throw light. Joan Robinson ([b], p. 141).

I Agricultural resources: Their ownership and co-ordination

Institutional arrangements

Institutional arrangements in agriculture assume a variety of forms depending, in part, on the pattern of resource ownership. Suppose for the moment that agricultural production utilizes only the services of land and labour. A critical consideration is the pattern of ownership of these resources, in particular whether they are owned by one group or by distinct groups. The simplest institutional arrangement is the 'pure' peasant proprietorship where the ownership of both resources is vested in one group: each peasant household cultivates its own land using its own labour. However, under some other system, there may be distinct landowning and labouring classes. Even with only two resources, more complex patterns of ownership are possible. Thus there may be a group which owns only land, another which owns only labour and yet another group which owns both land and labour. In particular, the agricultural sector may exhibit a dualistic structure, with one sub-sector involving a division between landowners and labourers and the remaining sub-sector comprising pure peasant proprietorships.

Of crucial importance is the precise locus of decision taking. While all participants take decisions of some sort, we are particularly interested in who assumes responsibility for what may be described as the activity of co-ordination, that is, the activity of deciding precisely how the different input services are to be co-ordinated and deployed in production activities. Following Wicksell, the person who does so may be referred to as the 'entrepreneur'. Under peasant proprietorships, the locus of these types of decisions is clear: they are taken by heads of households. Where, however, resources are under separate ownership, precisely who assumes the co-ordinating activity may vary. The entrepreneurial role may be undertaken by landowners. It may be undertaken by labourers. Entrepreneurial decisions may be taken jointly: landowners and labourers may enter into more or less formal partnerships. Furthermore, as Wicksell observed, the entrepreneurial role may even be undertaken by agents who do not own any of the physical resources used in the production process.

Where resources are owned separately, there will necessarily be some sort of formal or informal contractual arrangement involving transfers of rights of use. The simplest case would be a contractual arrangement where one person transfers an unrestricted right to use the services of a resource which he owns to another person for a specified period of time in return for a stipulated payment. Thus a landowner may lease land to a tenant, the latter being free to determine its precise use, in return for an agreed rental payment. Alternatively, a labourer may enter into a contract with a landowner, transferring to the landowner a right to use his labour time in return for a wage payment. The hiring of labour and leasing of land are not, of course, confined to situations where there are distinct landowning and labouring classes. Under a system of 'impure' peasant proprietorships, one peasant family may rent land or hire labour services from another family.

Freedom of use, in fact, is usually restricted. The ways in which one person may use another person's labour or land may be restricted by external constraints of a legal or social nature. Moreover, the contractual arrangement itself may restrict the rights and behaviour of the contracting parties. Thus land may be leased subject to restrictive covenants, the person acquiring the rights of use accepting constraints on the ways in which he can use the land. Where such restrictions form part of the contractual arrangement, this can be regarded as a type of joint decision-taking, though it differs in nature from a partnership involving more or less continuous joint decisions.

Physical and financial capital

Most agricultural activities involve the use of physical capital, that is, of produced means of production. Such capital goods include circulating capital, such as seed, manure and chemical fertilizers, and fixed capital, such as simple tools and complex machinery. The presence of capital complicates matters, not simply because of the familiar difficulties of drawing a precise distinction between land and capital. Its presence increases the number of possible institutional arrangements, depending on who produces the produced means of production. Where capital comprises only simple items, such as seed and simple tools, the additional complications may be relatively minor. Thus the peasant household itself may retain part of its own produce for use as seed and construct tools with its own labour, so that the household both produces the capital and decides on its utilization. In contrast, the producers of modern machinery or chemical fertilizers are typically not directly engaged in agricultural activities. Chemical fertilizers will invariably be sold to those who use them. Producers of machinery may lease the services of machines to users. But more commonly they will also sell these outright. The ultimate owners of these physical capital goods may or may not constitute a group distinct from the owners of land and labour. In England in the late eighteenth and early nineteenth centuries, the tenant farmers owned and contributed the physical capital – or the 'farm stock' – and did constitute a distinct class. Those who own and provide physical capital are often those who undertake the entrepreneurial role, as in the English system, though this is not inevitable. They may hire out the services of durable capital goods to some other agent. What the presence of physical capital goods of diverse types does imply is the greater likelihood of a complex system.

In addition to physical capital, command over financial capital may play a vital role depending on institutional arrangements regarding the nature and timing of payments for the use of resource services. Financial capital is likely to assume considerable importance where physical capital goods are widely employed in agricultural production and where they are produced 'outside' the agricultural sector. But even if land and labour are the only physical inputs, financial capital may be necessary to lubricate the production process. If the entrepreneurial role is assumed by someone who does not contribute any physical resources he will still require access to financial capital if resource services have to be paid for prior to their use. Though even this he may borrow. In any event one group may be involved in agriculture simply because of its ownership of and control over financial capital.

The ensuing analysis will not be confined to one particular system. Indeed, we are specifically interested in comparing different institutional arrangements. We will pay particular attention to the role of financial capital. We will not, however, specifically consider the decisions of producers of capital goods where these are produced outside the agricultural sector, though we will, of course, take into account the terms on which farmers can acquire them.

II The ownership structure and the operating structure

Neither the Classical nor the conventional Neo-classical treatments of land are satisfactory for our purposes. The inevitable abstraction and simplification that accompanies the Classical tendency to regard the agricultural sector as one large farm would obscure many of the issues which concern us. But at least the abstraction involved in this approach has the merit of being self-evident. However, the conventional Neo-classical approach involves a similar degree of abstraction but in a way that seems to have attracted little, if any, attention and to have caused remarkably little disquiet. This abstraction entails the analysis of ownership and rental markets for land on the assumption that land comprises perfectly divisible and homogeneous acres.

The objection to this approach is not based on the observation that agricultural land differs in fertility. This is typically acknowledged. Rather the objection is that the conventional approach ignores the spatial dimension of land. The necessarily different location of different acres of land means that it is inappropriate to start an analysis with the assumption that land is homogeneous. A prospective purchaser of oranges might say to a Walrasian auctioneer: 'At that price I would like to buy five oranges of that particular type. I do not mind which particular five oranges of that type you arrange for me to have.' But a prospective purchaser of land would *never* say to a Walrasian auctioneer: 'At that price I would like to buy one hundred acres. I do not mind which particular hundred acres you arrange for me to have.' The point is more than that location matters in the sense that he may prefer his hundred acres to be relatively close to a market for his produce, thus minimizing transport costs. That location matters in this sense has been understood since the work of Von Thünen. Rather the point is that the spatial relations between the hundred acres will matter. Typically he will prefer one connected plot of one hundred acres to one hundred spatially disparate plots each of one acre. By overlooking this the conventional approach conveys a most deceptive impression of the functioning of land markets.[1]

We will employ a framework suggested by Kelso in 1941. Although his recommendation appears to have attracted very little attention, this framework provides a most useful heuristic device for considering the various issues relating to property rights in agricultural land. The essence of this framework will now be explained.

An area of land will be defined as comprising an 'ownership unit' if and only if that land is owned by some individual or group as a single unit. The land comprising an ownership unit need not necessarily be contiguous; a unit may be composed of two or more physically separate sub-units. We will assume that it is possible to partition the agricultural land of a country into a set of mutually exclusive and exhaustive ownership units. The 'ownership structure' of agricultural land is then defined as the particular configuration of ownership units. The ownership structure can be identified solely in terms of a particular configuration of areas on a map. The identity of the owners of particular ownership units is irrelevant for this purpose, except in so far as, by definition, no person may own more than one ownership unit. Alienation of land through sale, gift or bequest may or may not alter the ownership structure. There would be a change in the ownership structure if, say, a landowner buys additional land. However, there would be no change if, say, someone who does not own land purchases the ownership unit of another.

An area of land will be defined as comprising an 'operating unit' if and only if it is 'farmed' as a single unit by some individual or group. The land comprising an operating unit need not be contiguous. We will assume that it is possible to partition the agricultural land of a country into a set of mutually exclusive and exhaustive operating units. The 'operating structure' of agriculture at a particular point in time is then defined as the particular configuration of operating units. The operating structure can be defined solely in terms of areas on a map. The identity of the operators of particular operating units is irrelevant for this purpose, except in so far as, by definition, no person may operate more than one unit.

It must be acknowledged that, in practice, it might not be possible to partition unambiguously all the agricultural land of a country into a set of mutually exclusive and exhaustive ownership units, on the one hand, and into a set of mutually exclusive and exhaustive operating units, on the other. For example, with respect to the ownership of land, it is possible for two persons, each being the sole owner of a separate plot of land, to own jointly a third plot of land. Similar possibilities exist with respect to the farming of land. However, these complications will largely be ignored. The ownership and operating structures are merely useful heuristic concepts designed to provide an underlying 'scheme' for considering various aspects of land tenure.

The relationship between the ownership and operating structures will depend on forms of land tenure. Under a system of universal owner-occupancy, the two structures would necessarily coincide. However, if there is the possibility of leasing land, farming can be separated from landownership. Consequently, the two structures need not coincide. Indeed, although in practice there *is* a close connection between the two structures, there is no *necessary* relationship between them.

The significance of the ownership and operating structures should emerge from the following chapters. However, a few brief prefatory comments are appropriate. Consider the significance of the operating structure. It is surely incontrovertible that the size, compactness and connectedness of an operating unit will determine the production possibilities available to the farmer and thus influence his activities. Consequently, the performance of the agricultural sector as a whole will depend on the nature of the operating structure – on the number of operating units between which the total stock of agricultural land is allocated and on the layout of those units. In view of the recurrent debates as to the respective merits of large versus small farms, we should not expect to arrive at any consensus amongst economists as to the 'optimal' operating structure for agriculture. Indeed, most economists would surely agree that it would be meaningless to refer to the optimal operating structure in a vacuum. Nevertheless, most economists would accept that the nature of the operating structure is likely to have a critical impact on the performance of agriculture, that it is important to understand the process of change over time in the structure and that, on the basis of certain criteria, particular types of changes may be preferable to others.

Consider the significance of the ownership structure. This structure is of interest because of its indirect relationship with the performance of the agricultural industry. Because of the close connection between the two structures, changes in the ownership structure are likely to have repercussions on the operating structure and perhaps on the performance of the industry. In particular, undesirable changes in the operating structure may be impelled by changes in the ownership structure. The nature of the ownership structure in any country is typically of widespread interest directly, particularly where land is the principal form of wealth. In the United Kingdom, the New Domesday Survey of 1872 was instigated by Lord Derby in order to discredit the widespread belief that the ownership of agricultural land was heavily concentrated. In fact, the exercise backfired since it revealed that, while over one million persons owned some land, eighty per cent of the land was owned by less than 7,000 people. The pattern of land ownership continues to attract curiosity and concern.

III Types of decisions

It is appropriate at this point to illustrate briefly the sorts of decisions which agents may have to take. One reason – a very important reason – for doing this is to emphasize at the outset the complicated nature of the issues we are examining. This serves to indicate both the inevitability of drastic abstraction for any theoretical analysis and the need for caution in interpreting any theoretical propositions.

Consider briefly the decision problem confronting some particular individual who owns agricultural land. One decision is whether to sell the farm or whether to retain possession. If he keeps possession, he must decide whether to retain the land in agricultural use or whether to use the land for some non-agricultural purpose. If he retains it in agricultural use, he must decide whether to farm the land himself or lease it to a tenant farmer. If he withdraws it from agricultural use, he must decide which use to make of it – forestry, development, amenity or idleness. If he sells the farm, he must decide what to do with the proceeds from the sale; he must decide whether to re-enter farming as a tenant; and so on.

It should not be supposed that there is necessarily a simple temporal sequence to the various decisions – that first he decides whether or not to sell, then he decides ... All the various decisions are closely interconnected. If anything it might be better to reverse the sequence in which the decisions have just been presented. Thus we might suppose that before he can sensibly decide whether or not to sell, he must decide what use he would make of it if he did not sell; that before he can sensibly decide whether to use it in agriculture or not, he must decide whether, if he did, he would farm it himself or lease it to a tenant farmer. We will, in fact, tend to approach matters roughly in this way. However, there is no suggestion that the chosen sequence is in some sense 'correct', any other being 'incorrect'.

It must be emphasized that, if the above characterization of the decision problem of a landowner seems enough to be going on with, it is still extremely simplistic. One reason is that units are divisible. Thus he must decide not simply whether or not to sell the whole ownership unit but whether or not to sell part of his land. Similarly he may have the option of farming part of his land and leasing the remainder to one or more tenant farmers. Moreover, his best course of action may involve his entering the land market both as a buyer and as a seller: it may pay him to sell part or all of his land and buy some other plots of land. These sorts of qualifications should always be borne in mind, even if the reader's attention is not continually being drawn to them.

IV   A concluding comment

Before embarking on our inquiries, an important *caveat* is in order. Our purpose throughout is, in Joan Robinson's words, to attempt 'to set up a scheme that simplifies the problem so as to make it manageable without eliminating the essential character of the situation on which it is intended to throw light'. The justification for the assumptions which we employ in any particular context will not be that they are 'realistic' in some absolute sense but that they are appropriate and reasonable for the purposes at hand. The reason for employing the framework suggested by Kelso is that it assists our deliberations by enabling us to organize our thoughts and shift the focus of our attention in some coherent manner. If we are to make any progress at all, simplifications and abstractions are unavoidable. However, it must be emphasized that the various aspects of land tenure are closely inter-connected. It is not our purpose to detract from the complexity of the issues involved; nor is it our purpose to pretend that there are simple answers to particular problems.

4

Farming and investment decisions under owner-occupancy

Private property, in every defence made of it, is supposed to mean the guarantee to individuals of the fruits of their own labour and abstinence. John Stuart Mill (p. 129).

I Introduction

This chapter considers the decisions of farmers who own the land they cultivate. The term 'owner-occupancy' encompasses a wide variety of farming arrangements. Some further classification is desirable. Of the possible classifications, we will focus on the source of labour. We will designate as 'capitalist' farmers those who rely *entirely* on hired labour to perform the farm work. We will describe as 'peasant' farmers those who employ family labour. Peasant farmers may or may not hire additional labour. On this basis virtually all the world's farmers would be 'peasants'. Very few indeed would be 'capitalists'. Nevertheless this distinction is useful from an analytical point of view. Moreover, it accords quite closely with a distinction to be found in the history of economic thought between, on the one hand, the capitalist of Classical economics and the profit-maximizing farmer of Neo-classical economics and, on the other, the pioneering analysis of Chayanov and the relatively recent extension of Neo-classical utility maximization to farm-families as exemplified by Nakajima.

The subsequent analysis explicitly acknowledges that agricultural activities take time. By the use of period analysis, we avoid the unfortunate tri-partite separation between production, investment and finance characteristic of the conventional theory of the firm. The treatment of financial capital follows closely the type of approach employed by Carlson in his classic but neglected work *The Pure Theory of Production*, published in 1939. Rather than building upon this work, the mainstream Neo-classical theory of the firm has become enmeshed in an essentially atemporal framework.

In this chapter we will assume not only that the farmer owns all the land he cultivates but also that he cultivates all the land he owns. We will assume that he is content to remain the owner of his land. Thus we will not consider the possibilities of his entering into land transactions either in the ownership market or in the rental market.

We will not explicitly evaluate the proposition that owner-occupancy is an 'efficient' form of land tenure. We will defer consideration of efficiency until a subsequent chapter.

II Capitalist farmers

Terminal wealth maximization

In essence, this section considers the behaviour of the capitalist farmer of Classical economics, with the difference that he is an owner-occupier rather than a tenant. As such he is a particular type of individual whose driving motive is the accumulation of wealth. As in the Classical model, he relies entirely on hired labour to perform the farm work.

We will suppose that there is a well-defined production period, a plausible assumption for agriculture. At the beginning of the period the farmer enters into contractual obligations with the suppliers of productive resources. During the period these resource services are used in production. At the end of the period the perishable produce is sold at prevailing market prices. We will assume that the farmer owns only land and financial capital. He may hire the services of fixed capital for the duration of the production period but he is excluded from acquiring full ownership of such resources. He can, of course, purchase circulating capital, that is, inputs which are entirely used up during the process of production. Initially we will assume that agricultural activities during the period have no impact on the terminal state of the property.

A critical consideration is the timing of payments for resource services and of receipts from the sale of produce. In the spirit of the Classical analysis, we will assume that the farmer pays for all inputs at the *beginning* of the production period; in particular, he advances wages to workers. He receives the proceeds from the sale of the produce at the *end* of the period. It follows from these assumptions about timing that financial capital plays a crucial role. Whether or not there are opportunities for borrowing and lending will be of decisive importance. In recognition of this, we will develop two polar cases. The first model assumes that there is no opportunity for borrowing or lending. The second model assumes that there is a perfect market for financial capital.

The farmer's outlay of financial capital at the outset of the tth period, K_t, is given by

$$K_t = \sum_{i=1}^{n} P_{it} X_{it}$$

where X_{it} is the quantity of the ith input purchased by the farmer – the n inputs may include farm labour of different types, seed, fertilizer, the hire of machinery – and P_{it} is the price per unit of the ith input. We will assume that the farmer can purchase as much of any input as he likes at its market price, each input being perfectly divisible. The farmer is also assumed to be a price-taker for products.

At date t the farmer has a given initial financial wealth, $\overline{W}_t$. At date t, assuming that there is no opportunity for borrowing or lending, he must decide how much to set aside for consumption expenditure, how much to save and how much to use for the acquisition of input services. In the spirit of the Classical analysis, we will assume that the amount he sets aside for his own consumption is predetermined, say, by the customary standard of living of his family. If we denote this by $\overline{C}_t$, then the farmer's fund of own financial capital, $\overline{K}_t$, is given by

$$\overline{K}_t = \overline{W}_t - \overline{C}_t$$

This fund establishes a constraint on his capital advances:

$$K_t \leqq \overline{K}_t$$

The farmer's terminal financial wealth will be

$$W_{t+1} = Z_{t+1} + (\overline{K}_t - K_t)$$

where Z_{t+1} represents his revenue from the sale of the produce and $(\overline{K}_t - K_t)$ constitutes what he saves out of the initial fund.[1] We will define the farmer's 'profit' as

$$\pi_t = Z_{t+1} - K_t$$

Note that π_t represents his profit for the tth period. It is not associated with one particular date. It is the difference between receipts and payments at different dates.[2] His rate of profit for the tth period may be defined as

$$r_t = \frac{\pi_t}{K_t}$$

The objective of the capitalist farmer is to maximize his terminal financial wealth subject to the constraint on his capital outlay.[3] This is equivalent to maximizing his total profit for the tth period subject to the financial capital constraint. Note, however, that it is *not* equivalent to maximizing the rate of profit, as defined.

The decision problem can be decomposed into two stages. First, terminal wealth maximization implies that the farmer must maximize total revenue corresponding to any level of capital advances. The necessary first-order condition for the optimal allocation of funds between inputs is that, for all inputs employed in strictly positive quantities, the ratio of the marginal contributions to revenue of any two inputs equal the corresponding input price ratio. The resulting relationship between maximum total revenue and the level of capital advances is given by

$$Z_{t+1} = Z_{t+1}(K_t)$$

The precise form of this relationship will, of course, depend on the prices of inputs, the prices of outputs and on techniques of production. We are not interested in the details of which particular products he chooses to cultivate, in what quantities and by which methods. We will assume that the marginal contribution of capital outlay to total revenue is positive but diminishing.

The second stage is to maximize terminal financial wealth by the appropriate choice of a feasible level of capital advances. The corresponding first-order conditions are derived in Appendix 4.1. The condition with respect to the optimal level of capital advances may be summarized as follows: Let $\tilde{K}_t$ designate the level of advances at which their marginal revenue product would equal one. Then the optimal level of capital advances, K_t^*, is given by

$$K_t^* = \min \{\tilde{K}_t, \bar{K}_t\}$$

There are three possible cases: where $\bar{K}_t$ is less than $\tilde{K}_t$; where $\bar{K}_t$ exceeds $\tilde{K}_t$; and where, by coincidence, $\bar{K}_t$ just equals $\tilde{K}_t$.

Figure 4.1 illustrates the first two cases. In Figure 4.1(a), where OZ represents the relationship between total revenue and the level of capital advances, the capital constraint is binding. The farmer is unable to advance capital up to the point where its marginal contribution to revenue is equal to one. In other words, if, say, hired labour is the only non-land input, he is unable to employ labour up to the point where its marginal revenue product is equal to the wage rate. He employs the maximum possible labour given his capital fund. The case where the capital constraint is not binding is illustrated in Figure 4.1(b). The farmer advances capital up to the point where the marginal contribution to total revenue is equal to one and saves the remainder of his fund.

Consider now the case where the farmer is able to borrow or lend as much as he likes for the duration of the production period at a given market rate of interest, ρ_t. His terminal financial wealth will be

$$W_{t+1} = Z_{t+1} + (\bar{K}_t - K_t)(1 + \rho_t)$$

where $(\bar{K}_t - K_t)$ represents his *net* lending at date t. Letting $\hat{K}_t$ denote the

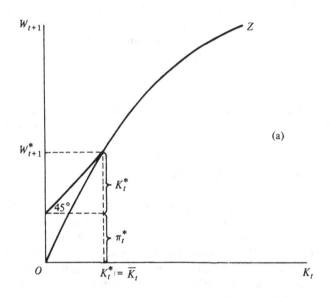

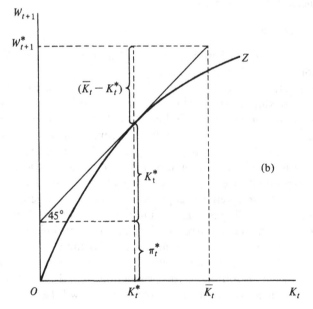

Figure 4.1. Capitalist farmer with no opportunity for borrowing or lending

farmer's *own* funds employed in farming, then

$$\hat{K}_t \equiv \min (K_t, \bar{K}_t)$$

If he employs all his funds in farming, so that $\hat{K}_t = \bar{K}_t$, his profit from farming is

$$\pi_t = Z_{t+1} - (K_t - \hat{K}_t)(1 + \rho_t) - \hat{K}_t$$

In the case where he does not employ all his funds in farming, so that $\hat{K}_t = K_t$, his profit from farming is

$$\hat{\pi}_t = Z_{t+1} - \hat{K}_t$$

In *both* cases his profit from farming may be expressed as

$$\pi_t = \{Z_{t+1} - K_t(1 + \rho_t)\} + \rho_t \cdot \hat{K}_t$$
$$= \pi_t^\varepsilon + \rho_t \cdot \hat{K}_t$$

where π_t^ε represents 'excess profit', that is, total revenue less the *effective* cost of inputs. His rate of profit from farming may be defined as a rate of return on his *own* funds employed in farming:

$$r_t = \frac{\pi_t}{\hat{K}_t} = \frac{\pi_t^\varepsilon}{\hat{K}_t} + \rho_t$$

The necessary first-order condition for maximizing terminal financial wealth is derived in Appendix 4.1: he must employ inputs up to the point where the marginal revenue product of capital outlay is equal to its effective marginal cost $(1 + \rho_t)$.

Figure 4.2 illustrates the case where the farmer does not employ all his initial fund in farming. By construction, the slope of AC is equal to $(1 + \rho_t)$, the marginal opportunity cost of funds. The optimal level of capital advances is $K_t^* = \hat{K}_t^*$, where the marginal contribution to revenue of capital advances is equal to $(1 + \rho_t)$. He lends the remainder of his funds, receiving back at the end of the period $(\bar{K}_t - \hat{K}_t^*)(1 + \rho_t)$. This, together with his total revenue, constitutes his terminal financial wealth. His profit equals the interest forgone on the funds he uses in farming plus excess profit. In interpreting Figure 4.2, where this decomposition is illustrated, it should be noted that, by construction, the slope of AD is equal to ρ_t.

The cases of no financial capital market and of a perfect financial capital market are, of course, polar extremes. It is quite likely that some form of market will exist but involve some type of 'imperfection'. For example, in the light of transaction costs, the rate of interest at which a farmer can borrow may well exceed the rate at which he can lend.

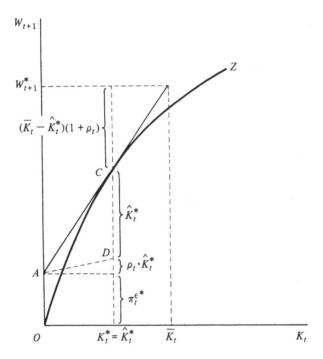

Figure 4.2. Lending by the capitalist farmer

Furthermore, since lending institutions often indulge in some form of credit rationing, there may be limits on borrowing. A farmer may well find that the average rate of interest depends on how much he wishes to borrow, the rate perhaps rising the more he seeks to borrow. Such imperfections would not pose any formidable analytical difficulties. For example, in the case where the borrowing rate, ρ_t^B, exceeds the lending rate, ρ_t^L, it could easily be shown that the optimal level of capital advances would involve a marginal contribution to revenue not greater than $(1+\rho_t^B)$ nor les than $(1+\rho_t^L)$.

An important consideration is that whether the precise level of the farmer's initial capital fund exercises an influence over his behaviour depends on whether or not there is a perfect market for financial capital. If there is a perfect market then the level of this fund is immaterial: irrespective of the size of $\bar{K}_t$ the farmer will advance capital, whether his own or borrowed, up to the point where its marginal revenue product is equal to $(1+\rho_t)$. If, however, there is no market at all or an imperfect market then the level of his initial fund will matter. Whether he is relatively wealthy or poor will affect his production behaviour.[4] In the case of no opportunity for borrowing or lending it clearly matters whether his initial fund is greater than or less than the level of capital advances at which the marginal revenue product equals one. In the case where the borrowing rate exceeds the lending rate, not only whether it would be appropriate for him to borrow, lend or do neither but also the resulting level of capital advances would depend on his initial fund. In the case of an imperfect market, there may be a further influence, since the farmer's initial capital may affect the terms on which he can secure credit.[5]

Consumption expenditure

Whereas the assumption that the farmer's consumption expenditure is determined by his habitual standard of living would probably have been acceptable to the Classical economists, it would be unlikely to find favour amongst many Neo-classical economists. It ignores the possibility of an inter-temporal trade-off, the possibility of the farmer forgoing some current consumption in order to use funds productively.

The analysis can be modified relatively easily to treat consumption expenditure endogenously. Assume that the objective for the farmer is to maximize utility, where utility depends on consumption expenditure at the beginning of the period and on terminal financial wealth:

$$U_t = U_t(C_t, W_{t+1})$$

where U_t is utility at the beginning of the period.[6] The farmer would maximize utility subject to the constraint imposed by his initial financial wealth. Whether or not there exist opportunities for borrowing or lending and, if so, on what terms would be crucial in determining the set of feasible combinations of consumption and terminal wealth.

A famous proposition – the Fisher decomposition – is that if there exists a perfect financial capital market the production decision can be separated from the consumption decision. The optimal level of capital advances will not depend on the nature of the farmer's utility function. The marginal revenue product of capital advances will equal $(1 + \rho_t)$. If, however, there is no market for financial capital or if there is an imperfect capital market, such a simple decomposition will not be legitimate. Production decisions will depend on the farmer's utility function.

Some implications of uncertainty

Of the assumptions which we have made, the most disquieting is surely the assumption that the farmer is perfectly certain about the relationship between actions and their outcomes. Agriculture is a notoriously uncertain occupation. For most commodities, yields depend not simply on the farmer's activities but also on the weather and on disease, that is, on forces which the farmer can neither fully control nor entirely anticipate. Furthermore, given that production takes time, the farmer has to take decisions before he knows what the market prices of agricultural products will be at harvest time.

The Classical economists were aware of the significance of uncertainty but did not attempt a formal analysis of its implications. When Neo-classical economists did develop formal analyses of individual behaviour, uncertainty was largely ignored. This was perhaps in part attributable to the fact that, rather than adopting as their temporal framework the period analysis of Classical economics, they employed a static framework which did not even recognize that production takes time. With such an approach it is that much easier to ignore the implications of uncertainty. It is only relatively recently that there have been attempts to incorporate uncertainty into the theory of the firm. It is on this recent literature that this section will draw.[7]

For our purposes it is sufficient to consider the simplest case of uncertainty. Suppose that the farmer produces a single perishable product; that he has an initial fund $\bar{K}_t$; and that there exists a perfect financial capital market. His terminal financial wealth is given by

$$W_{t+1} = P_{t+1} \cdot Q_{t+1} + (\bar{K}_t - K_t)(1 + \rho_t)$$

where Q_{t+1} represents the output and quantity sold of the product at the end of the period and P_{t+1} represents its price per unit. Assume that the relationship between maximum output and the level of capital advances is certain. The sole source of uncertainty relates to the price of the product. The farmer bases his decisions on expectations about this price, as represented by a non-degenerate subjective probability density function. Thus, corresponding to each level of capital advances is an associated subjective probability density function of terminal wealth. The farmer's decision problem is to choose the level of K_t with the most desirable probability density function of terminal wealth.

The farmer's decision criterion is to maximize the expected utility of terminal wealth. As is well known, acceptance of a number of axioms, relating in this context to the individual's preferences among alternative probability density functions of wealth, implies the existence of a von Neumann–Morgenstern utility of wealth function, $U(W_{t+1})$. Thus, corresponding to any probability density function of wealth is an expected utility of wealth. Furthermore, behaviour in accordance with the axioms requires that the farmer maximize expected utility; that is, he is required to select that level of capital advances which has the probability density function of terminal wealth with the highest expected utility.

The properties of the utility function are crucial. Assume that the function is continuous, twice differentiable and strictly increasing over the relevant range, so that

$$U'(W_{t+1}) > 0$$

The sign of the second derivative is particularly significant. If the utility function is linear over the relevant range, so that

$$U''(W_{t+1}) = 0$$

the farmer would be indifferent to a 'fair' gamble. Accordingly he would be described as 'risk neutral'. If the utility function is strictly concave over the relevant range, so that

$$U''(W_{t+1}) < 0$$

the farmer would decline a fair gamble. Accordingly he would be described as 'risk averse'. If his utility function is strictly convex, he would be described as 'risk loving'.

For a risk neutral farmer, expected utility maximization implies the maximization of expected terminal financial wealth. Consequently he would equate the *expected* marginal revenue product of capital advances to their marginal opportunity cost $(1 + \rho_t)$. Given a perfect market for financial capital, his decision would *not* depend on his initial fund, $\bar{K}_t$. If the assumption of risk neutrality was acceptable, incorporation of uncertainty would be straightforward. However, many economists would argue that farmers are likely to be averse to risk. For a risk averse farmer, expected utility maximization implies that the expected marginal revenue product of capital advances will be *strictly greater* than its marginal opportunity cost. This proposition, which is perhaps to be expected on intuitive grounds, is demonstrated formally in Appendix 4.2. Moreover, in general, the optimal level of capital advances *will* depend on the farmer's initial fund.[8]

Extending the analysis to a multi-product farmer facing uncertainty regarding the prices of those products would raise additional complications. For heuristic purposes, we could separate the decision problem into three stages. The first stage would be to determine the precise way in which the farmer would employ any given bundle of inputs. His choice would depend on his attitudes to risk, the nature of his expectations, the cost of the input bundle, and so on. The second stage would be to determine which bundle of inputs the farmer would purchase for each level of K_t: this would determine the most desirable subjective probability density function of terminal wealth for each level of K_t. The final stage would be to determine the optimal level of K_t. Similar complications would arise in the case of yield uncertainty. Even in the single product case, the farmer might have an effective choice as to how to use a given bundle of inputs. One manner of input use might result in a lower expected output but one which was less 'risky' – less susceptible to the vagaries of the weather or to disease – than some other use. A formal analysis of these issues is not necessary for our purposes. We will, however, have occasion to refer subsequently to the scope for decision taking in the face of uncertainty. For the present we will simply note that the scope for decision taking under uncertainty is greater where there are various products and various alternative techniques of production.

Investment in land improvements

So far we have assumed that the activities of the farmer have no effect on the state of his property. However, many, if not most, agricultural activities do have an impact on the characteristics of the land. These effects may be adverse or beneficial. They may be the incidental side-effects of cultivation or they may be the results of deliberate activities. An owner-operator will be concerned not only with the revenue he receives at the end of the period but also with the terminal value of his property.

There is likely to be some sort of trade-off. Suppose that the farmer has a certain sum of money to spend on inputs. If he were to decide on input acquisition and utilization solely with an eye to maximizing revenue this would quite probably lead to the depletion of the fertility of his land. By forgoing some revenue he could maintain the fertility of his land. By sacrificing still more revenue he might well be able to enhance the value of his property. This trade-off may arise both in regard to which inputs to acquire and in regard to how to use particular inputs. Deliberate attempts at improvement will frequently be associated with the purchase of durable capital goods which are then embodied in the land, as for example with fences or buildings. But investment need not necessarily imply the acquisition of particular types of inputs. The simplest case is where hired labour can be deployed either in the cultivation of crops or in digging ditches to improve drainage.

The analysis can easily be modified to allow for the effects of farming operations on the state of the land. We can still employ our single-period framework. Let V_{t+1} be the terminal value of the property. If the farmer intends to sell the property at the end of the period, V_{t+1} would represent the net proceeds from its sale. If he intends to retain ownership this value would depend on the prospective profitability from farming the land in subsequent periods. Suppose that the farmer is ultimately interested in his aggregate wealth, defined as the sum of his financial wealth plus the value of his property. Assuming a perfect financial capital market, the farmer will wish to maximize terminal aggregate wealth corresponding to any outlay on inputs. The relationship between revenue, property value and outlay on inputs is given by an implicit function:

$$G(Z_{t+1}, V_{t+1}, K_t) = 0$$

Any trade-off between revenue and property value will be reflected in this function. Appendix 4.3 derives the necessary conditions for maximizing terminal aggregate wealth for a given outlay on inputs. The relevant condition is

$$\frac{\partial G/\partial Z_{t+1}}{\partial G/\partial V_{t+1}} = 1$$

that is, input acquisition and utilization must be such that the marginal rate of transformation between revenue and property value equal one.[9]

In the absence of opportunities for borrowing and lending, the situation might be somewhat more complicated. A farmer might not be indifferent as to the *composition* of aggregate wealth. In particular, he may be disinclined to have too high a proportion of his wealth tied up in the value of his property if this leaves him short of funds for operating the farm.

III Peasant farmers

Consider now the behaviour of a peasant household which owns the land it farms. The household relies, at least in part, on family labour to cultivate the land. In addition to land and labour, the household may own physical capital goods, such as animals, seed or implements. The household may produce commodities solely for sale. Or it may consume part of its produce itself. The feasible courses of action available to the household will depend on the nature of markets for productive resources. This will determine both its access to other inputs to supplement those it owns and the alternatives to using its own resources in farming. In addition, institutional arrangements in these markets will determine the timing of payments for resource services and thereby the need for financial capital. As with the capitalist farmer, whether or not there are opportunities for borrowing and lending and, if so, on what terms will be of crucial significance.

Various analyses could be developed depending on the assumptions chosen. For our purposes we will focus on the labour decision of the household assuming that all non-labour resources are fixed. We will also assume that the household sells all its produce at given market prices. We will employ the temporal framework employed in the last section and suppose, for simplicity, that the household is perfectly certain about prices and yields and that agricultural activities have no effect on the characteristics of the land.

Even with labour as the only variable input there are several possible situations depending on whether there exist opportunities for part-time off-farm employment and/or opportunities for hiring supplementary labour and, if so, whether wages are received or paid at the beginning or the end of the period. Initially we will consider the case where there are no opportunities either for part-time off-farm employment or for hiring labour.[10]

Let L_t represent the level of labour input decided at date t and utilized, in accordance with that decision, during the tth period. Let Z_{t+1} represent total revenue received at date $(t+1)$ from the sale of the produce of the tth period. The relationship between total revenue and any level of labour input will depend on the particular commodities which the household produces and on the precise way it deploys its labour. We will simply assume that the household maximizes total revenue for any level of labour input, the relationship between maximum total revenue and labour input being given by

$$Z_{t+1} = Z_{t+1}(L_t)$$

The specific form of this relationship will, of course, depend on the non-labour resources owned by the household, on the techniques for producing the various products and on product prices. We will assume that the marginal revenue product of labour is positive but diminishing.

At the beginning of the period the household must decide, not only the level of labour, but also its consumption expenditure. Assuming no opportunities for borrowing or lending, the household's consumption expenditure is constrained by its initial financial wealth:

$$C_t \leqq \bar{W}_t$$

The household's terminal financial wealth will comprise the revenue it receives from the sale of its produce and any savings. In addition, we will allow for the possibilities that at the end of the period the household may receive some autonomous income from a source other than the sale of its produce or that it may be obliged to pay a predetermined sum, such as a land tax or mortgage repayment. Let $\bar{A}_{t+1}$ represent the net value of these autonomous receipts and payments. Then

$$W_{t+1} = Z_{t+1}(L_t) + (\bar{W}_t - C_t) + \bar{A}_{t+1}$$

We will assume that the household's preferences can be represented by a differentiable, strictly quasi-concave utility function

$$U_t = U_t(L_t, C_t, W_{t+1})$$

where utility is strictly increasing in both consumption expenditure and terminal wealth but strictly decreasing in labour. The specific form of the utility function will depend on the size and composition of the household, notably on the numbers of 'workers' and 'dependants'.[11] The utility function is defined over a 'consumption set' involving non-negative consumption expenditure and levels of labour which are non-negative but no greater than some maximum level of labour, $\bar{L}_t$.[12]

The decision problem of the household is to choose a level of consumption expenditure and a level of labour so as to maximize utility subject to its wealth constraint and to the choice being in the consumption set. The necessary first-order conditions are derived in Appendix 4.4. For *interior* solutions the conditions are as follows. First, the marginal contribution of labour to revenue, and therefore to terminal financial wealth, must equal the marginal rate of substitution between wealth and leisure. Second, the marginal rate of substitution between consumption and terminal financial wealth must equal one. Finally, the marginal rate of substitution between consumption and leisure must equal the marginal revenue product of labour.

Henceforth, in the interests of simplicity, we will asume that the household spends *all* of its initial wealth on consumption expenditure, so that $C_t = \bar{W}_t$. This assumption, which permits a two-dimensional representation, is by no means implausible. Very many peasant households in poor agrarian economies are never in a position to indulge in the intertemporal trade-off of Neo-classical economics. On the basis of this assumption, Figure 4.3 illustrates the labour–wealth choice for the peasant household. The curve XX' represents the household's terminal financial wealth as a function of the level of labour input. The intercept OX represents net autonomous receipts, $\bar{A}_{t+1}$. Each indifference curve represents, for the given consumption expenditure, combinations of labour and wealth between which the household is indifferent. The positive slope of each indifference curve implies that an increase in wealth is required to compensate for an increase in labour. Combinations of labour and wealth on I_3 are preferred to combinations on I_2; and so on. The optimum for the household occurs where the wealth–labour curve XX' is just tangent to the highest attainable indifference curve, I_2. The optimal level of labour input is L_t^*; the corresponding terminal financial wealth is W_{t+1}^*.

Consider briefly certain comparative static propositions. First, suppose that there is an increase in net autonomous receipts. Solely on the basis of our earlier assumptions the effect is indeterminate. However, it can be shown that, provided that both wealth and leisure are 'normal' commodities over the relevant range, the impact would be a lower level of labour input – that is, more leisure – and a higher level of terminal financial

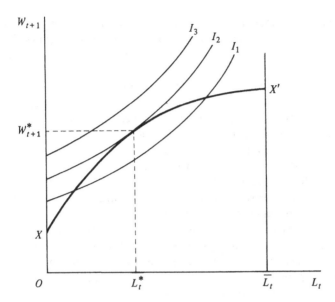

Figure 4.3. Labour–wealth choice for a peasant household

wealth. This implies, for example, that increased land taxes or increased mortgage payments would induce the household to work harder. Second, consider a change in the relationship between revenue and labour. This could arise as a result of changes in product prices, in the levels of non-labour resources or in technology. In general, the directional effect of such a change on the level of labour is indeterminate. Consider an increase in farm size. Given the plausible assumption that the marginal revenue product of each level of labour would be higher at the higher farm size, the substitution effect would increase the level of labour. However, the lump sum 'wealth' effect would reduce the level of labour if leisure is normal. The two effects would work in opposite directions. The net effect might be a higher, the same or a lower level of labour input.[13]

Part-time off-farm employment

Consider now the case where the household has the option of undertaking part-time off-farm employment. Assume that the household is free to decide what time to devote to off-farm employment at a given wage rate, the wages to be received at the end of the period. Terminal financial wealth is given by

$$W_{t+1} = Z_{t+1}(\hat{L}_t) + w_{t+1}(L_t - \hat{L}_t) + \bar{A}_{t+1}$$

where L_t represents total labour, $\hat{L}_t$ represents labour on the farm, so that

$(L_t - \hat{L}_t)$ represents off-farm work, and w_{t+1} represents the off-farm wage rate.

The household must determine not simply the total amount of labour but also its allocation between the two types of employment. Assuming that the household is indifferent between the two types of employment *per se*, a prerequisite for utility maximization is that the household maximize the earnings associated with any level of total labour. If the household undertakes *both* on-farm and off-farm work, the necessary condition is that the marginal contribution to terminal financial wealth must be the same for both forms of employment. Thus the marginal revenue product of farm labour must equal the off-farm wage rate, the latter constituting the marginal opportunity cost of farm labour over the relevant range.

The optimal choice for the peasant household is illustrated in Figure 4.4. The curve $XX'X''$ represents the relationship between terminal financial wealth and household labour if all labour is devoted to farming. Given the opportunity for part-time off-farm employment, the maximum level of terminal financial wealth for any level of labour is given by $XX'Y$, where the slope of $X'Y$ equals the off-farm wage rate and where $X'Y$ is tangent to $XX'X''$ at X', in accordance with the condition that the marginal revenue product of farm labour equal the off-farm wage rate. The optimal choice for the household involves a total labour supply of L_t^*, of which $\hat{L}_t^*$ is farm labour and $(L_t^* - \hat{L}_t^*)$ is off-farm labour. The corresponding terminal financial wealth is W_{t+1}^*, of which $(W_{t+1}^* - Z_{t+1}^* - \bar{A}_{t+1}) = w_{t+1}(L_t^* - \hat{L}_t^*)$ constitutes wages from off-farm employment.

A significant consideration is that we can develop a number of more definite comparative static propositions for a household which does undertake part-time off-farm employment. First, it is clear that an increase in the off-farm wage rate will lead to a reduction in the level of labour devoted to farming. If the wage rate rises sufficiently the household will cease farm work entirely. Second, we can now determine the qualitative impact of certain changes in, say, farm size or technology. Specifically an increase in farm size, such that the marginal revenue product of labour increases for each level of farm labour, will lead to higher farm labour, provided that off-farm employment continues to be undertaken. For a sufficiently large increase in farm size the household will cease off-farm employment altogether, the effects of subsequent increases in farm size on the level of labour thereafter being indeterminate. 'Output-increasing' technological change, which increases the marginal revenue product of labour for each level of farm-labour, would have similar effects.

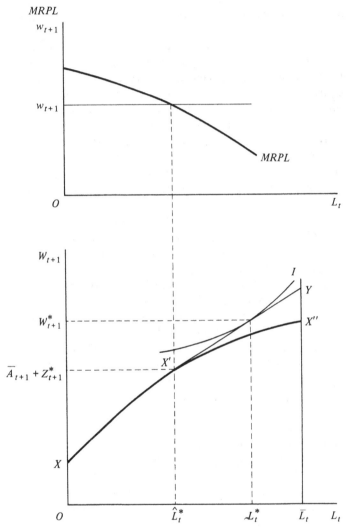

Figure 4.4. Labour choice for a peasant household with opportunity for part-time off-farm employment

Labour hiring

Consider now a 'semi-capitalistic' peasant household which hires labour to supplement its own labour. Assume that the household is able to employ whatever quantity of labour it wishes at a given wage rate – there are no institutional rigidities such as standard working weeks – and that wages are paid at the end of the period. Assume also that hired labour is equivalent in terms of quality and productivity to own labour. Terminal financial wealth is given by

$$W_{t+1} = Z_{t+1}(L_t + H_t) - w_{t+1} \cdot H_t + \bar{A}_{t+1}$$

where L_t represents own labour, H_t represents hired labour, so that $(L_t + H_t)$ represents total labour used during the production period, and w_{t+1} represents the wage rate for hired labour.

A prerequisite for maximizing utility is that the household maximize terminal wealth for any level of its own labour. If the marginal revenue product of that level of labour is greater than the wage rate of hired labour it will pay the household to hire supplementary labour until the marginal revenue product of labour equals the wage rate. In Figure 4.5, the curve $XX'X''$ represents the relationship between terminal financial wealth and the level of own labour assuming that the household relies entirely on its own labour. The curve $YX'X''$ represents the maximum level of terminal financial wealth for each level of own labour given the possibility of hiring labour. The slope of the linear segment YX' is equal to the wage rate of hired labour; it is tangent to $OX'X''$ at X', the point at which the marginal revenue product equals the wage rate. The optimum for the household involves a total labour input of $(L_t^* + H_t^*)$

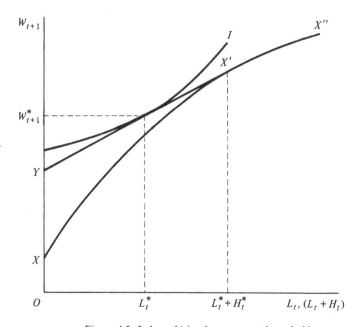

Figure 4.5. Labour hiring by a peasant household

and a level of own labour of L_t^*. After paying the wages of hired labour, the household is left with a terminal financial wealth of W_{t+1}^*.

For a peasant household which does employ labour certain comparative static propositions could be demonstrated. First, a reduction in the wage rate would increase the total labour used on the farm. Assuming that leisure is a normal commodity, the level of own labour would fall, implying *a fortiori* an increase in the level of hired labour. Second, an increase in farm size which increased the marginal revenue product of farm labour would increase the total level of labour. Assuming that leisure is a normal commodity, the level of the household's own labour would fall implying *a fortiori* an increase in the level of hired labour. For sufficiently low wage rates or for sufficiently high farm size the household might cease to use its own labour at all and become 'capitalist'.

The analysis could easily be extended to the case where there are possibilities both for part-time off-farm employment and for hiring labour. Nakajima considers the situation where the off-farm wage equals the wage rate for hired labour. In this event the marginal revenue product of farm labour will necessarily equal that wage rate. The assumption of equal wage rates is, however, a very restrictive one. Propositions derived from it should be treated with caution. In view of transaction costs, travelling costs and income taxes, the wage rate of hired labour may well exceed the wage rate for off-farm employment. Because of such divergencies a peasant household may well neither undertake part-time off-farm employment nor hire supplementary labour even though possibilities for both do exist.

One particular limitation of the foregoing analysis must be acknowledged. We have disregarded the precise seasonal application of labour during the production period. The labour requirements of agricultural activities vary from time to time within a production cycle. In order to accommodate this phenomenon, we could distinguish different types of labour according to sub-periods within the overall production period. For example, we could analyse the household's decision with respect to March labour, April labour, and so on. We will not undertake a formal analysis. However, a formal analysis is not needed for us to appreciate that a household might well undertake casual off-farm employment during seasons of relative inactivity in farming, if opportunities are available, and also that it might well hire casual labour at critical times in the agricultural year, if opportunities for that are available.[14]

As a postscript to this section it is worth emphasizing that the sorts of decisions we have been considering – whether to undertake part-time off-farm employment or whether to hire labour – may not be taken solely on the basis of narrow economic considerations. For example, it has been claimed that in certain countries there are social pressures on peasant households to employ landless labourers and that they do so even though it is uneconomic. In other countries peasant households may be disinclined to hire workers, possibly on ideological grounds, even though it would be economic for them to do so. In addition, there is the question of supervision of hired workers. A certain amount of effort may be required to ensure that hired workers perform their work satisfactorily.

Physical and financial capital

Consider briefly the case where inputs other than labour are variable. Provided that the household can buy some input, such as fertilizer, in divisible units at a given price and provided that it pays for them at the end of the period, the extension of the analysis is straightforward. The household will purchase the input up to the point where the marginal revenue product of the input equals its price. If, however, inputs have to be paid for at the beginning of the period, financial capital will yet again play a crucial role. If there is a perfect market for financial capital the household will purchase a perfectly divisible input up to the point where the marginal revenue product of that input equals its price compounded according to the rate of interest. If, however, the household is unable to borrow or is only able to borrow on highly unfavourable terms, the purchase of inputs may only be possible at the expense of consumption expenditure. If the household is barely able to meet its subsistence requirements, profitable opportunities may not be exploited. This is particularly likely to occur with indivisible inputs. Even where there are opportunities for borrowing, many peasant households in under-developed countries only borrow if forced to do so to meet *consumption* requirements. It has frequently been observed that even relatively affluent farm-families in developed countries exhibit a definite aversion to borrowing money.

Appendix 4.1 Maximization of terminal financial wealth

Assuming no opportunities to borrow or lend, the farmer's objective is to

> maximize $W_{t+1} = Z_{t+1}(K_t) + (\bar{K}_t - K_t)$
> subject to $K_t \leq \bar{K}_t$

The augmented objective function is

$$Z_{t+1}(K_t) + (\bar{K}_t - K_t) + \lambda_t(\bar{K}_t - K_t)$$

where λ_t is a Lagrange multiplier. The corresponding first-order conditions are

$$\frac{dZ_{t+1}}{dK_t} - 1 - \lambda_t \leqq 0 \tag{4.1.1}$$

$$K_t \left\{ \frac{dZ_{t+1}}{dK_t} - 1 - \lambda_t \right\} = 0 \tag{4.1.2}$$

$$(\bar{K}_t - K_t) \geqq 0 \tag{4.1.3}$$

$$\lambda_t (\bar{K}_t - K_t) = 0 \tag{4.1.4}$$

$$K_t \geqq 0 \text{ and } \lambda_t \geqq 0 \tag{4.1.5}$$

Assume $K_t > 0$. From (4.1.2)

$$\frac{dZ_{t+1}}{dK_t} = 1 + \lambda_t \tag{4.1.6}$$

Consider the case where he would not use all his funds in farming. From (4.1.4), $\bar{K}_t > K_t$ implies $\lambda_t = 0$. Thus, from (4.1.6)

$$\frac{dZ_{t+1}}{dK_t} = 1$$

Thus, in the case where the tenant does not use all his funds, the marginal revenue product of the optimal level of capital advances must equal one.

Consider now the case where $\lambda_t > 0$. From (4.1.4), this implies $\bar{K}_t = K_t$, so that the farmer employs all his available funds in production. From (4.1.6), $\lambda_t > 0$ implies

$$\frac{dZ_{t+1}}{dK_t} > 1$$

In this case the farmer is unable to advance funds up to the point where its marginal revenue product equals one. Note from (4.1.6) that

$$\lambda_t = \frac{dZ_{t+1}}{dK_t} - 1$$

Thus λ_t is equivalent to Carlson's 'marginal rate of return'. It represents the marginal addition to maximum profit of a small increase in $\bar{K}_t$. Thus $(1 + \lambda_t)$ represents the marginal addition to maximum terminal wealth of a small increase in initial capital.

Assume now that the farmer is able to borrow or lend as much as he likes at a market rate of interest, ρ_t. The objective of the farmer is to

$$\text{maximize } W_{t+1} = Z_{t+1} + (\bar{K}_t - K_t)(1 + \rho_t)$$

The corresponding first-order conditions are

$$\frac{dZ_{t+1}}{dK_t} - (1+\rho_t) \leqq 0 \qquad (4.1.7)$$

$$K_t \left\{ \frac{dZ_{t+1}}{dK_t} - (1+\rho_t) \right\} = 0 \qquad (4.1.8)$$

Assume $K_t > 0$. From (4.1.8)

$$\frac{dZ_{t+1}}{dK_t} = (1+\rho_t) \qquad (4.1.9)$$

Thus the optimal level of capital advances involves a marginal revenue product equal to its 'effective' cost. Note from (4.1.9) that

$$\frac{dZ_{t+1}}{dK_t} - 1 = \rho_t$$

that is, the marginal rate of return equals the market rate of interest.

Appendix 4.2 Capitalist farmer and price uncertainty

Suppressing time subscripts, the farmer's objective is to

$$\text{maximize } E\{U[P \cdot Q + (\bar{K} - K)(1+\rho)]\}$$

Provided that $K > 0$, the necessary first-order condition is

$$E\{U'(W)[P \cdot Q'(K) - (1+\rho)]\} = 0 \qquad (4.2.1)$$

Condition (4.2.1) may be expanded as

$$E[U'(W)(P - \mu_P)Q'(K)] + [\mu_P \cdot Q'(K) - (1+\rho)]E[U'(W)] = 0 \quad (4.2.2)$$

where μ_P is the expected product price. Consider the first term on the left-hand side of (4.2.2). Since $U'(\mu_W)$ is non-random for a given level of K, where μ_W is expected terminal financial wealth,

$$E[U'(W)(P - \mu_P)Q'(K)] = E\{[U'(W) - U'(\mu_W)](P - \mu_P)Q'(K)\} \qquad (4.2.3)$$

If $P > \mu_P$ then $W > \mu_W$ so that, for a risk averse farmer, $U'(W) < U'(\mu_W)$. If $P < \mu_P$ then $W < \mu_W$ so that, for a risk averse farmer, $U'(W) > U'(\mu_W)$. Therefore, from (4.2.3), the first term on the left-hand side of (4.2.2) is negative. Therefore

$$[\mu_P \cdot Q'(K) - (1+\rho)] \cdot E[U'(W)] > 0$$

Since $E[U'(W)] > 0$

$$\mu_P \cdot Q'(K) > (1+\rho)$$

Appendix 4.3 Capitalist farmer and investment in improvements

To maximize terminal wealth subject to a given outlay on inputs, $\hat{K}_t$, the farmer's objective is to

maximize $Z_{t+1} + V_{t+1}$

subject to $G(Z_{t+1}, V_{t+1}, \hat{K}_t) = 0$

The augmented objective function is

$$Z_{t+1} + V_{t+1} + \lambda_t \cdot G(Z_{t+1}, V_{t+1}, \hat{K}_t)$$

where λ_t is a Lagrange multiplier. For an interior optimum, the necessary first-order conditions are

$$1 + \lambda_t \cdot \frac{\partial G}{\partial Z_{t+1}} = 0 \tag{4.3.1}$$

$$1 + \lambda_t \cdot \frac{\partial G}{\partial V_{t+1}} = 0 \tag{4.3.2}$$

$$G(Z_{t+1}, V_{t+1}, \hat{K}_t) = 0$$

From (4.3.1) and (4.3.2)

$$\frac{\partial G / \partial Z_{t+1}}{\partial G / \partial V_{t+1}} = 1$$

that is, the marginal rate of transformation between revenue and property value must equal one.

Appendix 4.4 Utility maximization for a peasant household

The peasant household's objective is to chose non-negative values for L_t and C_t so as to

maximize $U_t(C_t, L_t, W_{t+1})$

subject to $C_t \leqq \bar{W}_t$

and to $L_t \leqq \bar{L}_t$

where $W_{t+1} = Z_{t+1}(L_t) + (\bar{W}_t - C_t) + \bar{A}_{t+1}$

The augmented objective function is

$$U_t(C_t, L_t, W_{t+1}) + \mu_t[\bar{W}_t - C_t] + \lambda_t[\bar{L}_t - L_t]$$

where μ_t and λ_t are Lagrangian multipliers. The corresponding necessary first-order conditions are

$$\frac{\partial U_t}{\partial L_t} + \frac{\partial U_t}{\partial W_{t+1}} \cdot \frac{\partial W_{t+1}}{\partial L_t} - \lambda_t \leq 0 \tag{4.4.1}$$

$$L_t \left\{ \frac{\partial U_t}{\partial L_t} + \frac{\partial U_t}{\partial W_{t+1}} \cdot \frac{\partial W_{t+1}}{\partial L_t} - \lambda_t \right\} = 0 \tag{4.4.2}$$

$$\frac{\partial U_t}{\partial C_t} + \frac{\partial U_t}{\partial W_{t+1}} \cdot \frac{\partial W_{t+1}}{\partial C_t} - \mu_t \leq 0 \tag{4.4.3}$$

$$C_t \left\{ \frac{\partial U_t}{\partial C_t} + \frac{\partial U_t}{\partial W_{t+1}} \cdot \frac{\partial W_{t+1}}{\partial C_t} - \mu_t \right\} = 0 \tag{4.4.4}$$

$$(\bar{W}_t - C_t) \geq 0 \tag{4.4.5}$$

$$\mu_t(\bar{W}_t - C_t) = 0 \tag{4.4.6}$$

$$(\bar{L}_t - L_t) \geq 0 \tag{4.4.7}$$

$$\lambda_t(\bar{L}_t - L_t) = 0 \tag{4.4.8}$$

$$L_t \geq 0, \ C_t \geq 0, \ \mu_t \geq 0 \text{ and } \lambda_t \geq 0 \tag{4.4.9}$$

Assume

$$\bar{L}_t > L_t > 0$$

From (4.4.1) and (4.4.8)

$$\frac{\partial U_t}{\partial L_t} + \frac{\partial U_t}{\partial W_{t+1}} \cdot \frac{\partial W_{t+1}}{\partial L_t} = 0$$

so that

$$\frac{\partial W_{t+1}}{\partial L_t} = -\frac{\partial U_t/\partial L_t}{\partial U_t/\partial W_{t+1}}$$

or

$$\frac{dZ_{t+1}}{dL_t} = -\frac{\partial U_t/\partial L_t}{\partial U_t/\partial W_{t+1}} \tag{4.4.10}$$

This condition states that the marginal revenue product of labour must equal what Nakajima would describe in the present context as 'the marginal valuation of household labour in terms of terminal financial wealth'. This condition may alternatively be interpreted as involving equality between the marginal revenue product of labour and the marginal rate of substitution between terminal financial wealth and *leisure*.

Assume

$$\bar{W}_t > C_t > 0$$

From (4.4.4) and (4.4.6)

$$\frac{\partial U_t}{\partial C_t} + \frac{\partial U_t}{\partial W_{t+1}} \cdot \frac{\partial W_{t+1}}{\partial C_t} = 0$$

so that

$$\frac{\partial U_t}{\partial C_t} = -\frac{\partial U_t}{\partial W_{t+1}} \cdot \frac{\partial W_{t+1}}{\partial C_t} \tag{4.4.11}$$

Now

$$\frac{\partial W_{t+1}}{\partial C_t} = -1$$

Therefore, from (4.4.11)

$$\frac{\partial U_t / \partial C_t}{\partial U_t / \partial W_{t+1}} = 1 \tag{4.4.12}$$

that is, the marginal rate of substitution between terminal financial wealth and current consumption expenditure must equal one.

Note that (4.4.10) and (4.4.12) imply

$$\frac{dZ_{t+1}}{dL_t} = -\frac{\partial U_t / \partial L_t}{\partial U_t / \partial C_t} \tag{4.4.13}$$

This condition states that the marginal revenue product of labour must equal 'the marginal valuation of household labour in terms of current consumption expenditure'. This condition may alternatively be interpreted as involving equality between the marginal revenue product of labour and the marginal rate of substitution between consumption and *leisure*.

5

Farming and investment decisions under tenancy

If a farmer cannot look to the future with security, little can be hazarded by him beyond the expenses which the returns of the year will defray; and not only will all great improvements, but even the most common works of the season, be imperfectly performed. If we shall deny to the farmer that security of possession which is essential to the safe and profitable application of his funds, we may rest assured that his capital will be sparingly expended on another man's property. Low (p. 9).

I Introduction

This chapter examines the farming and investment decisions of agricultural tenants and their landlords. We are primarily concerned with the impact of tenancy arrangements on their behaviour. In essence, a tenancy arrangement entails an agreement whereby the owner of the land transfers the right of use to the tenant in return for some payment. Beyond that, however, there have been, and still are, bewildering varieties of tenancies in different countries. Some tenancies involve formal contractual agreements. Others do not. The duration of a tenancy may be agreed at the time the tenancy is created, as in a lease for a fixed term of years. Alternatively the precise duration may not be stipulated *ex ante* but rather left to the subsequent discretion of the parties, as in a tenancy-at-will. Rents may be paid in cash or in kind. The contract of tenancy may or may not provide for compensatory payments between the parties at the termination of the tenancy.

This chapter does not attempt a formal theoretical analysis of all the various possible types of tenancy agreement. Rather the main objective is to highlight general principles. The fact that we are concerned with general principles does not, of course, preclude the use of specific illustrations. This chapter will draw heavily on past and present tenure arrangements in England. Indeed, section IV considers explicitly the development of the English Agricultural Holdings Legislation. This legislation is worth examining not simply for illustrative purposes. With some justification, it has been regarded as model legislation which many other countries would do well to emulate.

II Tenant farmers

In studying the behaviour of a tenant farmer we can draw on the analysis of capitalist and peasant owner-operators developed in the previous chapter. The fundamental difference is that, rather than enjoying permanent ownership of the property, the tenant has only a right of temporary occupation in return for which he pays rent to the owner. In general terms, the behaviour of the tenant will depend on his proprietary rights and obligations under the leasehold for two main reasons. First, the nature of property rights may affect the set of legally feasible courses of action available to him. Second, property rights will influence the nature of incentives, that is, the extent to which the costs and benefits of particular activities accrue to him, rather than to the landowner. Of these the latter is the more crucial. The extent to which costs and benefits are internalized will depend on the nature of rental payments, on the duration and security of tenure and on the form of provisions, if any, for compensatory payments at the termination of the tenancy.

Rental payments

Historically the main forms of agricultural rental payments have been labour services, farm produce and cash. Labour services have generally been associated with feudalistic systems whereby the peasant is allotted a plot of land to farm on his own account in return for working on the lord's home farm. Although the precise manner of work may be at the discretion of the lord, the length of time the peasant has to work for the lord during the various agricultural seasons is normally stipulated.[1] As such, these labour services constitute a fixed and certain imposition on the peasant household's time.[2]

Produce and cash rents may or may not be fixed and certain. Consider the simple case where the farmer produces a single commodity, the rent to be paid at the end of the production period. There are various possibilities. First, the contract may specify that the farmer pay the landowner a stipulated money rent, irrespective of the harvested output and the realized price. Second, the contract may stipulate that the farmer deliver to the landowner a certain quantity of the commodity, irrespective of the harvested output. Third, the contract may stipulate that the farmer pay the landowner in cash the market value of a specified quantity of the commodity. The rental payment will depend on the market price of the commodity but not on the harvested output.[3] Fourth, the contract may stipulate that the farmer pay the landowner an agreed share of the output, say, one half of the output. Fifth, the contract may stipulate that the tenant pay the owner the market value of an agreed share of the output.[4]

Under the first and second arrangements, the rental payment is both fixed, in the sense of being *independent of the tenant's behaviour*, and certain. Under the third arrangement, the rental payment is fixed, provided at least that the tenant's behaviour does not affect market price. However, if there is uncertainty as to the market price at harvest time the precise level of money payment will be uncertain *ex ante*. Under the fourth and fifth arrangements, that is, the share-rental arrangements, the rental payments *will* depend on the behaviour of the tenant. In addition, to the extent that there is yield and price uncertainty the precise levels of rental payments will be uncertain.

We have already encountered the proposition that share-rental agreements impair the tenant's incentives. The essence of this argument can be demonstrated quite simply by employing our earlier analysis of a capitalist farmer who has perfect foresight and who seeks to maximize his terminal wealth. Assuming a perfect financial capital market, his terminal financial wealth is given by

$$W_{t+1} = (1-r) \cdot Z_{t+1} + (\bar{K}_t - K_t)(1 + \rho_t)$$

where r is the share of his total revenue which he is committed to pay the landowner as rent. The optimal level of capital advances must satisfy the condition

$$(1-r) \cdot \frac{dZ_{t+1}}{dK_t} = (1 + \rho_t)$$

Note that, provided the rental share is positive, the marginal revenue product of capital is strictly greater than the marginal opportunity cost of funds. The tenant chooses that outlay on inputs at which *his* share of the marginal revenue product equals the marginal opportunity cost of funds. With a share-rental agreement of this sort, the net benefits of the tenant's farming activities are not fully internalized. He would select a lower level of capital advances than if he were paying a fixed rent to his landlord.

Now it must be acknowledged that share-rental institutions are normally to be found in comparatively poor agrarian economies, for which wealth or profit maximization models may be inappropriate. An interesting question – one which seems to have been seldom, if ever, considered – is whether the disincentive proposition applies in the case of a utility-maximizing peasant household which relies entirely on its own labour and has no opportunities for part-time off-farm employment. In this case the disincentive proposition can no longer be maintained, at least on *a priori* theoretical grounds. A household committed to paying a prescribed share of its total revenue as rent may devote more, the same or less labour to cultivation than if it were allowed to farm the land free of charge. Likewise a marginal increase in the rental share could quite possibly lead to an increase in farm labour, the impact depending on the relative strengths of substitution and wealth effects. It also follows from this indeterminacy that it cannot be asserted that input and output levels will necessarily be lower under a share-rental tenancy than under a fixed-rent contract. The disincentive proposition could be reinstated if we assumed that the household undertook part-time off-farm employment or that it employed supplementary hired labour. But we have already cautioned against too much credence being attached to propositions based on these assumptions. The disincentive proposition also loses its *a priori* appeal once we allow for uncertainty. In the face of uncertainty with respect to prices or yields, cultivation may be more intensive under a share-rental agreement than it would be under a fixed-rental agreement. These remarks are not intended as an attempt to 'rehabilitate' share-tenancy as an 'efficient' form of tenure. They should not detract from the basic insight of Adam Smith that incentives may be impaired. They are directed rather at the tendency to suppose that propositions derived on the assumption of profit maximization are somehow of universal validity.

A similar tendency to claim generality for a proposition which has really only been demonstrated for the case of a profit-maximizer with perfect foresight is the common assertion that under a fixed-rent tenancy the precise level of cash rent does not affect tenant behaviour. Once the contract has been concluded, rent is in the nature of a fixed cost. Since, it is asserted, bygones are bygones, the level of rent will not influence production decisions. This proposition stands in stark contrast to the old adage: 'An increase in rent is as good as a dressing of manure.' There may well be more to that saying than to that particular theory. Under more realistic assumptions, the level of rent will, in general, matter. Thus – and this is surely what the adage has in mind – for a peasant household which relies entirely on its own labour an increase in rent would 'normally' induce the family to work harder.[5]

Rent levels may matter for another reason, one which is bound to be overlooked in an atemporal analysis. Given imperfect financial capital markets, the level of rental payments may well affect the *ability* of a tenant farmer to finance the production process. If rents are paid at the outset of the production period they constitute a deduction from the farmer's fund of working capital. If they are paid at the end of the period, there will be an impact in the next period. This was something which the Classical economists readily appreciated. According to Low (p. 15):

To take away the tenant's profit is to produce the hazard of trenching upon his capital, and to trench upon his capital is to lessen or cut off the source from which the landlord's rent must be derived ... It is rarely that a landlord profits by a system of rack-rents rigidly enforced. For a few years he may gain by exhausting the capital stock of his tenants, but almost always, sooner or later, the injurious effects become apparent, in the ceasing of improvements, the failure of tenants to fulfil their obligations, and the general deterioration of the property in condition and character.

Duration of leases and security of tenure

A tenant farmer will typically have a choice between various ways of employing his labour, his real capital and his financial capital. There are two particularly important characteristics of activities. First, different types of activities have different types of net benefit streams. Certain types of activities promise more or less immediate pay-offs. For example, the benefits from the purchase of fertilizer accrue relatively soon after its application. Other types of activities promise benefits spread over long periods of time. For example, the benefits from the purchase of a tractor or from improved drainage are likely to be spread over a number of years. This distinction is, of course, closely related to the distinction between circulating capital and fixed capital.

The second characteristic of activities is that they differ in the extent to which they are tied to a particular holding. Thus, if a tenant farmer were to invest in, say, a new tractor, he could easily take it with him if he moved to a new holding. Alternatively, if he purchased a certain type of building, legal considerations aside, he might be able to move it to another location but at a significant cost. If, however, he invested in drainage improvements these would be embodied in the land; to enjoy the benefits from the improvements would require continued occupation of the holding. These distinctions are, of course, closely related to the Physiocratic distinction between *avances primitives* and *avances foncières*.

We would expect that the sort of activities a tenant farmer would pursue would depend on the duration and security of his tenure. Consider a farmer on a short-term lease who has no desire to remain on the holding at the expiration of the lease. In the absence of any provisions for compensatory payments, the farmer will have no interest in the terminal state of the property. He will be interested solely in his own revenue. We would expect him to concentrate on types of activities which promise benefits in the relatively near future and on types of activities the benefits from which would not require the continued occupation of his present holding. He would have no incentive to undertake improvements to the property, since all or most of the benefits would accrue to the landowner. Indeed, he may well have an incentive to behave in ways which would lead to exhaustion of the soil.

If a tenant on a short-term lease hopes to renew the lease at the end of the period, he does have an interest in the state of the property at the end of the current lease. It might seem that the tenant has an obvious interest in the holding being in a good state at the end of the term. The better the state of the land the greater the prospective profitability of farming the land in the future. Moreover, he may expect that taking care of the land will enhance his chances of securing a renewal of the lease. However, a tenant who does undertake improvements to his landlord's property at his own expense runs a risk. Such improvements would increase the open-market rental value of the property. He might end up paying twice. He might not only bear the costs of the improvement but also suffer higher rents in consequence. If the burden of the costs of the improvement were such that he was unable to pay higher rents – or if he simply refused to do so – he might face eviction. A system whereby tenant improvement might lead to increases in rent would have a disincentive effect similar to share rents and tithes. Walter Blith wrote in 1649:

If a tenant be at ever so great pains or costs for improving of his land, he doth thereby but occasion a great rack upon himself, or else invest his landlord with his cost and labour gratis, or at best lies at his landlord's mercy for requital, which occasions a neglect of good husbandry to his own, the land, the landlord and the kingdom's suffering.[6]

That some landlords were unscrupulous enough to exploit improvements undertaken at the expense of their tenants accounts for the old warning:

> He that havocs may sit,
> he that improves must flit.

Clearly much depends on the tenant's perception of his own security of tenure and of the integrity of his landlord. Even without legal security of tenure, he may feel he has a certain *de facto* security. This may be derived from a confidence in his own ability as a tenant farmer or from a reliance on his relationship with his landlord. On this basis, Mingay (p. 170) has argued that eighteenth- and nineteenth-century commentators exaggerated the benefits from leases:

The main ground on which contemporary agricultural experts joined in advocating leases was that no improvements could be expected from farmers who lacked security of tenure. In this they seemed to overlook the evidence, even in their own works, that the satisfactory tenants of reputable proprietors enjoyed in practice great security of tenure, although it may be that they were only on annual tenancies. Such farmers expected to be undisturbed for life, and frequently passed on their farms to sons, daughters and widows, and were not averse to making improvements at their own expense.

However, most of the 'contemporary agricultural experts' did appreciate this possibility. Certainly Low was familiar with this sort of argument. But he was not impressed. Low's admirable observations are worth citing at some length:

The only fitting security for a man who has capital to employ in the cultivation and improvement of land, is a written covenant, subsisting for a definite and adequate period. Tenancy at will, it must be apparent, so much extended over the richest parts of England, is in no degree an adequate substitute for the lease, insuring to the tenant his right of possession for a determined period. Habit, indeed, may reconcile the tenantry of a country to such a species of tenure, and a kind of confidence may arise that a tenant will not be capriciously dispossessed, nor an unfair advantage be taken of his expenditure; but this confidence, however great, is not to be compared, as the means of inducing men to expend capital on land, with that sense of security and independence which is the soul of industry and exertion. It is impossible to divest the tenant at will of the knowledge, that every improvement which he makes upon his farm gives it a higher value to another, and adds to the means of raising the rent against himself. He may have all confidence in the honour of a landlord who is known to him, but what can he know of the feelings of those who, in the course of nature may inherit the property in which he has invested his capital and earnings; of creditors and legal managers, or even of ordinary agents, on whom in fact he is more directly dependent than upon the landlord himself? All the confidence, therefore, which this species of tenancy can inspire, can never afford that security which a man of sense and prudence will require, in order that he may lay out his acquired funds largely in the hope of a distant return (pp. 9–10).

It should be emphasized that, even if leases for a fixed term of years, say twenty-one years, were universal, this would not mean that at any point in time all tenant farmers would be operating with such a long-term planning horizon. Those who were just beginning their tenancies would have every reason to adopt a long-term outlook. However, some tenants would be nearing the expiration of their term. To the extent that they did not anticipate renewal of their leases, they would have little incentive to undertake permanent improvements. Indeed, they would have a definite incentive to deplete the land. In the past, English landlords employed a variety of devices to protect their properties from abuse. One method was the adoption of leases of twenty-one years certain, with an additional seven year period at the option of the landlord. Under this arrangement, if the tenant exhausted the fertility of the land during the normal period of tenure, he could be forced to stay on and suffer the consequences himself.

A device which was once common-place in England was to

incorporate into the contract of tenancy restrictive covenants which limited the set of legally feasible courses of action available to the tenant. Thus the contract of tenancy might prevent the tenant from ploughing up meadow land or removing manure from the land. The contract might even dictate the cropping pattern the tenant should follow. On long leases the restrictions often applied to the last few years of the term of the lease. Many arguments have been advanced both in favour and against the use of restrictive covenants. On balance, the case against is more persuasive. Particularly at times of rapid development of new techniques, such restrictions prevented tenant farmers from responding appropriately to changing circumstances. To abandon the use of restrictive covenants does not necessarily leave the way open for unscrupulous tenants to deplete the soil. The objective of such covenants can be achieved in another manner: by providing for compensatory payments at the termination of the leasehold.

Compensatory payments

A tenant farmer contemplating some long-term improvement to his holding might enjoy more or less complete security of tenure. He might be confident that his rental payments would not be increased as a result of the improvement. And yet he may still not have an adequate incentive to undertake that improvement, notwithstanding that the improvement might, in some sense, be a beneficial one. The reason is that the improvement might promise benefits after the time he expects to have quit the holding. The lifetime of the improvement may exceed the expected duration of his tenancy. The older a tenant, the greater the variety of activities for which this is likely to be true. Security of tenure is not itself sufficient to guarantee that tenant farmers will reap the full benefits of their investment activities.

A method whereby the costs and benefits of a tenant's activities can be internalized is to provide for compensatory payments at the termination of the tenancy. Specifically, if the tenant's activities have an adverse impact on the property he would be obliged to compensate the landowner. If the tenant improves the property he would be entitled to compensation for any unexhausted improvements. The basis for compensation would be the difference between the market value of the property as it stands at the termination of the tenancy and what its market value would have been at that time if the tenant's activities had not affected the state of the property.

This can be illustrated for the case of a capitalist tenant farmer, with perfect foresight, who seeks to maximize his terminal wealth. The duration of his tenancy coincides with the production period. Assuming a perfect financial capital market, his terminal financial wealth is given by

$$W_{t+1} = Z_{t+1} + (\bar{K}_t - K_t)(1 + \rho_t) + (V_{t+1} - \bar{V}_{t+1}) - \bar{R}_{t+1}$$

where V_{t+1} is the terminal market value of the property, $\bar{V}_{t+1}$ is what the market value would be if his activities did not affect the state of the property and $\bar{R}_{t+1}$ is a fixed cash rent to be paid at the end of the period. As for the owner-occupier, terminal wealth maximization would require that the marginal rate of transformation between revenue and property value equal one. Under this arrangement the tenant would bear the full costs and reap the full benefits of his activities. In principle at least, the landlord would be unaffected.

III Landlord behaviour

Certain activities may be obligatory for a landlord. The contract of tenancy, or statutory legislation, may impose an obligation on the landlord to undertake certain specified acts of repair, maintenance or replacement. What we will now consider briefly is whether the landlord will undertake non-obligatory improvements to his property. We will consider both the nature of inducements to undertake improvements and factors which may affect his ability to undertake improvements.

Investment incentives

Consider a landowner contemplating undertaking some investment project which would enhance the productive potential of his land. If the landowner is solely motivated by pecuniary considerations, he will compare the anticipated benefits from the investment with the associated costs. Assuming perfect foresight and a perfect financial capital market, he will undertake the project if the appropriately discounted benefits to him exceed the appropriately discounted costs.

If he were an owner-occupier he would enjoy the benefits of the investment directly through an increased net income from farming. However, as a landlord, any economic benefits which accrue to him – assuming he continues to retain ownership – will come indirectly in the form of higher rental payments. A crucial consideration from the landlord's point of view is whether there is a sitting tenant and, if so, what are the terms of the tenancy arrangement. If there is no sitting tenant the landlord could secure for himself any enhancement in the rental value of the property attributable to the improvement on leasing the property. However, if there is a sitting tenant on a lease of fixed duration the landlord may be unable to secure an increase in rental payments until the expiration of the lease. He could, of course, bargain with the tenant for increased rent *prior* to undertaking the improvement. But he would not generally be able to complete the improvement and then automatically secure, on demand, an appropriate increase in rent. To this extent the incentive to undertake the improvement may be impaired: the benefits of the landlord's activities may not be fully internalized. This 'distortion' will be greater the longer the unexpired term of the lease. As a consequence of such a distortion the landowner may well delay implementing the improvement until the termination of the tenancy.

Ability to undertake improvements

It is worth noting that even if a landowner has every incentive to pursue a particular activity he may still not be able to implement it. The set of feasible activities open to a landlord may be restricted by legal considerations.

England provides a particularly important historical example. The complex land laws admit of different degrees of ownership. The 'owner' of a property might, in fact, only own a life-tenancy in the land. As a life tenant, his powers were restricted by the common law. For example, he was unable to cut down timber or plough up ancient meadow land. His powers to mortgage the property were curtailed. Moreover, the life tenant had extremely limited powers of alienation: he could only sell to another person an interest in the land which would terminate on his own death.

These restrictions on the powers of a life tenant were based on the recognition that the successor's interests in the property could be jeopardized by the selfish actions of the present occupier. A life tenant who was interested solely in the time profile of his own consumption expenditure might well have an incentive to behave in ways which would deplete the value of the property. The costs and benefits of his actions were not internalized.

The large landowning families evolved a process of 'settlements', whereby the present incumbent was only a life tenant and not the full owner of the family estate.[7] They sought to prevent the present incumbent from destroying the family heritage. By this process land was tied up in families for generation after generation. The consequence of this process was that life tenants often found themselves in possession of impoverished estates, frequently burdened with provisions for various relatives, and with very limited rights to decide how to use the land. Judicious estate management was frequently impossible. They were often unable to undertake improvements or even to maintain their properties in a reasonable state. Legislation during the late nineteenth and early twentieth centuries sought to mitigate the harmful effects of settlements by giving the life tenant as much power as possible to sell, lease, mortgage or otherwise deal with the property, subject to the interests of others entitled under the settlement being protected. For example, suppose the tenant for life wished to sell part of the land. The purchaser would deposit the money either with trustees or in court. This money would then be used for the benefit of the life tenant and the other persons entitled under the settlement.

It is also worth noting that, in the absence of a perfect financial capital market, the availability of funds will determine the set of financially feasible investment projects. There may be a further link between rents and improvements. One link, as we have argued, is that the anticipation of future increases in net rental payments provides the basic incentive for improvements. Another link is that the levels of past and present net rental payments may affect the landlord's ability to finance improvements. This latter link has been particularly prominent in the arguments of defenders of agricultural landlords. They have perhaps exaggerated its significance. Of greater importance is probably the relationship between improvements and property values. Not only are improvements undertaken in the expectation that they will increase the value of the property. In addition the market value of a property will typically exert a very significant influence on the ease with which the owner can borrow money to finance long-term improvements.

IV Tenancy in England: the Agricultural Holdings Acts

In eighteenth-century England, various types of tenancy coexisted. Many tenants farmed under leases for fixed terms. Terms of seven years, fourteen years and twenty-one years were common. Other farmers were tenants-at-will. A tenant-at-will was someone who occupied land as long as both he and his landlord wished it. A tenant-at-will could quit whenever he wished to. More importantly, his landlord could eject him whenever he wished to; the tenant had only a reasonable time to leave. Another arrangement – one which had increased considerably in popularity since its appearance in the sixteenth century – was the 'tenancy from year to year'. Such a tenancy, by agreement between the parties, continued from year to year until it was terminated in the appropriate manner by either party. Depending on the date at which a notice to terminate the tenancy was served, it could be anywhere between six and eighteen months before either party could effectively terminate the arrangement against the will of the other.

The rights and obligations of landlord and tenant during the term of a tenancy were frequently stipulated in detail in the contract of tenancy. Leases might specify the amount and the date of rent payments; the undertaking of the tenant not to sublet or assign his interest to some third party without the written permission of the landlord; the repairs which were the responsibility of the landlord; the taxes which the landlord undertook to pay; the taxes which the tenant undertook to pay; the right of the landlord and his friends to enter the premises for the purposes of sport; the obligation of the tenant not to sell manure off the farm and so on. A notable feature of leases, both for tenancies from year to year and for tenancies for fixed terms of years, was that they frequently restricted the husbandry activities of the tenant farmer, perhaps even obliging him to follow specific types of rotation.

Leases frequently specified the rights and obligations of landlords and tenants at the termination of tenancies. Contracts of tenancy often detailed what outgoing tenants could and could not take with them on quitting their properties. If outgoing tenants were prohibited from removing certain things, such as manure and straw, the leases might indicate whether they were entitled to compensation and, if so, how the sum was to be calculated. Similarly, leases might specify whether or not outgoing tenants were entitled to compensation for permanent improvements embodied in the land and, if so, how the sum was to be calculated.

A tenant without such provisions in his lease could expect little from the common law. Whereas a landlord enjoyed a common law right to compensation if the tenant's activities led to a deterioration in the state of the property, a tenant had no general common law right to compensation if he improved the property. The basic maxim of ownership was *quicquid plantatur solo, solo cedit* – whatever is planted in or annexed to the land belongs with the land. A tenant without provisions for compensation in his lease *might* still be entitled to compensation according to 'customs of the country'. These were certain practices which evolved over generations in particular areas and which became so embedded that they came to have the force of law. Although they were described as customs of the country – custom being something 'to which the memory of man runneth not to the contrary' – they were, in fact, localized. Two of the more famous customs were the Evesham custom and the North Lincolnshire custom. Under the Evesham custom, the outgoing tenant would himself find an incoming tenant who would be willing to compensate him for all his improvements, including the fruit trees he had planted. Provided that the landlord approved the new tenant, the entire transaction was between outgoing and incoming tenants. Under the North Lincolnshire custom, tenants might get compensation for improvements such as draining, marling, liming and chalking the land. The amount of compensation was assessed on the basis of the initial cost of the improvement, its expected life and the number of years since the work was completed. These local customs did *not* override freedom of contract. They were implied into an arrangement between landlord and tenant only if they were not explicitly excluded by the contract of tenancy and if the contract was 'entirely silent as to the terms of quitting'.

A common conception of the traditional English landlord–tenant system was that it entailed a partnership involving well-defined roles. Tenants were supposed to provide working capital, livestock and durable capital items such as machinery. Landlords were supposed to undertake investments embodied in the land, such as drainage, and to construct and maintain fixed capital in the form of buildings. Writing in 1893, Shaw Lefèvre (p. 4) described the system:

The complete separation of the three classes of landowners, farm tenants, and labourers, has become the distinctive characteristic of the English rural system; differing in this respect from more or less every other country in the world. Under this system the landowners supply the land and the capital required for all permanent improvements, for draining and fencing it, for planting, for the erection of houses and buildings of all kinds necessary for the farm operations, and for the labourers' cottages. The tenants have no permanent interest in the land; they hire their farms generally on yearly tenancies, not under leases for years; they expend nothing on permanent improvements; they supply only such capital as is necessary for the ordinary cultivation of the land, for the growing of crops and for manure, for stocking it with cattle and sheep, and for supplying farm horses and implements. Their capital can be transferred to other farms, except so much as is sunk in the growing crops and in unexhausted manures. The labourers, on their part, supply only their labour. They have no permanent interest in the land.

The distinction between roles was, in fact, often blurred, practices differing from estate to estate. Indeed, it was only really during the depression after 1815 that the distinction became clearly marked between the responsibilities of landowners and tenants. As a result of the chronic depression tenants were left with little capital. They had developed a profound distrust of long leases and yet, in the absence of security of tenure, they were unwilling to undertake permanent improvements. Landlords were obliged to provide funds for investment. They often did so in lieu of rent reductions.

By the latter part of the nineteenth century, it had become clear that many landlords could not perform their tasks of improving and maintaining the land and fixed equipment, while many of those who could would not. Many landowners were restricted by settlements. Many were only interested in the social prestige and political influence conferred by landownership anyway. They preferred docile tenants. This inability or unwillingness of landlords to fulfil their customary role led to the Agricultural Holdings Legislation. The burden of long-term improvements could conceivably have been shifted to tenant farmers by a process of freedom of contract without the necessity for statutory intervention. But this would have involved considerable negotiation, contracting and enforcement costs. Moreover, it might have been a long drawn-out process, given the apparent apathy of many landowners.

The first statutory measure was the Agricultural Holdings Act of 1875. This Act entitled tenants to compensation for unexhausted improvements, permitted tenants to remove certain fixtures and provided for one year's notice to quit yearly tenancies instead of six months. The Act had one fatal defect. Landlords could contract out of its provisions. And virtually every landlord did, including the person who had been responsible for drafting the provisions of the Act! The Agricultural Holdings Act of 1883 remedied this defect. It invalidated contracting out by the landlord unless the lease gave the tenant terms at least as favourable as the statutory provisions. This was the first of a series of Acts which have virtually eliminated freedom of contract.

The present legislation is based on the Agricultural Holdings Act of 1948, subject to a number of later modifications, notably in the Agriculture Act of 1958. The salient features of this legislation will be described briefly. Most agricultural tenancies are deemed to be or become tenancies from year to year. A tenant enjoys considerable security. *Provided that the tenant understands his rights*, a landlord can only eject a tenant against his will under certain specified circumstances. Examples of such circumstances are where the tenant has been previously certified as guilty of bad husbandry; where the tenant has become bankrupt; where the land is required for a non-agricultural purpose for which planning permission has been granted or is not required. In these cases the notice to quit is automatically effective. In other cases – for example, if the landlord claims that termination of the tenancy is in the interests of the good husbandry of the holding itself or of the sound management of the estate as a whole – he must convince the Agricultural Land Tribunal, to whom disputes are referred. Even if the case falls within one of the latter categories, the Tribunal must withhold consent if, in the light of all the circumstances, it appears that 'a fair and reasonable landlord would not insist on possession'. Until recently an English landowner could only be sure of regaining vacant possession on the death of the tenant. But even this guarantee has disappeared. New legislation has given the sons of tenant farmers a right to inherit tenancies provided that certain stipulated conditions are satisfied.

Landlord and tenant re-negotiate the rent as they see fit. In the event of a dispute, either party can refer the matter to arbitration. The basis for 'rent properly payable' is the rent at which the holding might reasonably be expected to let in the open market. The arbitrator is expressly charged with disregarding any increase in rental value attributable to the adoption by the tenant of a particularly beneficial system of farming; any increase attributable to any improvements undertaken at the tenant's expense and not required by the contract of tenancy; and any decrease in rental value due to dilapidations or damage resulting from the activities of the tenant. Rents may, of course, be increased as a result of improvements undertaken at the landlord's expense.

The legislation provides for various compensatory payments at the termination of the tenancy. The landlord is entitled to compensation for any deterioration or damage to his property attributable to the tenant's activities. Compensation for specific damage is based on the cost of rectification. Compensation for any general deterioration is based on the decrease in the value of the holding.

The tenant may be entitled to compensation for disturbance if he leaves the holding as a result of a notice to quit served by his landlord. This compensation is designed to cover the cost of selling or removing implements, fixtures, farm produce and farm stock. The tenant may be entitled to compensation for 'high farming' if he has enhanced the value of the holding by a particularly beneficial system of farming. The amount of compensation is equal to the increase in the value of the holding. The tenant may also be entitled to compensation for specific unexhausted improvements.[8]

The provisions for compensation for unexhausted improvements are complex. For various traditional 'tenant-right' matters, such as seed already sown, compensation is based on their value to the incoming tenant. For various short-term or medium-term improvements – such as chalking and liming land – the tenant is entitled to compensation without his having obtained the prior consent of his landlord to their execution. Compensation is based on their value to an incoming tenant. For certain long-term improvements – such as the planting of orchards – the prior consent of the landlord to their execution is necessary. This category comprises somewhat unusual activities which might fundamentally alter the nature of the holding. For certain other types of improvements – such as the erection of buildings or installation of drainage – if the landlord refuses to consent, the tenant may appeal to the Agricultural

Land Tribunal. If the Tribunal approves the improvement, the landlord himself may execute the improvement. If he does not do so, the tenant may go ahead. The amount of compensation for long-term improvements is the increase in the value of the holding attributable to the improvement.

This legislation constitutes a classic attempt to internalize the costs and benefits of activities. The general principle is that the landlord should not be affected by the activities of his tenant. The use of the value of the holding as the basis for calculating compensation for unexhausted long-term improvements accords with this principle. One possible departure from this principle concerns the assessment of compensation for traditional tenant-right matters and for short- and medium-term improvements on the basis of value to incoming tenants. As Pigou pointed out in his *Economics of Welfare*, the landlord may be affected if the land is unlet for a time at the interchange of tenants. In practice, however, the landlord is usually unaffected in so far as the incoming tenant frequently negotiates with and pays the outgoing tenant directly. Indeed, it may be that, in practice, the landlord is more likely to be affected in the case of long-term improvements. The legislation can only provide guidelines for assessors and arbitrators. However expert they may be, valuers must rely on personal judgments. Moreover, they are not only valuing a property in its actual state. They are also valuing it in some hypothetical state. We would not expect that the spirit of the law would always be implemented with total precision.

6

Rental market: fixed rent tenancies

We heartily pray thee to send thy holy spirit into the hearts of them that possess the grounds, pastures and dwelling-places of the earth, that they remembering themselves to be thy tenants, may not rack and stretch out the rents of their houses and lands, nor yet take unreasonable fines and incomes, after the manner of covetous worldlings ... but so behave themselves in letting out their tenements, lands and pastures, that after this life they may be received into everlasting dwelling places. A Prayer for Landlords from *A Book of Private Prayer set forth by Order of King Edward VI. 1553.*[1]

I Introduction

This chapter considers the operation of the market for the leasing of agricultural land. We are primarily concerned with the factors which determine whether operating units are farmed by their owners or leased to tenant farmers and, if they are leased, what the terms of the tenancy contracts will be. In this chapter we will confine our attention to tenancy contracts involving fixed cash rental payments. We will defer the analysis of share rent tenancies until the next chapter.

The tenancy market and the ownership market are inevitably closely interrelated. We will explore this connection in Chapter 8. For the moment we will regard the ownership of land as predetermined and suppose that all owners of land are content to remain so. The ownership structure is therefore predetermined and invariant. In addition, for simplicity, we will assume that the operating structure is also predetermined and invariant. The simplest case is where the ownership and operating structures coincide. Transactions in the rental market determine for each unit whether it will be farmed by its owner or leased to a tenant.[2] In contrast to the conventional treatment of the rental market for agricultural land, transactions in our analysis relate to indivisible units and *not* to perfectly divisible acres of land.

In the next section we develop a simple model, based on the familiar reservation price and limit price framework, designed to indicate how, in a situation where all units are initially vacant, the decisions of landowners and prospective tenants interact to determine who farms the units and, where they are farmed by tenants, what rents they pay to their landlords. The treatment of the operation of the rental market is based on the Edgeworth process of contracting and recontracting.[3] Initially we employ a patently unrealistic assumption in order to develop the analysis in a manageable form. This is the assumption that all operating units are identical in all relevant respects. Section III considers how the analysis might be extended to more than one type of operating unit and discusses some implications of heterogeneity. Section IV examines the impact of security of tenure on the operation of the rental market and considers ways in which security of tenure and flexibility of rents can be reconciled. Finally, Section V considers some implications of market power and of market imperfections and draws attention to the possible significance of non-economic considerations.

II A simple model of the rental market

In this section we will assume that operating units are identical in all *relevant* respects; that is, any prospective tenant farmer is indifferent between operating units at the same rent. This assumption enables us to conduct the analysis in terms of a representative unit.

Transactions in the market involve bilateral contracts whereby the landowner transfers to a tenant the right to use a unit for a stipulated period of time in return for an agreed rental payment to be paid by the tenant to the landowner at some specified point in time. Thus leaseholds are assumed to be of fixed and certain duration, so that they are automatically terminated at the end of the period. The two parties might subsequently agree to enter into a new arrangement for the ensuing period but there would be no obligation on either party to do so. We will assume that the duration of leaseholds is a year and that rents are paid at the end of the year. We will also assume that farming will not affect the characteristics of the land.

The outcome of the interaction between landowners and prospective tenant farmers will clearly depend on what rents owners are prepared to accept and what rents prospective tenants are prepared to pay.[4] We will assume that each owner has some 'reservation rent', defined as the minimum rent he is prepared to accept for leasing his unit, and that each prospective tenant farmer has some 'limit rent', defined as the maximum rent he would be prepared to pay for a representative operating unit. We must now consider the determinants of reservation rents and limit rents. It is convenient to consider limit rents first.

The limit rents of prospective tenant farmers

The limit rent of a prospective tenant farmer is that level of rent which would result in the same level of welfare as he would enjoy if he did not enter into a tenancy agreement for the period in question. Let $\bar{U}$ represent his maximum utility if he does not enter into a tenancy contract. This level of utility will depend on the resources he owns and on the precise nature of the feasible choices with respect to the use or disposal of those resources if he does not enter into a tenancy contract. Let $U^I(R)$ represent maximum utility if he does enter into a tenancy contract as an indirect function of the level of rent. His limit rent, R^I, is then the level of rent such that

$$U^I(R^I) = \bar{U}$$

Since the indirect utility function will be strictly decreasing in the level of rent, his limit rent will be lower the higher is $\bar{U}$.

Consider a peasant whose sole asset is his labour. His limit rent will depend on the wages which that labour could command in the best available alternative occupation. This might involve becoming a hired farm worker or working outside agriculture. In order to illustrate this, we can employ the analysis developed in Chapter 4 for a peasant household. For simplicity, we will assume that the peasant will spend all his initial financial wealth on consumption; that the best alternative to farming is employment in some particular occupation at a given wage rate, $\bar{w}_{t+1}$, where wages would be received at the end of the period; and that he is indifferent between the two types of work *per se*. In Figure 6.1, OB, with a slope equal to that wage rate, represents the level of terminal financial wealth corresponding to each level of labour if he were to follow that employment. In this event, he would choose a level of labour of L_t^* with an associated terminal financial wealth of W_{t+1}^*. He would thus be on indifference curve, $\bar{I}$.

In Figure 6.1, OX represents the relationship between terminal financial wealth and the level of his labour if he were to take on an operating unit at a zero rent. If he were able to obtain the farm at a zero rent he would choose to do so in this case, since he would be able to reach an indifference curve preferred to $\bar{I}$. In order to determine his limit rent, we simply vertically displace the wealth–labour curve until it is just tangent to $\bar{I}$. At the wealth–labour curve YY', he would be just as well off as a tenant working $\tilde{L}_t$ and receiving $\tilde{W}_{t+1}$ as he would be if he were to pursue the alternative employment. His limit rent is given by the distance OY. Given his utility function, his limit rent clearly depends on the pro-

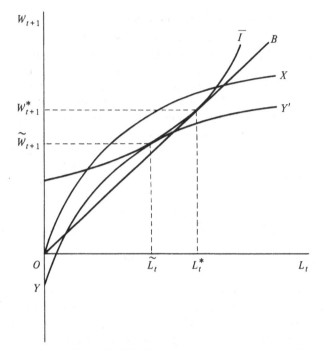

Figure 6.1. The limit rent of a prospective peasant farmer

ductivity of his labour in farming relative to what it would earn outside farming.[5] *Ceteris paribus*, the higher the relevant off-farm wage rate the lower will be his limit rent.

This simple illustration should not detract from the fact that limit rents for prospective peasant farmers will depend on a variety of complex inter-related factors. Thus resources other than labour will be important. If the peasant owns animals or farm machinery then his limit rent will depend on the terms on which he can sell or lease them if he does not enter into a tenancy contract. If he does not own animals, machinery or other resources essential to farming, his limit rent will depend on his access to them if he does become a tenant. If the markets for these resources are imperfect – so that acquisition prices exceed salvage prices – the peasant's initial ownership of these resources will affect his limit rent. Similarly access to credit will be important if inputs have to be paid for in advance of their use or if the peasant is obliged to borrow to finance current consumption. Moreover, tenant farming will typically involve significant uncertainty, whereas wage labour may involve little or no uncertainty. In this case his limit rent will depend on his attitude to uncertainty: the more averse he is to risk the lower his limit rent.

Furthermore, his limit rent will depend on the nature of living accommodation on the farm and on the cost of obtaining accommodation if he takes up some other form of employment.

It should be emphasized that even though the tenancy contract is assumed to relate to a relatively short period of time a prospective tenant will typically need to determine his limit rent in the light of long-term considerations. The decision to transfer from one occupation to another will not be taken lightly. There are costs entailed in switching occupations. These costs may be particularly significant if it entails moving between rural and urban areas. Moreover the system of wage payments is often such that wage rates increase as skills are acquired. For these reasons, someone deciding whether to leave farming for some other type of work will need to take into account long-term prospects in both occupations.

Consider now the limit rent of a prospective capitalist tenant farmer. Assuming certainty, his limit rent would be such as to just leave him with what he regards as the minimum acceptable total profit from farming. Assuming a perfect market for financial capital, this minimum profit level could be hypothesized to be the interest he would forgo on the funds he would employ as capital advances if he did become a tenant farmer. In other words, his limit rent would be the level of rent at which excess profit would be zero. Note that his limit rent in these circumstances does *not* depend on his initial own capital fund. This contrasts with the case of an imperfect financial capital market where, in general, his limit rent would depend on his initial capital fund. If we now admit uncertainty his attitude to risk will be relevant. If he is risk averse he will require a positive expected excess profit from farming if he is to enter into a rental contract. Finally he may require additional recompense to the extent that managing the farm and supervising hired workers entail some effort.

It should be clear from this discussion that different prospective tenants are likely to have different limit rents. There are many reasons why this should be so. Even within the restrictive analysis of Figure 6.1 there are three reasons. First, prospective tenants are likely to have different preferences as between wealth and leisure. Second, they are likely to have different alternative employment opportunities. Third, for any level of rent the wealth–labour relationship for any particular prospective tenant is likely to depend on factors such as his experience of farming. It is unlikely that, even with the same land and fixed equipment, the wealth–labour relationship for any level of rent would be the same for each prospective tenant. Once we leave the confines of that analysis the list of additional reasons why limit rents might differ is virtually endless.

The reservation rents of landowners

When we turn to the reservation rents of landowners, we are immediately confronted by the difficulty that agricultural landowners are a notoriously heterogeneous collection of individuals and institutions. To suppose that each landowner must decide whether to farm the land himself or whether to lease it to a tenant farmer conceals a variety of different types of effective choice. For one landowner, the effective choice may be between farming his land himself, on the one hand, and leasing his land and taking up non-farm employment, on the other. For another landowner, the relevant choice may be between continuing to farm his land, on the one hand, and leasing it and retiring, on the other. For another landowner – such as an absentee or institutional landowner – the effective choice may be between leasing land and employing a farm manager.

We will not consider all the possible variations. We will simply consider, as an example, the choice between leasing and installing a farm manager. If he employs a farm manager, the owner receives a residual income, that is, revenue less costs, including the salary of the manager, less any taxes. If this net income is subjectively certain then his re-servation rent might be hypothesized to be the level of rent which would yield an equivalent net income. In the more likely event that, as a residual claimant, his net income with a farm manager is uncertain, his reservation rent will be that level of rent which yields a utility of terminal wealth equal to the expected utility of terminal wealth under a farm manager. In the absence of taxation of rent, if the owner is risk averse, his reservation rent will be less than his expected net income from farming. The more averse he is to risk, the lower his reservation rent will be. Moreover, the lower his autonomous income from other sources – the less independently wealthy he is – the lower his reservation rent is likely to be.[6] Certainly a major attraction of leasing is that it offers the prospect of a more or less certain income in contrast to the uncertainty involved in farming. Leasing will be particularly attractive if it is difficult to find a reliable and competent farm manager.

Rental contracts

We will now consider the interaction between landowners and prospective tenant farmers in terms of a process of contracting and recontracting. The participants enter into contracts. These contracts are not binding. A subset of participants may recontract without the consent of others. They will do so whenever all members of the subset can benefit thereby. A 'final settlement' is a set of contracts between the participants such that it is impossible for any coalition to form which would lead to gains for all its members. The collection of final settlements is described as the 'core'.

We will assume initially that the costs of entering into contracts are zero. Moreover, we will initially consider a limited number of participants and subsequently generalize to the case of a large number of participants. Consider, therefore, the simplest case where there is just one landowner and one prospective tenant farmer. Let R^r represent the reservation rent of the landowner and R^l represent the limit rent of the prospective tenant. A necessary condition for there to be a basis for trade is clearly that R^l be at least as great as R^r. If R^l is strictly greater than R^r, a tenancy contract will be entered into. However, the precise level of the contract rent, R^*, is indeterminate. All we can say is that it will lie in the range

$$R^r \leqq R^* \leqq R^l$$

Its precise level within that range will depend on the relative bargaining strengths of the two parties.[7] If, by coincidence, the limit rent of the prospective tenant equals the owner's reservation rent, then, if the two parties do enter into a tenancy agreement, the contract rent is clearly determinate: the contract rent will equal R^r and R^l. However, in this case there is another form of indeterminacy: since both parties are indifferent as to whether or not a contract at that rent is agreed, whether the unit will be leased or not is indeterminate.

Consider now the case of one owner of a unit and two prospective tenant farmers. Let R^r be the owner's reservation rent, R_a^l the limit rent of prospective tenant A and R_b^l the limit rent of prospective tenant B. Suppose that $R_a^l > R_b^l > R^r$. In this case the unit will be leased to A. Any preliminary contract involving B would be 'blocked' by a recontract between A and the owner. Whatever the rent in such a preliminary contract, A could improve on it. However, the presence of B is significant since it narrows the range within which the final contract rent can lie. Specifically the final contract rent cannot be less than B's limit rent. If A entered into an initial contract with the owner at a rent below R_b^l, this would be blocked by a recontract between B and the owner. Moreover, it can be shown that it is impossible for A and B to collude in such a way as to allow one of them to obtain the unit at a rent below R_b^l. Consequently the core consists of settlements which involve A leasing the unit at a contract rent within the range

$$R_b^l \leqq R^* \leqq R_a^l$$

Suppose now that $R_a^l = R_b^l > R^r$. In this case the unit will be leased to one of the prospective tenants at a contract rent equal to his limit rent. However, whether A or B will take on the unit is indeterminate.

Consider now the case of two landowners and two prospective tenants. Let R_x^r be the reservation rent of landowner X, R_y^r the reservation rent of landowner Y, R_a^l the limit rent of prospective tenant A and R_b^l the limit rent of prospective tenant B. Suppose $R_a^l > R_b^l > R_x^r > R_y^r$. In this case the important feature is that the final settlement will involve both units being leased at the *same* contract rent. Any arrangement involving different rents would be blocked by a recontract involving the owner whose preliminary contract involves the lower rent and the prospective tenant whose preliminary contract involves the higher rent. The core consists, therefore, of those settlements involving both units being leased at the same rent, the level of rent falling within the range

$$R_x^r \leqq R^* \leqq R_b^l$$

This case is illustrated in Figure 6.2. The step supply function is $SS^IS^{II}S^{III}S^{IV}$.

The step demand function is $DD^ID^{II}D^{III}D^{IV}$. The set of possible final contracts – the core – is given by the intersection of the supply and demand functions, that is, by $S^{III}D^{III}$. This stretch corresponds to both units being leased at a contract rent between the reservation rent of X and the limit rent of B.

Consider finally the case of m owners and n prospective tenants. Let R_i^r

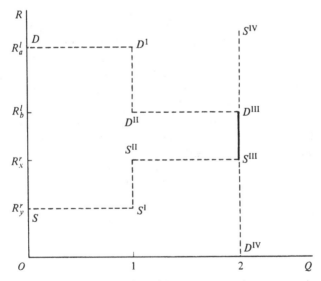

Figure 6.2. The rental market with two owners and two prospective tenants

be the reservation rent of the ith owner $(i = 1, 2, \ldots, m)$ and R^l_j be the limit rent of the jth prospective tenant $(j = 1, 2, \ldots, n)$. Without loss of generality, we can order owners and prospective tenants on the basis of their reservation rents and limit rents respectively:

$$R^r_1 \leqq R^r_2 \leqq \ldots \leqq R^r_m$$
$$R^l_1 \geqq R^l_2 \geqq \ldots \geqq R^l_n$$

We will assume that $R^l_1 > R^r_1$ so that there is a basis for trading. Any final settlement will necessarily involve the same rent for each unit leased. This level of rent must lie in a range set by the limit rents of the 'marginal' prospective tenants and the reservation rents of the 'marginal' owners. Specifically if a final settlement involves k tenancy agreements the contract rent must lie within the range

$$\max \ (R^r_k, R^l_{k+1}) \leqq R^* \leqq \min \ (R^r_{k+1}, R^l_k).$$

As in the case of two owners and two prospective tenants, we could construct a step supply function by ordering owners in terms of their reservation rents and a step demand function by ordering prospective tenants in terms of their limit rents. The intersection of the two functions constitutes the core. By construction, equilibrium is necessarily stable. Notice, however, that indeterminacy of some sort is inevitable. This indeterminacy may relate to the contract rent, the number of transactions or the identities of the final farmers. This indeterminacy is attributable to the indivisibility of operating units. It does not disappear however large the number of participants. However, it may well become of less practical significance as the number of participants increases. Consequently, provided that we bear in mind this indeterminacy, it is convenient to represent this case graphically in terms of smooth demand and supply curves as in Figure 6.3. The market demand curve for units is represented by DD. The supply curve of operating units available for rent is given by $SS^I S^{II}$. The equilibrium level of market rent is R^e. The number of units which would be farmed under the landlord–tenant system is Q^e; the number which would be farmed under owner-occupancy is $(\bar{S} - Q^e)$.

Some observations and implications

The basic implication of the foregoing analysis is that the level of agricultural rents will depend on the relative profitability of agriculture. The more profitable farming is relative to other comparable occupations the higher the rents prospective tenant farmers are likely to be prepared to pay and the higher the rents landowners are likely to require to induce them to lease their land. The broad background influences on rent would

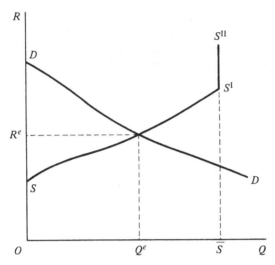

Figure 6.3. The rental market

thus be the sorts of factors which shape the relative profitability of farming – the stage of development, the rate of population growth, the rate of growth in *per capita* incomes, the nature of responses of demand for food at the farm gate to price and income changes and the rate of technological change.

The rental market will be closely related to other markets. In particular, there will be a close connection with the market for hired agricultural labour for at least two reasons. First, for prospective farmers who contemplate hiring workers the wage rate for agricultural labour will determine the profitability of farming. Second, for some prospective farmers the best alternative to farming may be to become hired farm workers. In both cases, the higher the wage rate of agricultural labour, the lower are likely to be the limit rents of prospective tenants and the reservation rents of landowners.

The level of agricultural rents may, of course, be influenced by government policies. Most developed countries pursue policies which involve market intervention designed to raise the prices received by farmers above their 'free market' levels or to reduce the price uncertainty confronting farmers. The methods employed include deficiency payments, support buying, import tariffs and import quotas. The typical effect of such policies is to increase agricultural rents. Consequently the usual beneficiaries are the owners of land, both owner-occupiers and landlords. Any benefits to tenant farmers are nullified provided that rents adjust relatively quickly to changing circumstances.

This familiar observation has prompted widespread criticism of government intervention in agriculture. It has been claimed that the usual justification for such policies, namely, that they benefit poorer farmers, is invalid. It is alleged that such policies benefit the better-off sections of the farming community but confer no real benefit on the poorer members. The post-war United Kingdom deficiency payment system has been criticized for another reason.[8] This criticism relates to the procedure for determining the levels of guaranteed prices. Specifically changes in guaranteed prices have traditionally been negotiated with industry representatives on the basis of changes in an index of farming costs, defined so as to include rents. Now it should be evident that, in the case of administered prices, rents are price-determined in the Smith–Ricardo sense and further that they are not really costs from the point of view of the agricultural sector as a whole. The absurdity of treating rents as costs is easy to see: an increase in guaranteed prices leads to increased rents, this leads to an increase in guaranteed prices, this leads to increased rents, and so on. It is not difficult to imagine what Smith and Ricardo would have made of such a procedure.

Proposals for the taxation of rent have received widespread support amongst economists over the years. It has often been suggested that a tax on rent would fall solely on landlords. In terms of the Ricardian analysis this proposition is correct. The implicit assumption of Classical economics that landowners would not consider farming themselves would imply a perfectly inelastic supply curve of units for rent. A tax on rent would have no effect on the rents paid by tenants; it would simply reduce the 'net' rents received by landlords. However, if the reservation rents of landowners differ and the limit rents of prospective tenants differ, the impact of a tax on rent will not be confined to landowners; tenant farmers will pay higher rents. The reason that tenants bear part of the burden is that the owners of land have the option of farming the land themselves. The imposition of the tax will induce some owners to withdraw their units from the market, thereby driving up market rent.[9]

A special case

It is worth briefly reconsidering the Malthus–Ricardo theory of rent in terms of the framework developed in this chapter. We will assume that landowners would never consider farming themselves, so that their reservation rents are zero, implying a perfectly inelastic supply of farms available for rent. The limit rents of prospective capitalist farmers will, as noted earlier, depend critically on whether or not there exist opportunities for borrowing and lending. Assuming a perfect financial capital market, a prospective tenant's limit rent will not depend on his 'wages fund'. His limit rent will be that level of rent at which his excess profit would be zero. Now, assuming that there are no differences in the revenue – capital advances relationships of different tenants, the limit rents of prospective tenant farmers will be the *same*, implying a perfectly elastic demand curve for farms. Thus each tenant farmer will actually pay his limit rent. His profit from farming will equal the interest forgone by employing his funds in farming. There will be no surplus. Each tenant farmer will earn the same *rate* of profit, though not necessarily the same total profit. This will be the Classical 'normal' rate of profit. Landowners will extract the 'surpluses' from intra-marginal applications of inputs.

III Heterogeneity of operating units

Extension of the analysis

So far we have assumed that all operating units are identical in all relevant respects. We must now recognize that operating units differ with respect to size, layout, fertility, location and the nature of permanent equipment. In order to indicate the modifications necessary to incorporate heterogeneity it is convenient to consider the simplest case where there are just two different types of operating unit. A prospective tenant is then faced with three mutually exclusive alternatives: he can rent a farm of the first type, rent a farm of the second type or seek off-farm employment. The maximum rent he would be prepared to pay for one particular type of unit will depend, in general, not only on the alternatives to farming but also on the rent at which he could obtain the other type of unit. In Figure 6.4, *ABC* represents the maximum rent he

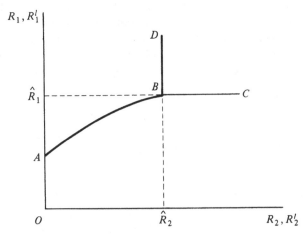

Figure 6.4. Limit rents of a prospective tenant farmer with two types of operating units

would be prepared to pay for the first type of unit for each level of rent for the second type of unit, given the alternatives to farming. Similarly, *ABD* represents the maximum rent he would be prepared to pay for the second type of unit for each level of rent for the first type of unit, given his off-farm opportunities. For rent combinations along *AB*, he is indifferent between the two types of unit.[10] For rent combinations exceeding $\hat{R}_1$ and $\hat{R}_2$ he would seek off-farm employment.

On this basis, for a given level of rent for one type of unit, we could derive the market demand curve for the other type of unit by ordering the limit rents of the prospective tenant farmers. In general, the markets would be closely interrelated on the demand sides. In addition, there may be a further type of connection between the two markets. For certain combinations of rent, an owner of one type of unit might decide to lease out his unit and become a tenant on one of the other type of unit. His reservation rent might therefore depend on the market rent for the other type of unit. Thus the market supply curve for one type of unit may depend on the market rent for the other.

Strictly, the market demand and supply curves will be step functions. However, they are represented as smooth in Figure 6.5 in the interests of simplicity. This figure depicts a situation of 'simultaneous equilibrium' in both markets. D_1D_1 represents the market demand for units to rent of the first type given that the market rent for the second type is R_2^e; $S_1S_1^I S_1^{II}$ represents the supply of units of the first type given that the market rent for the second type is R_2^e; and so on. For the *i*th type of unit, $(\bar{S}_i - Q_i^e)$ will be farmed by their owners, the rest being leased to tenant farmers, some of whom could conceivably be owners of the other type of unit.[11]

It should be recalled that the treatment of supply and demand curves as smooth conceals the problem of indeterminacy. Strictly, the indivisibility of units implies indeterminacy of some form, as in the case of

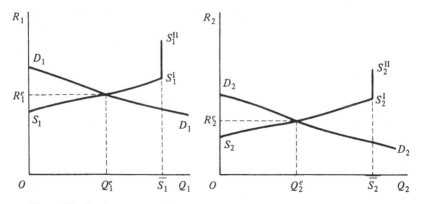

Figure 6.5. Simultaneous equilibrium in markets for two types of operating units

homogeneous units. If there are just two types of units and a large number of participants, this indeterminacy may be regarded as inconsequential. However, once we think in terms of extending the analysis to a large number of different types of units – the extreme case being where each unit is different – indeterminacy may become much more significant. Further, it becomes increasingly difficult to maintain the fiction of zero costs of contracting, perfect information and an absence of market power.

Some aspects of heterogeneity

Equilibrium rent differentials will clearly depend on differences in the physical characteristics of units, such as the properties of the soil, size, farm buildings, climatic conditions and location. However, in general, it will not be possible to rank different types of units in terms of 'fertility', in an economic sense, simply by studying these physical attributes. As Marshall (p. 133) observed: 'The term fertility has no meaning except with reference to the special circumstances of time and place.' Any such ranking is likely to depend on the prices of agricultural commodities, the wages of agricultural labour, costs of transportation and, perhaps above all, techniques of production.[12]

The possibility that changes in the relative prices of agricultural commodities might alter the relative attractiveness of different types of land is self-evident. However, even changes in absolute prices may do so. For example, as af Heurlin has observed, whereas at low agricultural prices poor quality accessible land may yield higher rents than high quality inaccessible land, the latter type of land may command higher rents than the former at higher agricultural prices.[13]

Technical developments are a particularly potent source of changes in rent differentials. New techniques will, of course, often involve investment embodied in the land, thus altering the physical characteristics of operating units. In this context it is worth recalling the familiar paradox: whereas an individual landowner may have an incentive to improve his property in the expectation of thereby increasing his rent, landowners *as a group* may suffer if sufficient numbers do so.

In our analysis we treated the markets for the two types of units as closely interrelated. To the extent that the primary difference between the two types of units was, say, one of size we envisaged prospective tenants as choosing which size of unit to rent. In this case, the presumption would be that the larger units would tend to end up being farmed by those with the greater assets or greater experience or greater zeal for farming. In many countries the differences in the sizes of units are fairly gradual. However, in some poorer countries there are readily identifiable polarizations between very large and very small units. The large units are farmed, either by their owners or by substantial tenants, on capitalist lines. The small units are farmed by peasant households. In this situation there may be relatively little inter-dependence between the two markets.

Under an extreme dualistic structure there is very limited scope for mobility of tenant farmers. However, where the gradations are less severe, intra-sector mobility of tenant farmers may be quite important. Over his working lifetime, a tenant farmer may move a number of times – he may perhaps start on a relatively small unit; once he has gained experience and acquired more tenant capital he may move to a larger and more challenging unit; as he nears retirement he may move to a small holding. The inducements for this sort of life-cycle are evident. However, against the benefits must be set the financial and psychological costs of moving. Indeed, these costs of moving *imply* a certain heterogeneity. In other words, costs of moving mean that a sitting tenant will be prepared to pay a higher rent to remain on his present holding than for some other operating unit which is otherwise indistinguishable with respect to such features as size, compactness, fertility and so on.

IV Security of tenure

Hitherto we have supposed that the leasehold arrangement between landlord and tenant lasted for a fixed and certain but relatively short period of time. The analysis would be most appropriate where the duration of leaseholds was a year and where there was some customary date of entry. We could think in terms of the market allocating operating units among prospective farmers at the customary date each year. In these circumstances there would be few institutional rigidities limiting the responsiveness of rents to changing economic conditions. Thus, if there was an underlying change in the relative profitability of agriculture *vis-à-vis* other pursuits, rents *could* respond accordingly. However, the actual response of rents might still be relatively sluggish. As we have seen, reservation and limit rents depend critically on the *expectations* of owners and prospective tenant farmers. These expectations may respond relatively slowly. It may take time to identify genuine underlying changes given the short-term fluctuations characteristic of agriculture.

Under a system of leaseholds of long duration at fixed rents the foregoing analysis would have to be modified accordingly. Thus prospective tenants would necessarily have to take a long-term view in determining what rents they would be prepared to commit themselves to paying each year. Similarly landowners would have to take a long-term view in deciding on their reservation rents. To the extent that expectations become less confident the further into the future the dates to which they relate the more important attitudes to risk would be. In this context expectations about future market rent levels may be important. Thus if a landowner expects the market rent of his type of property to increase, he may delay entering into a long-term contract at a fixed rent. A prospective tenant might also delay entering into a leasehold arangement if he expects market rent levels to fall. However, tenants will generally have less flexibility than landowners with respect to timing.

Under a system of leaseholds of long duration only a subset of units would fall vacant in any one year. Current market rents for vacant units might well diverge from the rents paid by sitting tenants for similar units. An obvious disadvantage of leaseholds of long duration at fixed rents is that they create a form of inflexibility. This inflexibility is the main reason why such an arrangement became unpopular with both tenants and landowners in England. Tenant farmers on long leases suffered considerably during the depression following the Napoleonic wars. Many had contracted to pay fixed rents on the basis of the abnormal wartime prosperity of agriculture. They were unable to meet these commitments in the ensuing depression. They were obliged to ask their landlords for help. Some landlords agreed reluctantly to permanent rent reductions. Others agreed to temporary rent abatements. But these reductions and abatements came too late for many farmers. Thereafter English farmers were extremely suspicious of long-term commitments. This suspicion was increasingly shared by landowners. They came to feel that the system entailed an unfair asymmetry: if there was an unanticipated depression they were obliged to reduce actual rents below nominal rents, whereas if there was an unanticipated boom – or if there was a general inflation – they had to wait until current leaseholds expired before they could secure rent increases. As a result of this general disenchantment with long leaseholds at fixed rents, they were superseded by tenancies from year to year.

The practice of granting rent abatements is by no means of historical interest only. It is quite a common phenomenon. In certain countries rent abatements are not confined to exceptional circumstances. Rather they are a normal response to the vagaries of agriculture. Sometimes they are symptomatic of an exploited tenantry. Nominal rents are geared to 'good' years, so that landowners forgo little or nothing in such years. The 'benevolent' rent abatements in 'bad' years have the effect of reducing tenants to a state of dependency on their landlords.

An important question is clearly whether security of tenure can be reconciled with flexibility of rents. Such an arrangement could result from freedom of contract between landlord and tenant. For example, both parties might agree on a formula which related rents to specified indicators of economic conditions in agriculture. In order not to impair the incentives of the tenant, rents would need to be independent of his behaviour. Furthermore the indicators would have to be readily identifiable so that once the contract was agreed its implementation would be mechanical. The difficulty is to find readily identifiable indicators on which a 'fair' rent could be based.

An obvious possibility would be to employ agricultural prices. The rental payment could be based on a stipulated bundle of agricultural commodities, converted into a money payment at ruling market prices. This arrangement was recommended by McCulloch as preferable to fixed rent tenancies. His main reservation was that this system would allow for price variability but not for yield variability. Rents might exceed 'fair' values in years when yields were low and prices high, and be less than fair values in years when yields were high and prices low. The problem is that even a system involving only prices might be complicated, particularly with mixed farming. An arrangement involving yields would inevitably be extremely complicated both to formulate and to implement.

The problem of reconciling security of tenure and flexibility of rent was confronted by the framers of the English legislation. As we have seen, the Agricultural Holdings Act of 1948 conferred on tenants considerable security of tenure. In the absence of any provision for adjusting the rents of sitting tenants there would have been a basic asymmetry: rents would have been flexible downwards but inflexible upwards. Accordingly, the framers of the 1948 Act sought to establish a formal procedure for the readjustment of rents. Specifically provision was made for arbitration with respect to rent. As we have seen, the instructions to arbitrators seek to internalize costs and benefits. Thus, in assessing the appropriate rent, arbitrators are required to ignore any beneficial or adverse effects of the activities of the tenant himself on the property. Initially, however, arbitrators were not given further instructions as to what constitutes 'rent properly payable'. They tended to implement a *de facto* rent control, typically setting rents below market rents for comparable vacant units. Widespread dissatisfaction led to a provision in the 1958 Agriculture Act directing arbitrators to use open-market value as the basis for assessment.

Duration and security of tenure are not the only dimensions of tenancy arrangements which may be important in the rental market. If we relax the assumption that tenant activities will not affect the value of the property, then whether or not there are provisions for compensatory payments at the termination of tenancies will, in general, affect the limit rents of prospective tenants and the reservation rents of landowners. For example, suppose that tenants were liable to compensate landlords for any damage to their properties but were not entitled to compensation for unexhausted improvements. Then, *ceteris paribus*, the limit rents of prospective tenant farmers would be lower than in the absence of such a provision.[14] The reservation rents of landowners would be lower. Market rents would be lower. If, in addition to being liable for damage, tenants were entitled to compensation for any unexhausted improvement, prospective tenants' limit rents would be higher, landowners' reservation rents would be higher and market rents would be higher than in the absence of such a provision.[15]

If there is complete freedom of contract, the respective rights and obligations of the parties will not be taken as given by the participants but will be determined in the rental market. Landlord and tenant decide on the provisions to be incorporated into the contract of tenancy. There will be an incentive for the parties to stipulate provisions for compensatory payments. Suppose that landlord and tenant have a choice between a contract which does involve provisions for compensatory payments, the basis for compensation being the difference in the terminal value of the property attributable to the behaviour of the tenant, and one which does not. Assuming that the negotiation and enforcement costs are the same for both types of contract, then given any contract without such provisions there would, in general, exist some contract incorporating compensatory provisions which 'dominated' it, in the sense that both parties would be better off. In the absence of compensatory provisions, the tenant's actions, calculated to maximize his own terminal wealth, would not, in general, result in the maximization of their joint terminal wealth. However, with such provisions, selfish behaviour on the part of the tenant would maximize joint terminal wealth. Given that joint terminal wealth would be higher there must exist some distribution of wealth which would dominate the outcome without compensation. There must exist some fixed rental payment which, combined with the compensatory payment, would achieve that distribution of wealth.

V Market power, market imperfections and non-economic considerations

Hitherto we have assumed that each landowner owns only one operating unit. This assumption is unacceptable for many countries. Frequently large estates comprise numerous tenant farms. Indeed, it is often alleged that the owners of large estates exercise considerable local monopoly power in dealing with peasant tenants.

The conventional treatment of monopoly power in the rental market for agricultural land assumes that a landowner exercises such power by restricting the quantity of land he makes available for leasing, thereby increasing rent per acre. It is assumed that each tenant will pay the same rent per acre. The possibility of discrimination between tenants is seldom admitted.

This would seem to be a very peculiar approach. If a landowner does enjoy local monopoly power there is no compelling economic reason why he should not discriminate between prospective tenants. Perhaps the use of the simple monopoly model is invoked as the easiest extension of the conventional treatment of the rental market in terms of perfectly divisible acres. However, once the analysis is cast in terms of indivisible operating units it seems natural to admit at once the possibility, and indeed the likelihood, of discrimination.

Consider the simplest case of one landowner, who owns two homogeneous units, and three prospective tenant farmers, A, B and C. Suppose that the owner's reservation rent is zero for each unit. Suppose that A's limit rent (for either unit) is 180, B's limit rent is 150 and C's limit rent is 100. The core then consists of the owner leasing his units to A and B, the corresponding contract rents falling within the ranges

$$100 \leq R_a^* \leq 180$$
$$100 \leq R_b^* \leq 150$$

The precise level of each contract rent will depend on the outcome of bilateral negotiations. There is *no* reason why R_a^* and R_b^* should be equal. This is in stark contrast to the situation where the two units were owned by separate individuals. In that case a process of contracting and recontracting would have ensured a final solution involving the same contract rents. It is evident, therefore, that where landowners do exercise local monopoly power there may well be rent differentials even with homogeneous farms.[16]

The analysis in this chapter involved a particular restrictive assumption. Specifically, the process of contracting and recontracting was assumed to be costless. Where the number of owners and prospective tenants is large, the number of contracts necessary to establish a competitive equilibrium may be extremely large. If such contracts are costless then the number of required contracts is immaterial. In practice, however, participants incur a variety of costs. For example, prospective tenant farmers encounter costs in locating farms available for rent and in verifying the characteristics of farms, such as the qualities of the soil, drainage, buildings and fences. Furthermore, the process of negotiation will involve costs. In practice, therefore, a prospective tenant farmer is likely to contact only a relatively small number of owners before deciding to enter into a final and binding contract. Similarly a landowner is likely to negotiate with relatively few prospective tenant farmers before doing the same. To this extent the final set of contracts may differ from what would obtain in the absence of transaction costs. Specifically the existence of transaction costs may alter the identity of the final farmers, the number of units leased and the levels of contract rents. In addition, in the light of such transaction costs it is no longer inevitable that homogeneous units will be leased for the same contract rent.

When considering the operation of the rental market, it must always be remembered that the relationship between landlord and tenant is a complex one. A landowner with a vacant farm will not necessarily select the tenant offering the highest rent. A prudent landowner will want to convince himself of the competence and integrity of an incoming tenant. He may believe that the person offering the highest rent has over-estimated the rent he can afford to pay while maintaining the land in good condition. Or he may believe that he has deliberately offered too high a rent in the hope of subsequently obtaining a reduction by re-negotiation or by arbitration. Or he may not like him. A landowner is likely to be particularly cautious where the tenant will enjoy considerable security of tenure.

In England, landowners are frequently introduced to prospective tenants by friends, relatives or other tenants. They see the recommendations of family, social and business contacts as invaluable guides to the competence and integrity of prospective tenants. Where they do resort to more formal procedures, they typically invite open tenders for farms rather than auctioning leaseholds. Under the open tender system landowners at least retain the ultimate power to decide on incoming tenants. In contrast, the auction system, whereby the tenant is selected and the rent determined by the auctioneer's hammer, is a highly impersonal procedure.

That the relationship between landlord and tenant is more than simply an economic one is particularly evident in the treatment of sitting tenants. For example, English landowners have often not extracted the highest possible rents from tenants. In some cases, this 'leniency' was designed to secure the goodwill of the local community at election time. In other cases, it was undoubtedly due to a sense of moral obligation or to a family tradition of being easy with the estate tenants. Many of the large landowning families displayed a paternalistic attitude towards their tenants. The situation in the eighteenth century has been described by Sutherland (p. 5):

The attitude of the big landlords towards their tenantry and employees was, by tradition, benign and paternal. They joined with them in country pursuits such as hunting and hawking, discussed their problems with them and called the most favoured ones by their first names. The wives of the squirearchy assumed the role of Lady Bountiful, visiting the sick and infirm, bearing with them well-meant gifts of calves' foot jelly. The parish poor might subsist at little above starvation level for most of the year, but on high days and holidays they would be invited to join in the mass celebrations at the squire's expense, when food and drink would be provided on a generous scale.

John Stuart Mill (p. 142) has provided a plausible explanation of why the purely economic aspects of landlord–tenant relationships have frequently been de-emphasized:

Landed property is felt even by those most tenacious of its rights, to be a different thing from other property; and where the bulk of the community have been disinherited of their share of it and it has become the exclusive attribute of a small minority, men have generally tried to reconcile it, at least in theory, to their sense of justice, by endeavouring to attach duties to it, and erecting it into a sort of magistracy either moral or legal.

A vivid illustration of the pressure on landlords to treat their tenants fairly is provided by the extract from a prayer for landlords cited at the beginning of the chapter.

The importance of non-economic considerations will, of course, vary from time to time, from place to place and from individual to individual. Our purpose is simply to indicate that they *may* be of significance.

7

Rental market: share-rent tenancies

In this most miserable of all modes of letting land, after running the hazard of such losses, fatal in many instances, the defrauded landlord receives a contemptible rent; the farmer is in the lowest state of poverty; the land is miserably cultivated; and the nation suffers as severely as the parties themselves. Young (p. 298).

I Introduction

This chapter considers the operation of markets for share tenancies. In order to highlight the really important features of share tenancies, various simplifying assumptions will be maintained throughout this chapter. We will assume that the ownership and operating structures are invariant and coincident; that operating units are perfectly homogeneous; that the characteristics of units are unaffected by the behaviour of tenants; that contracts last for a stipulated period of time which corresponds to the production period; and that rents are paid at the end of the period.

We have already noted the recurrent criticisms of share tenancies. However, contrary to predictions that they would be superseded by fixed rent tenancies, share tenancies continue to be employed in many countries. We must examine what sorts of considerations influence the choice of the form of tenancy arrangement. This will be investigated in Section III.

II The market for share tenancies

Certainty

We will assume, initially, perfect information on the part of both landowners and prospective tenants. Specifically both parties to a particular negotiation know what the absolute rental payment would be corresponding to any rental share. It is important to be clear what this means. This not only rules out uncertainty with respect to both product prices and yields. In addition, it requires that a landowner be perfectly certain as to how a prospective tenant would behave if he were to lease the farm to him.

Consider initially the simplest case whereby, if a prospective tenant does take on a farm, his behaviour will not depend on the rental share. Assuming that tenant labour is the only variable input, then, irrespective of the rental share, the tenant will devote a given amount of labour, $\bar{L}$, to farming.[1] The corresponding (maximum) total revenue will be $\bar{Z} = Z(\bar{L})$. The tenant will pay the landlord $r . \bar{Z}$ and retain for himself $(1-r) . \bar{Z}$, where r is the rental share stipulated in the contract. In this case the rental share serves only to determine distribution between landlord and tenant.[2]

Consider the case of one landowner and one prospective tenant farmer. The landowner, whose reservation rent may be assumed to be zero for simplicity, will wish to negotiate as high a rental share as possible. The prospective tenant's limit rental share may be assumed to be that share which would leave him with the equivalent of the wage payments which his labour would command if he did not enter into a tenancy contract. Therefore, the contract rental share, r^*, would fall within the range

$$0 \leqq r^* \leqq \frac{\bar{Z} - w . \bar{L}}{\bar{Z}}$$

where w represents the wage rate in the best alternative occupation. The location of the contractual share within that range would depend on relative bargaining strengths. There is no reason why the landowner would necessarily be able to force the prospective tenant to agree to his limit rental share.

Consider briefly the case of one landowner and two prospective tenants, A and B. Note that the landowner will not necessarily lease the unit to the prospective tenant with the higher limit rental share. He will also need to consider their respective labour endowments and any differences in their productivity. Specifically which prospective tenant he will lease his unit to will depend on

$$r_a^l . \bar{Z}_a \gtreqless r_b^l . \bar{Z}_b$$

where r_a^l is the limit rental share of A, $\bar{Z}_a$ is the total revenue which would result from A farming the unit, and so on. Suppose

$$r_a^l . \bar{Z}_a > r_b^l . \bar{Z}_b$$

Then the unit would be leased to A at a contractual share within the range:

$$r_b^l \cdot \frac{\bar{Z}_b}{\bar{Z}_a} \le r_a^* \le r_a^l$$

Consider now the case of two owners of identical farms and two prospective tenants. Suppose that both landowners have zero reservation rents. The units will be leased to the tenants. For each contract the rental share cannot exceed the limit rental share of the tenant involved in that contract. In addition, the contractual shares must imply the same *absolute* rental payments, that is

$$r_a^* \cdot \bar{Z}_a = r_b^* \cdot \bar{Z}_b$$

Any provisional arrangement implying different absolute rental payments would be blocked by a coalition involving the prospective tenant with the higher absolute rental payment and the landowner with the lower absolute rental payment. An important implication – one which applies to the case of many owners and many prospective tenants – is that, in general, rental shares will *not* be the same in the set of final contracts. This simple observation casts considerable doubt on the usefulness of analyses which assume that landowners and prospective tenants take the rental share as a parameter determined by the market. For example, Bardhan and Srinivasan, in their attempt to rehabilitate the view that cropsharing is an inefficient arrangement, base their analysis on the assumption that, under competition, each atomistic landlord and each atomistic tenant takes the rental share as given. Their approach neglects the fact that a landowner is concerned not simply with his rental share but also with the behaviour of the tenant, in so far as this will determine the magnitude of what he shares in. In the face of inter-tenant differences in labour endowments or productivities, a situation involving the same rental shares would not be an equilibrium one. Rather, in equilibrium, inter-tenant differences imply differentials in rental shares such that all landowners receive the same absolute rental payments.

Consider now the more realistic but somewhat more complicated case where tenant behaviour does depend on the rental share. In this case total revenue is an indirect function of the rental share. Suppose that this dependency arises because the tenant is able to undertake part-time off-farm employment.[3] His labour input, and therefore total revenue, will be a decreasing function of the rental share. Consider the case of one landowner and one prospective tenant. In contrast to the situation where tenant behaviour is independent of the rental share, the landowner will *not* wish to negotiate as high a rental share as possible. He must take into account the disincentive effect of an increase in rental share on labour input. If the landowner were to enjoy all the bargaining power he would set r so as to

maximize $r \cdot Z(r)$

where $Z(r)$ represents revenue as an indirect function of the rental share. The necessary first order condition is

$$r \cdot \frac{dZ(r)}{dr} + Z(r) = 0$$

that is

$$Z(r) \left[\frac{r}{Z(r)} \cdot \frac{dZ(r)}{dr} + 1 \right] = 0$$

Thus to maximize his rental payment the landlord would set the rental share so that the elasticity of revenue with respect to the rental share equals minus one.[4] The rental share which would be optimal from the point of view of the landlord is, of course, only an upper limit.[5] The tenant may succeed in negotiating a lower share.

Consider now the case of one owner and two prospective tenants. Let $\tilde{r}_a$ be the rental share which would maximize the landowner's rent if he were to lease the unit to A and $\tilde{r}_b$ be the rental share which would maximize his rent if he were to lease it to B. Then which prospective tenant he would lease to would depend on

$$\tilde{r}_a \cdot Z_a(\tilde{r}_a) \gtreqless \tilde{r}_b \cdot Z_b(\tilde{r}_b)$$

Suppose

$$\tilde{r}_a \cdot Z_a(\tilde{r}_a) > \tilde{r}_b \cdot Z_b(\tilde{r}_b)$$

Then the unit would be leased to A at a contractual rental share within the range

$$\tilde{r}_b \cdot \frac{Z_b(\tilde{r}_b)}{Z_a(r_a^*)} \leqq r_a^* \leqq \tilde{r}_a$$

Consider finally the case of two owners of identical farms and three prospective tenant farmers A, B and C. Suppose that the owners' reservation rents are zero and that

$$\tilde{r}_a \cdot Z_a(\tilde{r}_a) > \tilde{r}_b \cdot Z_b(\tilde{r}_b) > \tilde{r}_c \cdot Z_c(\tilde{r}_c)$$

The farms would be leased to A and B. The contractual shares, r_a^* and r_b^*, would fall within the ranges

$$\tilde{r}_c \cdot \frac{Z_c(\tilde{r}_c)}{Z_a(r_a^*)} \leq r_a^* \leq \tilde{r}_a$$

$$\tilde{r}_c \cdot \frac{Z_c(\tilde{r}_c)}{Z_b(r_b^*)} \leq r_b^* \leq \tilde{r}_b$$

In addition, the landowners would receive the same total rental payments, that is

$$r_a^* \cdot Z_a(r_a^*) = r_b^* \cdot Z_b(r_b^*)$$

The extension to the case of many owners and many prospective tenants is straightforward. As in the case where tenant behaviour is independent of the rental share, final contracts will generally involve different rental shares, reflecting inter-tenant differences in assets, productivities and opportunities. It is also worth noting that certain tenants will, in general, earn 'surpluses', in the sense that the share of revenue they retain will exceed the opportunity costs of farm labour. Assertions that such surpluses are incompatible with competition involve the implicit assumption of identical prospective tenants, that is, in the present context, that they are all equally skilled at farming and that they all face the same part-time off-farm employment opportunities. In the present context, even if this were true, so that each tenant paid the rental share which was optimal from the point of view of his landlord, each tenant would typically still be left with a surplus.

Imperfect information and uncertainty

The assumption that a landowner has perfect information as to how a tenant will behave if he leases the farm to him is clearly a very restrictive one, particularly where the tenant's behaviour will depend on the rental share. In the case where the tenant's alternative to farm work is leisure, $Z(r)$ will depend on the tenant's utility function as well as on his productivity. Hurwicz & Shapiro have analysed the decision problem of a landlord who is free to set the rental share but does not have perfect information about the utility function or the productivity of the tenant. The landlord is assumed only to know that these belong to specified '*a priori* admissable' classes. They demonstrate that for a broad class of cases the optimal strategy for the landowner is to set a rental share of 0.5, implying an equal division of total revenue.[6] This result is particularly interesting in view of the frequency of such a division in actual rental share agreements.[7]

The existence of imperfect information of this type has a potentially significant implication for the set of final contracts. We have seen that with perfect information there would generally be differentials in rental shares reflecting inter-tenant differences. Suppose, however, that land-owners are unable to discriminate *ex ante* between prospective tenants in the sense that they do not have access to any information about which tenants would be more industrious or more productive. In this case all contracts would involve the same rental shares. The assumption of no information at all is, of course, an extreme one.

Consider briefly the implications of uncertainty with respect to prices and yields. Under a share tenancy agreement, both landowners and tenants bear uncertainty. Expectations and attitudes to risk will clearly affect the rental shares tenants and landowners are prepared to agree to. Assuming that there are inter-tenant differences in assets, productivities, attitudes to risk and so on, and that landowners are able to identify such differences, the set of final contracts will again involve different rental shares. If all landowners are risk neutral, equilibrium will require that each of them has the same expected rental payment. However, if land-owners have different attitudes to risk, there will be differences not only in rental shares but also in expected rental payments. Equilibrium requires that each landowner's expected utility from his own contract be at least as high as it would be if he were to replace any other landowner in his contract.

III Choice of contract form

Certainty

We must now consider what factors are likely to determine the form of tenancy under a system of freedom of contract. We need only consider the case of one landowner and one prospective tenant. Initially we will assume that both participants have perfect knowledge.

It is convenient to approach the problem by supposing that the participants have entered into a provisional contract stipulating that the tenant pay the landlord an agreed share of the revenue from the sale of the produce of the holding. On this basis we will consider whether switching to some other form of tenancy would offer the prospect of mutual gains.

In the simplest case where the tenant will employ a given set of inputs irrespective of the form of tenancy (and of the level of the rental share) there is no prospect of mutual gains from switching to any other form of contract. Assuming that the recontracting process is costless, there exists

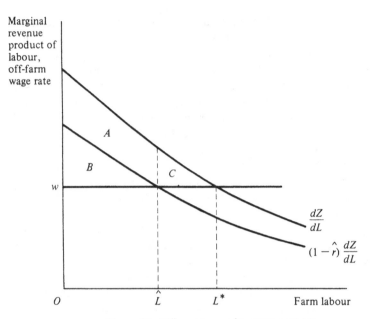

Figure 7.1. Different types of tenancy contract

a fixed absolute rental payment which is equivalent to the share-rental contract. This level of rent is equal to $\hat{r} \cdot \hat{Z}$, where $\hat{r}$ is the rental share in the provisional contract and $\hat{Z}$ is the (maximum) total revenue associated with the given input bundle.

Consider now the case where the tenant's inputs will depend on the form of tenancy. In this case there does exist the possibility of securing mutual gains from switching to a different form of contract. Specifically there exists a fixed rent contract which, provided recontracting is costless, would dominate the share tenancy agreement. This is illustrated in Figure 7.1 for the case of a peasant farmer who has the opportunity for part-time off-farm employment. Under the share-rental agreement, the tenant would equate his share of the marginal revenue product of farm labour to the off-farm wage rate. The corresponding level of farm labour would be $\hat{L}$. The combined surplus of revenue over the opportunity cost of that labour would be $(A+B)$. The tenant's share of that surplus would be B. If landlord and tenant switched to a contract involving a fixed rent, the benefits and costs of the tenant's activities would be internalized. He would respond by working L^* on the farm. The combined surplus of revenue over the opportunity cost of that labour would be $(A+B+C)$. Provided that the fixed rent, R, fell within the range

$$A < R < (A+C)$$

this recontract would dominate the share tenancy agreement: both land-lord and tenant would be better off.

Mutual gains from recontracting could be engineered in ways which preserved the share-rental format. One option would be an arrangement involving the sharing of costs as well as revenue. Suppose, in the present context, that the new contract stipulates that the tenant pay the landlord

$$r^*[Z(L) - w . L]$$

where r^* represents the new rental share and L represents the level of farm labour. Irrespective of the level of the new rental share, the tenant would respond by equating the marginal revenue product of labour and the off-farm wage rate. He would choose L^* in Figure 7.1. The surplus of revenue over the opportunity cost of the tenant's labour would be maximized. The rental share would simply play a distributive role: it would determine the respective shares in that surplus. There must exist a set of rental shares which would lead to mutual gains.[8]

Another option which would preserve the share-rental format would be for landlord and tenant to enter into a new contract which not only involved an agreed rental share but also stipulated the level of tenant input. In the case illustrated in Figure 7.1, both parties would have an incentive to stipulate L^*. They both would have an interest in maximizing the combined surplus of revenue over the opportunity cost of the tenant's labour. There would, of course, be conflict of interest over the precise level of the rental share. But there would exist a set of rental shares which would lead to mutual gains.[9]

The case where the tenancy contract stipulates the levels of tenant inputs has been given particular prominence by Cheung and by Hsiao. It is worth briefly considering a negotiation between landowner and tenant which involves this form of contract *ab initio*. In the case illustrated in Figure 7.1, if the landowner enjoyed all the bargaining power, his optimal strategy would be to stipulate the level of farm labour input L^*, thereby maximizing the total surplus of revenue over the opportunity cost of the tenant's labour, and then select the rental share in such a way that he would receive that surplus as rent, just leaving the tenant with his opportunity costs. The tenant's share would equal the elasticity of revenue with respect to the farm labour input.[10] If the tenant were to enjoy all the bargaining power, his optimal strategy would be to specify the level of labour input L^* and to stipulate a rental share which would yield a rent just equal to the landowner's reservation rent.[11] Whereas the location of the rental share would depend on the relative bargaining strengths of the two parties, the stipulated level of labour input would not. In the case of many landowners and many prospective tenants, the set of final contracts would involve landowners receiving the same rental payments. Inter-tenant differences would imply different rental shares and, in general, surpluses for certain tenants.

In this section we have demonstrated that, under certain assumptions, a share-tenancy arrangement which simply stipulates a rental share is dominated by a fixed rental agreement, by a partnership which involves the sharing of costs as well as revenue and by a share-rental contract which stipulates the levels of tenant inputs. The discussion has been conducted in terms of a peasant whose only contribution to production is his labour and who has opportunities for part-time off-farm employment. The proposition is, however, of general validity. It would apply to a peasant for whom the alternative to farm work is leisure; to a peasant who contributes inputs other than labour; and to a capitalist tenant farmer.[12] A concomitant implication of the analysis is that, under these same assumptions, contracts involving fixed rents, contracts involving the sharing of costs as well as revenue and share-rental contracts which stipulate the appropriate levels of tenant inputs are 'equivalent' in the sense that landlord and tenant would be indifferent between them. Given a provisional contract involving one of these forms there would be no prospect of mutual gains from switching to another form of contract. The combined surplus of revenue over the opportunity costs of tenant labour would already be maximized. The only feasible recontract would be one which resulted in the same tenant behaviour and the same rental payment, leaving both parties unaffected.[13]

The assumptions underlying these propositions are, first, that participants have perfect information and, second, that there are no costs involved in negotiating and enforcing contracts. We will consider now some implications of uncertainty, continuing to assume for the moment that there are no contracting and enforcement costs.

Uncertainty

Under a fixed rent contract the tenant alone bears any uncertainty with respect to either prices or yields. A share-tenancy arrangement offers the prospect of the sharing of risk between landowner and tenant. The existence of uncertainty provides by far the most plausible explanation of the prevalence of share tenancies.

Analysing the case of uncertainty is inevitably considerably more complicated than the case of certainty. However, we can bring out the factors involved by concentrating primarily on a relatively simple case, namely, the case where the tenant will devote a certain amount of labour to the farm irrespective of the nature of the tenancy arrangement. In contrast to the last section, we will assume that the landlord and tenant have entered into a provisional contract involving a fixed rent. We will consider whether switching to a simple share-rental contract offers the prospect of mutual gains.

We can easily identify one case where the share-rental format does offer the prospect of mutual gains. This is the case – admittedly an extreme one – where the tenant is averse to risk and the landlord is indifferent to risk. Suppose that the fixed rent in the preliminary contract is $\hat{R}$. Suppose that the tenant will use his endowment of labour to produce a single product in a particular manner, irrespective of the nature of the tenancy arrangement. Because of yield and price uncertainty, the resulting revenue from the sale of the produce is uncertain. We will assume that both landlord and tenant have the same subjective expectations about revenue. Under the fixed rent contract the tenant's terminal financial wealth would be

$$\hat{W} = Z - \hat{R}$$

with an expected value

$$E(\hat{W}) = E(Z) - \hat{R}$$

Suppose that the parties switch to a share-tenancy agreement which involves leaving the landlord's *ex ante* welfare unaffected.[14] Since the landlord is indifferent to risk, the rental share, $\tilde{r}$, which would accomplish this is the one which would yield an expected rent equal to the fixed rent, that is,

$$\tilde{r} \cdot E(Z) = \hat{R}$$

Under the new contract, the tenant's terminal wealth, $\tilde{W}$, would be

$$\tilde{W} = Z - \tilde{r} \cdot Z$$

with an expected value

$$E(\tilde{W}) = E(Z) - \tilde{r} \cdot E(Z) = E(Z) - \hat{R}$$

where we have used the condition that $\tilde{r} \cdot E(Z) = \hat{R}$. This recontract would leave the tenant's expected wealth unaffected, that is, $E(\tilde{W}) = E(\hat{W})$. However, from his point of view, the situation under share-tenancy would be less 'risky'. To see this, note that $Z > E(Z)$ implies $\hat{W} > \tilde{W} > E(W)$, whereas $Z < E(Z)$ implies $E(W) > \tilde{W} > \hat{W}$. Thus of the two subjective probability density functions for wealth, the one under the fixed rent tenancy would be more 'stretched' around the mean. Since, by assumption, the tenant is averse to risk, his expected utility of terminal wealth would be higher under the share-tenancy agreement. He would benefit from the recontract.[15]

It should not be inferred from this that under uncertainty there must exist a share-rental contract that would dominate any fixed rental contract. If the tenant was indifferent to risk and the landowner was averse to risk – admittedly an even more improbable case – there would be no prospect of mutual gains from switching to a share-rental contract. Indeed, it could easily be shown that switching to a share-rental contract which left the tenant's *ex ante* welfare unaffected would make the landowner worse-off. It is clear from these two extreme cases that which form of contract will be preferable will depend on the relative degrees of risk aversion of the two parties.

So far we have considered a straight choice between a fixed rental contract and a share-rental contract. But this begs a number of questions. Consider the case where the landowner is risk-neutral and the tenant is risk-averse. Given the assumptions we have been making, the share-rental contract would itself be dominated by an arrangement whereby the landowner hired the tenant's labour for a fixed wage. Under this arrangement, the landlord, who is indifferent to risk, would bear all the uncertainty and the 'tenant', or 'worker' as he might be more appropriately called, would bear none of the uncertainty.

There is a further possibility, one which is given prominence by Stiglitz. This is the possibility of a contract which involves sharing revenue in a stipulated manner combined with a fixed payment either from the tenant to the landowner or from the landowner to the tenant. This considerably increases the options available to the parties. Indeed, the other arrangements may be regarded as special cases of this.

In the analysis of this section we assumed not simply that the tenant will devote a predetermined amount of labour to the farm. We also assumed that the tenant would use this labour to produce a single commodity in a particular manner. The reason for this latter assumption was that if the tenant produced more than one commodity or if there was more than one way of producing a single commodity, the tenant would have a choice as to input allocation between commodities or as to techniques of production. Under a share tenancy agreement there might be a conflict of interest between landowner and tenant as to the appropriate choice, a conflict which would not arise under certainty. Consider again the case of a risk-neutral landowner and a risk-averse tenant. The landowner's interests would be best served by the decisions as to input allocation and techniques of production being taken with an eye to the maximization of expected revenue, whereas the tenant might prefer a production plan which entailed a lower expected revenue but offered the prospect of lower riskiness. This possible conflict of interest has been pointed out by Rao. He suggests that, for this reason, share-tenancies are more likely to be employed where the scope for this type of decision taking is relatively low, that is, in areas where the production of a single commodity predominates.

The case where tenant inputs are not predetermined is inevitably more complex. In the case of a choice between a fixed rent contract and a simple share rent contract there will typically be something of a trade-off. In contrast to a fixed rent tenancy, the share rental format offers the possibility of the sharing of risks. However, in contrast to the fixed rent tenancy, the share rental format does not involve the internalization of the costs and benefits of the tenant's decisions. In this case we cannot assert – even for the case of a risk-neutral landowner and risk-averse tenant – that, given a provisional fixed rental contract, there would exist a share-rental contract which would dominate it.[16] There would, however, be one form of recontract which would offer the prospect of mutual gains. This would be a share-rental contract which stipulated the levels of tenant inputs and, in the case of multiple products and multiple techniques, the precise manner of their use. That this format offers the prospect of mutual gains can be appreciated by noting that the contract could stipulate that the tenant deploy the same inputs in the same manner as he would do under the fixed rent contract. Invoking our earlier analysis, if the new contract then stipulated that rental share which would leave the landlord's *ex ante* welfare unaffected, the tenant would be better off under the recontract.[17]

Costs of negotiating and enforcing contracts

To the extent that there are costs entailed in negotiating and enforcing contracts, the critical consideration as regards the choice of contract form is whether there are differences in costs between forms. Consider the costs involved in negotiating and drawing up contracts. It seems likely that such costs would be similar for fixed rent contracts and for share rent contracts which only stipulate rental shares. However, as Cheung has suggested, it seems likely that they would be higher for share-rental contracts which detail the tenant's inputs. They would be even higher for contracts which stipulate the precise manner of use.

Consider the costs of enforcement. Under a fixed rent contract, violation of the terms of the contract, in the sense of the non-payment of rent, would be easily identified and presumably relatively easy to prove to the satisfaction of the courts. Under a simple share-tenancy arrangement, however, the tenant will have an economic incentive to defraud the landlord by understating the revenue from the sale of the produce of the holding. The landlord may incur significant costs in verifying that he does receive the rental payment to which he is entitled.[18] Where the contract stipulates the levels of tenant inputs, the costs of monitoring the behaviour of the tenant may be considerable, since the tenant has an economic incentive to violate agreements by reducing inputs below the contractually stipulated levels.[19] The costs of monitoring behaviour will typically depend on the choices available to the tenant. It may be relatively easy to check that the tenant is not spending less than the agreed amount of time on the farm in favour of additional part-time employment. But where the alternative to farm work is leisure it is likely to be extremely difficult to ensure that the tenant really does spend the stipulated amount of time actually working, rather than 'sitting on the stove'. The costs of enforcement are likely to be even higher where contracts stipulate the manner of input use, including the allocation of labour time between the cultivation of different crops.[20]

Certainly differences in negotiation and enforcement costs would seem to favour fixed rental contracts as compared to share-tenancies of one form or another. But perhaps the relevant comparison is not between fixed rent and share rent contracts. It may well be that the effective option to share-tenancies is wage-labour. Share-tenancies have one considerable advantage over wage-labour. The share-tenant does have a direct interest in the fruits of his labour. The wage-labourer does not. A landowner, who cannot be bothered to do any supervision at all, would prefer his land to be cultivated by a share-tenant than by a labourer who receives a fixed wage irrespective of the intensity of his work effort.

IV Custom

In this chapter we have analysed the operation of markets for share-tenancies and the choice of contract form on the assumption that all participants are motivated solely by economic considerations and that any possibility for economic gain will be exploited. It is important that the propositions which we have developed are qualified by the recognition of the importance of 'custom'. The not infrequent attempts to deny its importance are simply misplaced. People may follow customary practices either because it never occurs to them to do otherwise or because of social pressures to conform. Customary practices typically have some underlying rationale, at least initially. But they may be continued even after the rationale for them has disappeared.

In Section II we developed the proposition that in the face of inter-tenant differences the set of final contracts will involve different rental shares. The reason for developing this proposition was to show the implications of unfettered 'economic' behaviour on the part of participants and to highlight the flaw inherent in any analysis which *assumes* that each participant in a share rental market responds to a given rental share, *the level of which is determined by competitive forces.* We would not deny that, in certain instances, the rental share may be a given from the point of view of the participants. But, if this is so, it is because that share is customary, not because it is determined by a competitive market. The assertion that to assume that the rental share is predetermined by custom overlooks the fact that landowners and tenants are perfectly free to set whatever shares they wish to, itself overlooks the fact that the French term *métayage* means an arrangement whereby the tenant pays the landowner one half of the produce or of the revenue from the sale of the produce, as does the Italian term *mezzadria.*

The difficulties in pinning down the influence of custom have been admirably expressed in a different context by Ashley, an expert on the economic history of mediaeval England (p. 45):

Now mediaeval 'custom' is rather a deceptive thing: it is difficult to give it enough weight in our thoughts without giving it too much weight. On the one side there was certainly a strong and constant tendency to get into a groove; on the other hand changes were in actual fact made from time to time; and when once made, the new arrangement tended, in a curiously short time, to be itself regarded as of immemorial antiquity.[21]

8

Agricultural land values

The high preference for land was, of course, part and parcel of the mode of life and of the scale of values characteristic of peasants of most ages and most countries. To a peasant, whether wealthy or poor, ownership of land was an object to be pursued in all circumstances. To him land was not only a "factor of production", the means towards higher output and income, but also a "good" worth possessing for its own sake and enjoyed as a measure of family fortunes and a fulfilment and extension of the owner's personality. M. M. Postan (p. 151).

I Introduction

The objective of this chapter is to consider the operation of the market for the ownership of agricultural land. The ownership of land is constantly changing as a result of economic transactions, gifts or bequests, though the nature and rate of change in ownership naturally differ from time to time and place to place. We will be concerned with economic transactions.

In order to simplify matters, we will ignore changes in the ownership structure of agricultural land. Thus we will assume throughout the chapter that the only feasible transactions involve pure transfers of entire ownership units from one person to another. On this basis, Section II develops a simple competitive model designed to indicate how the decisions of landowners and prospective land purchasers interact to determine both the number of transactions and agricultural land values. As in the previous two chapters, we will consider the operation of the market in terms of a process of contracting and recontracting. In addition to assuming an invariant ownership structure, the simple model assumes that all ownership units are identical in all relevant respects; that is, each participant in the land market is assumed to be indifferent between alternative ownership units. Section III relaxes this assumption and considers how the analysis might be extended to more than one type of ownership unit. Finally Section IV considers the implications of market imperfections.

116

II A simple model of the ownership market

In this section we will assume that ownership units are identical in all relevant respects. Transactions in the market involve bilateral contracts whereby the owner of a unit transfers rights of ownership to a purchaser in return for an agreed payment. The outcome of the interaction between owners and prospective purchasers will clearly depend on the reservation prices of owners and the limit prices of prospective purchasers. We must therefore consider the determinants of reservation prices and limit prices.

The limit prices of prospective purchasers

The limit price of a prospective purchaser is defined as the maximum price he would be prepared to pay for a representative ownership unit. This limit price is likely to depend on a variety of complicated inter-related factors.

As a first step it is useful to determine the maximum price a prospective land purchaser would be prepared to pay in terms of the conventional present-value hypothesis. Consider a prospective buyer who would lease the land to a tenant farmer. The present-value calculation concentrates on the net economic benefits from purchasing the land. Assuming zero transaction costs, these economic benefits comprise, first, the stream of net income which accrues as a result of ownership of the land and, second, any net sum realized by the subsequent alienation of the land. The conventional calculation assumes that there is a perfect financial capital market and that the individual concerned has perfect foresight about the future or, at least, that he thinks he does.

Suppose that the individual were to buy now – at date 0 – and retain ownership for T periods. The associated present value, denoted by $P.V. (0, T)$, would then be given by

$$P.V.(0,T)= \sum_{t=1}^{T} \frac{Y_t}{(1+\rho_0) \dots (1+\rho_{t-1})}+\frac{P_T}{(1+\rho_0) \dots (1+\rho_{T-1})}$$

In this calculation, Y_t represents the net income accruing at date t, that is, at the beginning of the tth period. For a landlord, Y_t would be given by the gross rental payments from his tenants less any expenditure on repairs, maintenance, taxation and so on. P_T is the net price realized on the sale of the property at date T. The rate of interest during the tth period is represented by ρ_t. $P.V.(0, T)$ is a present sum of money which is 'equivalent' to the time profile of net receipts, including the proceeds from resale, which would result if he were to acquire the property and retain ownership for T periods: it is the maximum sum of money which could be borrowed now on the strength of that time profile or the minimum sum of money which could be loaned now in such a way as to yield that time profile. The simplest hypothesis, therefore, is that the individual's limit price is equal to this present value. Letting P^l denote his limit price

$$P^l = P.V.(0, T)$$

The present value represents the maximum sum of money he would be prepared to pay for an ownership unit.

An important extension of this simple hypothesis is to recognize that the ownership horizon itself is endogenous. Specifically the individual is free to determine the timing of his subsequent sale of the property. Letting $P.V.(0, h)$ denote the present value of a course of action involving the purchase of an ownership unit now and its subsequent retention for h periods, then

$$P^l = \max_h P.V.(0, h)$$

that is, his limit price would equal the present value of acquiring a unit now and retaining ownership for the 'optimal' length of time. Consequently, the prospective purchaser's limit price may depend on market prices at a series of subsequent dates. The link between future land prices and what prospective purchasers would currently be prepared to pay is further strengthened by the fact that an individual is also free to determine the timing of his purchase of an ownership unit. In other words, the relevant alternative to purchasing now may be to purchase a unit at a later date, rather than not to purchase one at all.

The conventional present value calculation is an over-simplification of the decision criterion of a prospective purchaser for a number of reasons. First, it presupposes that, for the tth period, the individual could borrow or lend as much as he likes at a given market rate of interest. However, financial capital markets are not perfect. Transaction costs imply that the cost of borrowing exceeds the return from lending. Moreover, banks, building societies and other financial institutions do not offer unlimited credit – they typically indulge in some form of 'capital rationing'. Either they set an upper limit on borrowing or they increase interest rates as the amount borrowed increases (or both). Consequently the limit price of a prospective purchaser will depend on the magnitude and form of his wealth, on the terms on which he can borrow additional funds – particularly on whether there are facilities for taking out mortgages – and on the specific alternative uses for his own funds. Second, the present value calculation assumes perfect certainty. However, someone contemplating purchasing agricultural land is inevitably uncertain about the prospective future time profile of net income from landownership. He is uncertain about the future market value of the land. He is uncertain about the prospective income flows from the ownership of assets other than land and of future changes in their capital values. In the face of uncertainty an individual's limit price will depend both on his expectations about the future and on his attitude to risk.

Finally, to suppose that the prospective purchaser of land is motivated in his calculations solely by anticipated economic benefits to himself, his family and his heirs – to portray the prospective purchaser as determining his limit price by comparing the economic net benefits from landownership with the economic net benefits from other feasible courses of action – does not do justice to the magnetic attraction of land. Land has always been much more than simply an economic asset. The most tangible non-pecuniary attractions arise from the various potential uses of land for residence, amenity and recreation. The most nebulous attraction is the frequently cited 'landownership *per se*'. Land purchase may be designed to secure the approval of others. Certainly in the heyday of landownership in England, 'social investment' was undoubtedly a powerful motive for acquiring land. Ownership of land was virtually a prerequisite for social acceptability.

Although our discussion has been confined to prospective purchasers who, if they did acquire the land, would normally expect to lease it to one or more tenant farmers, much the same sorts of considerations would be relevant for prospective purchasers who would normally expect to farm the land themselves. Thus we would expect the limit price of a prospective owner-occupier to depend on his anticipated income flow from farming; on his expectations about the future behaviour of land prices; on his initial wealth and the terms on which he could borrow and lend money; on the non-pecuniary facets of landownership; and so on. A particularly important feature of the prospective owner-occupier's decision is the nature of the alternatives to land purchase. For one individual the relevant alternative to purchasing land may be to rent land and use his wealth as tenant's capital to stock the farm. For another the relevant alternative may be non-farm employment and investment of his wealth outside agriculture. The specific nature of an individual's options to land purchase would influence his limit price.

It is worth emphasizing that different prospective buyers are likely to have different limit prices. The relative importance of prospective income flow and of prospective re-sale value may well differ from buyer to buyer. The longer the prospective purchaser expects to retain ownership of the land the less weight he is likely to attach to re-sale value. At one extreme, the acquisition of land may be an act of pure long-term investment and little or no significance may be attached to the prospect of re-selling the land. This would apply to an individual who intended to retain the land until his death and who had no interest in what happened after his death. Perhaps more significantly, it is alleged that many institutional investors are not motivated in their calculations by the prospect of re-selling the land. At the other extreme, the potential purchaser may be primarily concerned with the prospective re-sale value of land; little or no significance may be attached to the possible income stream from landownership. The classic example is the land speculator, whose motive for acquiring land is to secure a capital gain. Furthermore, in addition to differing relative emphasis on income and capital gains, prospective purchasers are likely to have different subjective expectations and attitudes to risk; different inter-temporal utility functions; different wealth; different access to financial capital; different valuations of the non-pecuniary facets of landownership.

The reservation prices of landowners

An extended discussion of the reservation prices of agricultural landowners would involve an unnecessary repetition of most of the factors considered in relation to the limit prices of prospective land purchasers. Thus the various motivations for land purchase would reappear as inducements to retain ownership; the alternatives to land purchase would reappear as alternatives to retaining ownership.

There is, however, one potentially significant difference between prospective buyers and owners. Whereas there are seldom legal restrictions on someone's ability to acquire land, there may be legal restrictions on someone's power to alienate land. The classic example was the strict settlement in England. As we have already seen, the essence of this device was to ensure that the current 'owner' of the land was merely a life tenant and therefore unable to alienate the land. It has been estimated that during the eighteenth and early nineteenth centuries well over half of the land in England was subject to strict settlement at any one time. Moreover, even if the owner of an estate was able to sell his land, he would be subjected to a variety of subtle pressures to retain ownership despite financial inducements to sell. Thompson (p. 6) has described these pressures:

Property in land was not merely immovable and therefore a guarantee that its owner would have an inescapable attachment to the concerns of a particular locality, but it also formed a real, tangible and visible domain, a territory naturally felt to be under the authority of its owner. The lawyers may have got into a tangle with their distinction between real property and personal property, and their language of hereditaments and chattels took them into a world of their own, but in the roots of their concept lay a distinction which seemed plain to ordinary men. The hereditary nature of the property was perhaps even more important, for it was this which conferred stability, permanence and continuity, this which established the landed family with its generations of tradition and its wide cousinhood, distinct from the mere passing single landed individual. It was this which fostered the idea, often honoured in the breach, that the owner of an estate for the time being was steward of a trust for unborn generations and temporary recipient of the fruits of his forebears' endeavours.

Land transactions

Consider now the interaction between owners and prospective purchasers in terms of a process of contracting and recontracting. We will assume that transaction costs are zero. Since the analysis is essentially the same as that applied to the rental market, a relatively brief treatment should suffice. Consider the case of three owners and four prospective purchasers. Figure 8.1 illustrates the step supply curve and step demand curve, where owners and prospective buyers have been ordered in terms of their reservation prices and limit prices respectively. The set of final contracts must lie within the core, CC'. This entails the two owners with the lowest reservation prices selling their properties to the two prospective buyers with the highest limit prices. Any final settlement must involve the same price for each unit. In this case price must fall within the range

$$P_2^r \leqq P^* \leqq P_2^l$$

The other owner will retain ownership of his unit.

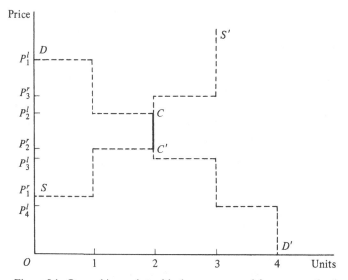

Figure 8.1. Ownership market with three owners and four prospective buyers

As in the rental market, some form of indeterminacy is inevitable. This indeterminacy may relate to price, as in the foregoing example, or to the number of transactions or to the identity of the final owners. Clearly if the number of transactions is indeterminate, the identity of final owners will necessarily be so. Moreover, if both the number of transactions and price are determinate, the identity of final owners will be indeterminate. This is illustrated in Figure 8.2, where the second and third prospective buyers have the same limit price. Whereas one unit will be sold to the prospective buyer with the highest limit price, the other unit may be sold to either the second or the third prospective buyer. Indeterminacy does not disappear however large the number of participants, although its practical significance may diminish.

Observations and implications

The conclusion to be derived from the simple competitive model is that a variety of factors, both pecuniary and non-pecuniary, influence agricultural land values. The fundamental economic influence is likely to be the relative profitability of agriculture. As we have seen in previous chapters, the relative profitability of agriculture will affect the levels of agricultural rents. We would expect this to have an impact on agricul-

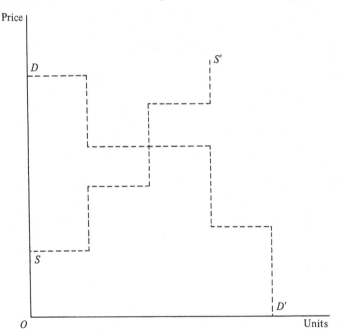

Figure 8.2. Ownership market where identity of final owners is indeterminate

tural land values since the prospective net income flows from leasing land will typically influence the limit prices of potential landlords and the reservation prices of existing landlords. In addition, the relative profitability of agriculture will have a direct impact on agricultural land values in so far as it will influence the limit prices of prospective owner-occupiers and the reservation prices of existing owner-occupiers.

The fundamental linkage between rents and land values is based on the fact that ownership of land enables a landlord to obtain a stream of net income in return for allowing some farmer to employ the flow of services from the land. Thus, as we have just argued, current rent levels and expectations about future rent levels will generally influence the values placed on agricultural land by owners and by prospective purchasers. It is this sort of 'model' which has prompted economists to state that land prices are determined by rents, but that rents do not depend on land prices. This assertion is substantially valid. Certainly it is correct to dispel any misconceptions that landlords have to charge high rents because land prices are high. However, the complex interrelationship between rents and land prices should not be over-simplified. The relationship between the rental market and the ownership market is not simply uni-directional. Even under a predominantly landlord/tenant system, the level of rents could be influenced by the state of the ownership market. Thus a landowner's effective choice may be between leasing or selling. His reservation rent may depend on the level of land prices. With owner-occupancy, the linkages between the two markets are more complex. Thus someone wishing to take up farming may purchase land or become a tenant farmer. His limit rent may therefore depend on the market price of land. Similarly for certain configurations of rents and prices, an existing owner-occupier may prefer to sell his property and become a tenant farmer. The extreme example of inter-connection between the rental and ownership markets is the sale-and-leaseback operation whereby the owner sells his property and simultaneously enters into a leasehold arrangement. Consequently, for a variety of reasons, the interrelationships between the rental market and the ownership market may be quite complex. Once we have emphasized this complexity, however, it is surely legitimate to claim that the major direction of influence is from rents to land values.

That there are popular misconceptions concerning the relationship between rents and land values is evidenced by the frequency of assertions that rents are 'too low' in the sense that they do not yield a 'fair' rate of return. In England it has even been suggested that the commitment in the 1947 Agriculture Act to ensure 'an adequate return on capital invested in the industry' implies a government commitment to ensure that net rents provide an 'adequate' return to capital invested in land-ownership. A basic problem with this revolves around the definition of a 'fair rate of return'. We may suppose that this means that the rate of return on capital invested in landownership should, in some sense, be comparable to rates of return elsewhere. But should the calculation of the rate of return on capital invested in landownership be based on the current market values of land or should it be based on historical costs?

Consider the possibility of calculating the rate of return on the basis of the purchase price to the landowner, with appropriate allowance for improvement expenditure. Although the legitimacy of landed property is often justified in terms of a historical cost argument, this is perhaps not what the proponents of the view that net returns to landowners are inadequate have in mind. For one thing it would be much more difficult to substantiate the claim that the net income from leasing land has provided a relatively low rate of return. Thus for someone who bought land twenty years ago present rent levels would seem to provide an attractive rate of return relative to purchase price, even after allowance for inflation. Once one takes into account that the owner has been receiving an income stream from the land for the past twenty years and that he owns an asset which even in real terms is now worth considerably more than he paid for it, he has hardly been treated 'unfairly'. For another thing, if one subscribes to the historical cost basis for calculation, this position would typically imply different levels of rent for indistinguishable operating units.

Suppose that, instead of using historical expenditure, the rate of return is calculated on the basis of current market values. It is certainly true that, since the second world war, the rate of return in this sense has been relatively low. It has been claimed that on this basis rents are too low. An objection to this is that this low rate of return has been offset by substantial increases in capital values. However, the relevant counter-argument in the present context is that the rate of return is low because landowners are prepared to accept that rate of return. As both Hallett and Ward have observed, this is precisely why it is nonsense to claim that the government should seek to ensure that net rents provide an 'adequate' rate of return on the current market value of land. If the government were to raise the absolute levels of net rents this would lead to an increase in land prices. There is no reason why the eventual rate of return should exceed the original rate of return.

The rate of return on land has always tended to be relatively low. This phenomenon was explained by Low (p. 33) in 1844:

There is no stock in this country which is computed to yield so small an interest as land, with relation to the purchase price. The inducements to acquire this species of property are, the security which it is supposed to possess, the fair expectation of a future increase of value, and the many pleasing associations connected with the solid and enduring possession of a landed estate. The value of landed property may be expected to vary with the progressive accumulation or decrease of capital and wealth in the country. When large capitals are to be invested, they will naturally flow towards the land, as the safest security.

III Heterogeneity of ownership units

Extension of the analysis

The analysis of the previous section was based on the assumption of perfectly homogeneous ownership units. In practice, of course, ownership units differ with respect to size, layout, fertility, location, permanent equipment and so on. These differences in characteristics mean that participants in the land market have very different preferences as between different units.

Essentially the same approach can be applied to the case of more than one type of ownership unit. The various sub-markets would be closely related on the demand side. Thus the limit price of a prospective land purchaser for a particular type of ownership unit would depend on the prices at which he could acquire the other types of unit. The various sub-markets might also be related on the supply side. Thus, for certain configurations of prices, a landowner might wish to sell his unit and purchase one of the other types of unit. His reservation price might therefore depend on the prices of the other types of unit.

The set of final contracts would necessarily involve the same price for ownership units of a given type. In general, there would be differences in prices between different types of units, reflecting differences in fertility, size, permanent equipment and so on.

Premium for vacant possession

As an illustration of heterogeneity, it is instructive to consider the emergence of a premium for vacant possession where sitting tenants enjoy security of tenure. Suppose that certain owners could, if they chose to sell their land, offer their land with vacant possession, either because they have been farming the land themselves or because previous tenancy arrangements have been terminated. Suppose that the remaining units have sitting tenants, all on long leases with the same unexpired terms. Ownership units are assumed to be otherwise indistinguishable in terms of size, fertility and so on. There are therefore two sub-markets comprising units with vacant possession and units with sitting tenants.

It is evident that a vacant possession premium could emerge if vacant units could be leased to tenants at higher rents than the rents paid by sitting tenants. A prospective purchaser who was interested in leasing land would be prepared to pay more for land with vacant possession than for land with sitting tenants. This could be one factor explaining the vacant possession premium in England between 1948 and 1958, since during this period arbitrators tended to set rents below their open-market levels. However, a vacant possession premium persisted after the instruction to arbitrators to base rents on open-market levels. In order to understand this phenomenon, we will assume in the present analysis that the rents paid by sitting tenants are adjusted over the period of their leases in accordance with the movement in open-market rents.

The two sub-markets will be very closely related. In general, the supply and demand curves for each type of unit will depend on the market price of the other type of unit. To appreciate this, consider prospective purchasers of land who are solely interested in leasing land. They will not be prepared to pay more for a vacant unit than the market price of a unit with a sitting tenant; nor will they be prepared to pay more for a unit with a sitting tenant than the market price of a vacant unit assuming that it is costless to install a tenant. Thus the demand curve of this group for vacant units will be of the form shown in Figure 8.3, where P_I represents the price of vacant units and P_{II} represents the price of tenanted units. For simplicity the decreasing stretch of the demand curve is represented as smooth rather than as a step function. The demand curve of this

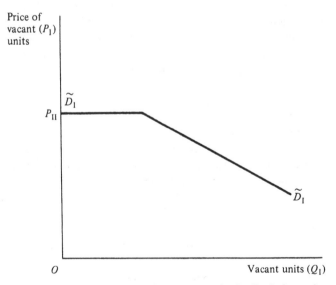

Figure 8.3. Demand curve for vacant units by prospective landlords for a given market price for tenanted units

group for tenanted units would be of a similar form, with a perfectly elastic stretch at the market price for vacant units.

Figure 8.4 depicts a situation of simultaneous equilibrium in both markets. The demand curve $D_I D_I$ represents the demand curve for vacant units by both prospective landlords and prospective owner-occupiers, given that the market price of tenanted units is P_{II}^e. It is obtained by horizontal aggregation of the demand curves of these two groups. The supply curve $S_I S_I$ represents the supply curve for vacant units by both those owners who, if they retained ownership, would farm the land themselves and those who would lease their land. This curve is also based on a price for tenanted units of P_{II}^e. The perfectly elastic stretch reflects the fact that if the vacant possession price exceeded the market price of tenanted units those owners of vacant possession land interested in leasing would sell their units, buy tenanted units and thereby realize a capital gain. The curve $D_{II} D_{II}$ represents the demand curve for tenanted units by prospective purchasers interested in being landlords. It is perfectly elastic at the market price of vacant units because, as we explained earlier, they would not be prepared to pay more than that price for tenanted units. Finally $S_{II} S_{II}$ represents the supply curve of tenanted units. The perfectly elastic stretch reflects the fact that the reservation prices of the owners of such units cannot exceed the vacant possession price. If the price of tenanted units exceeded the vacant possession price they could secure a capital gain by selling their tenanted units, purchasing vacant units and installing tenants.

Simultaneous equilibrium involves Q_I^e vacant units being sold at a price P_I^e, the purchasers being exclusively prospective owner-occupiers,

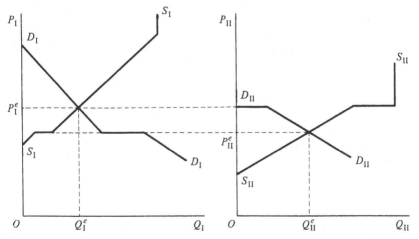

Figure 8.4. Simultaneous equilibrium in the markets for vacant units and for units with sitting tenants

and Q_{II}^e tenanted units being sold at a price P_{II}^e. The price differential $(P_I^e - P_{II}^e)$ constitutes the premium for vacant possession. It is attributable to the fact that prospective owner-occupiers are confined to the market for units with vacant possession. It should be noted at this point that this analysis involves the implicit assumption that sitting tenants would incur costs of moving to other farms. These costs of moving establish an upper-limit on the vacant possession premium. If the vacant possession premium were to exceed these costs it would pay someone wishing to sell his unit to bribe his sitting tenant to quit so that he could then secure the vacant possession price. Similarly it would pay a prospective owner-occupier to purchase a tenanted unit and bribe the sitting tenant to quit rather than pay the vacant possession price.

There is a further implicit assumption, namely, that we have ruled out the possibility of a sitting tenant himself purchasing his landlord's unit. If we admit this possibility, there is a further reason why the vacant possession premium could not exceed the costs of moving. If it did, each sitting tenant would have an incentive to purchase his landlord's unit at the market price for units with sitting tenants, resell at the vacant possession price, obtain a tenancy elsewhere and thereby realize a capital gain. Even if the vacant possession premium is less than the costs of moving, a sitting tenant may choose to purchase his unit and thereby change his status to that of owner-occupier. However, from an analytical point of view, this complicates matters by introducing an additional element of heterogeneity. We can no longer conclude that all tenanted units would command the same price in the set of final contracts. The owner of a tenanted unit might be able to negotiate a higher price from the sitting tenant than he could obtain from other prospective purchasers.

This analysis is a simplistic representation of the impact of security of tenure on the ownership market for other reasons. In practice, units with sitting tenants will be differentiated, in the minds of current owners and prospective purchasers, according to the length of time sitting tenants are likely to remain in occupation. If there are leases of fixed duration, unexpired terms will differ. If, as in England, tenants enjoy statutory security of tenure, the age of the current tenant and whether or not he has a son who satisfies the conditions conferring a statutory right to inherit the tenancy will be relevant. Such differences between sitting tenants may result in price differentials between tenanted units.

Certainly the existence of security of tenure complicates the operation of the ownership market and the rental market. The presence of a vacant possession premium may well influence decisions regarding the timing of sales. Thus a landowner contemplating selling his property may delay doing so if he expects his tenant to quit since this would enable him to obtain a higher price. Similarly a landowner who has not been contemplating selling may do so if his tenant unexpectedly quits or dies. He may be reluctant to install a new tenant since this would immediately reduce the value of his property. He may decide to sell at the vacant possession price.

IV Transaction costs

We may differentiate between two types of transaction costs. First, there may be costs of actually implementing final contracts, such as conveyancing fees. Formally such costs can be accommodated quite simply in the analysis by recognizing that these costs will influence the limit prices of prospective purchasers and the reservation prices of landowners. Specifically such costs will reduce limit prices and increase reservation prices. The impact of such costs will be to reduce the number of transactions. The effective price received by sellers, after paying these costs, will be lower. The effective price paid by buyers, including these costs, will be higher. However, the impact on the price paid by buyer to seller is indeterminate. It will depend on the precise nature of these costs and on the relative costs incurred by buyers and sellers.

Second, establishing contacts and preliminary negotiations will be costly. Thus a prospective land purchaser will incur costs in searching for suitable properties, verifying their characteristics and negotiating with owners. Similarly landowners will incur costs in locating and negotiating with prospective buyers. As in the case of the rental market, these costs mean that units of a given type need not necessarily command the same price. Where there are very many participants, the number of contacts needed to ensure this cannot be relied on to take place. Thus transactions may take place which would be blocked if contacts were costless. These types of transaction costs explain the emergence of estate agents who act as intermediaries between sellers and prospective buyers. These costs also explain the use of auction systems. Rather than engage in direct negotiations with a number of prospective purchasers a seller may elect to oblige prospective buyers to compete in the auction room.

9

The operating and ownership structures

The preference for keeping estates intact on their transference was a sound financial reflection of their social and political value. An estate was more than the farms and cottages which composed it, and was therefore more than their sum ... The one essentially indivisible asset of an estate in being was that it was the functioning centre of influence, the territorial basis of a social entity in which the strands of respect and deference led to the owner and at one and the same time the·source of the landowner's weight in the community and the means by which he exercised it. This quality could not survive the partition of an estate into its constituent properties and hence the value attached to it would be lost by any such action. F. M. L. Thompson (pp. 40–1).

I Introduction

In the previous three chapters, both the ownership structure and the operating structure were treated as invariant. This abstraction afforded a considerable simplification but at the cost of ignoring a most important phenomenon. This chapter focuses on the various factors which determine the nature of and rate of change in both the operating structure and the ownership structure.

Section II examines the conventional treatment of the markets for the flow of services from land and for the ownership of the stock of agricultural land. In contrast to our earlier analyses of these markets in terms of indivisible units, the traditional analysis is conducted in terms of perfectly divisible acres of land. It will be argued that this approach conveys a most deceptive impression of the functioning of these markets.

An important phenomenon is the movement of land into and out of agriculture. Given our definitions, any change in the amount of agricultural land involves a change in both the ownership and operating structures. These sorts of 'external' changes generally involve somewhat different considerations from 'internal' changes, that is, from those changes which involve a re-drawing of boundaries but no alteration in the aggregate amount of land used for agricultural purposes. It is convenient to consider them separately. Consequently, Sections III and IV will be concerned solely with internal changes; external changes will be considered in Section V.

II Conventional analysis of land markets

In the conventional treatment of the rental market for agricultural land, participants are assumed to respond to a competitively determined market rent per acre. Each participant decides how much land he would like to lease or to rent at each level of market rent. The equilibrium level of rent per acre is determined by supply and demand. It is that level of rent at which the excess demand for acres is zero.[1] As well as determining the level of rent, interaction between participants determines the number and sizes of farms, though this is not usually considered explicitly.

In deciding how much land to rent, each tenant farmer, provided that there is no uncertainty, equates the marginal revenue product of land to rent per acre. This is the optimal decision rule for a peasant family and for a capitalist farmer. Similarly in deciding how much land to lease or to rent, owners of land compare the marginal revenue product of land and rent per acre. If it pays an owner to farm some land himself – whether this involves reserving part of his land for his own use and leasing the remainder or whether it involves using all his own land and renting additional land – the marginal revenue product of the land that he does farm equals the market rent. The analysis could be modified to accommodate uncertainty. Tenants could be assumed to choose that acreage which would maximize their expected utilities. If tenants were indifferent to risk they would equate the expected marginal revenue product of land and rent per acre. However, for a risk averse tenant the expected marginal revenue product of land would exceed rent per acre.[2] The existence of uncertainty would have implications for both the equilibrium level of market rent and the resulting farm structure.

The conventional treatment of the rental market typically suggests that there is no particular connection between, on the one hand, the pattern of land ownership and, on the other hand, the equilibrium level of rent and the ensuing operating structure. A connection could be introduced by recognizing transaction costs. Thus we might suppose that, in view of such costs, the price at which a landowner can rent additional land exceeds the price at which he can lease land – or, in Glenn Johnson's terminology, that the acquisition price exceeds the salvage price. This extension would explain why a landowner might not participate in the rental market: he would not do so if the marginal revenue product of the acreage he owns lies between the acquisition price and the salvage price. In the absence of such costs, he would not participate only in the extreme coincidence that the marginal revenue product of his landholding just happened to equal market rent.

For our present purposes, the most important defect of the conventional analysis is that it treats land not only as perfectly divisible but also as 'homogeneous' in a particular sense. Specifically it assumes that a prospective tenant farmer is indifferent between renting, on the one hand, fifty separate plots of one acre and, on the other, one connected plot of fifty acres. This is clearly an unreasonable assumption. The conventional approach does not provide an explicit mechanism which ensures that the acreage which any participant ends up with is connected. Presumably those who employ this approach are not implying that a competitive rental market operates 'as if' there was a Walrasian auctioneer who not only determined the equilibrium rent by a *tâtonnement* process but also determined the operating structure so as to ensure the connectedness of the constituent units.

Precisely the same objection can be levelled at the conventional treatment of the market for the ownership of agricultural land. Each participant decides how many acres he would like to buy or sell at a competitively determined price per acre. Interaction between the participants determines the equilibrium market price, the associated transactions and the resulting pattern of landownership. The implicit assumption is that a prospective purchaser is indifferent between, on the one hand, one connected plot of one hundred acres and, on the other hand, one hundred separate plots of one acre. Whereas the homogeneity assumption may be satisfactory for analysing the markets for certain commodities, it is not satisfactory in the case of agricultural land, even if all land has the same chemical properties, enjoys the same climatic conditions, and so on.

III The operating structure

In this section, taking the ownership of land as given, we will consider the sorts of factors which may affect the nature of the operating structure. We will assume throughout that all agricultural land has the same chemical properties, enjoys (or suffers from) the same climatic conditions, and so on. In view of our criticisms of the conventional approach, we must be explicit about the spatial characteristics of operating units. We have already suggested that it is desirable that the land comprising an operating unit be connected.[3] We will go further and assume that for farming purposes, an operating unit should ideally be of rectangular shape. We will employ extremely simple examples.

Two landowners

Consider two peasant landowners, whose ownership units are rectangular and adjacent, as shown in Figure 9.1(a). The size of A's unit is $\bar{N}_A$ acres. The size of B's unit is $\bar{N}_B$ acres. Each family has, in addition,

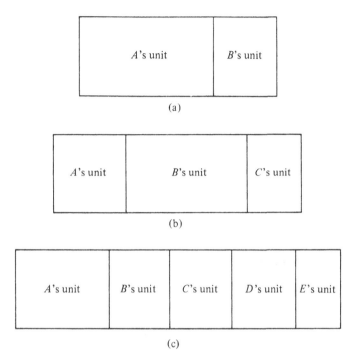

Figure 9.1. Ownership structures

a certain amount of labour to use in cultivation, the amounts being $\bar{L}_A$ and $\bar{L}_B$. We will suppose that these peasant families are entirely isolated from the rest of the world. Using only labour and land, they produce corn for their own consumption. We will assume that the corn production functions of the families are identical, strictly quasi-concave and linear homogeneous. The production function for an operating unit is given by

$$C = C(L, N)$$

where C represents the (maximum) output of corn at the end of the production period, L represents the amount of labour employed on the operating unit during the production period and N represents the size in acres of the operating unit. It must be emphasized that this production function is applicable provided that the operating unit is rectangular. If it was of some other shape the maximum output might be less than this function would imply.

We will use the familiar Edgeworth-box construction, as shown in Figure 9.2. The overall dimensions of the box correspond to the total amounts of the two factors, namely, $(\bar{N}_A + \bar{N}_B)$ acres of land and $(\bar{L}_A + \bar{L}_B)$ units of labour. Point I in the box represents the ownership of the resources. In the absence of any form of trade between the two households, point I would also represent the allocation of resources between the two operating units; that is, family A would use $\bar{L}_A$ units of labour to cultivate its $\bar{N}_A$ acres, and likewise for B. Family A would reach the isoquant labelled $\bar{C}_A$; that is, its (maximum) output would be $\bar{C}_A$ units of corn. Similarly family B would reach the isoquant labelled $\bar{C}_B$; that is, its (maximum) output would be $\bar{C}_B$ units of corn.

We are interested in whether there exists a basis for trade and, if so, what form trade will take. We can identify two possible types of trade. One form of trade would involve one of the families leasing land to the other for the duration of the production period in return for a stipulated payment of corn at the end of the period. The other form of trade would involve one of the families working for a stipulated amount of time for the other family in return for an agreed wage payment of corn at the end of the production period. These two types of trade are not mutually exclusive: the families may enter simultaneously into a wage-labour contract and into a tenancy contract.

Assuming that there no transaction costs, there will be an economic

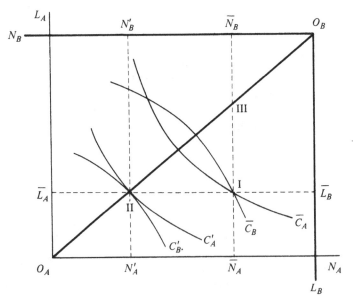

Figure 9.2. Trade between neighbouring landowners

basis for trade if the maximum possible *combined* output of corn exceeds the combined output which would result from their acting independently. Given our assumption of identical, strictly quasi-concave, linear homogeneous production functions, it is particularly simple to determine whether there is a basis for trade. There is a basis for trade if their labour/land endowment ratios differ, that is, if

$$\frac{\bar{L}_A}{\bar{N}_A} \neq \frac{\bar{L}_B}{\bar{N}_B}$$

The reason is that with this production technology the maximization of combined output requires the same labour/land ratio on each operating unit.[4] Furthermore this is all that is required. In other words, any allocation of resources between the units will maximize the combined output provided that the labour/land ratios on the units are the same.[5] Thus any allocation of resources along $O_A O_B$ will result in the maximum combined output.

Suppose that the families elect for a tenancy arrangement. The only undominated pure tenancy contract would involve family A leasing $(\bar{N}_A - N'_A) = (N'_B - \bar{N}_B)$ acres of land to family B, the agreed rental payment being no less than A's reservation rent and no greater than B's limit rent. A's reservation rent for that amount of land equals $(\bar{C}_A - C'_A)$, that is, the fall in its own output which would result from forgoing the use of the leased land. B's limit rent for the amount of land equals $(C'_B - \bar{C}_B)$, that is, the increase in its own corn output which would result from the use of the additional rented land. It would, of course, be necessary that the actual land leased be the land adjacent to the land B owns. It would be in their mutual interest to ensure that the two resulting operating units were rectangular.

Rather than entering into a tenancy contract, the two families could enter into a pure wage-labour contract. The only undominated pure wage-labour contract would involve family B working $(\bar{L}_B - L''_B) = (L''_A - \bar{L}_B)$ units of labour time for family A, where

$$\frac{L''_A}{\bar{N}_A} = \frac{L''_B}{\bar{N}_B}$$

The resulting allocation of resources would be at III in Figure 9.2. The stipulated wage payment would not be less than B's reservation wage, $(\bar{C}_B - C''_B)$, nor greater than A's limit wage, $(C''_A - \bar{C}_A)$, where C''_A and C''_B represent what the corn outputs on the two units would be if the transaction were to take place.[6] Alternatively the two families could enter into a mixed contract, involving both the leasing of land and the hiring of labour. Any mixed contract which resulted in an allocation of resources along $O_A O_B$ would be undominated.

A significant implication of this simple analysis is that, in the case of identical linear homogeneous production functions, land-leasing and wage-labour are alternatives. Combined output can be maximized either by the pattern of land use adapting to the pattern of labour ownership or by the pattern of labour use adapting to the pattern of land ownership. With constant returns to scale, scale as such does not matter. Without some other assumption about the respective costs of negotiating and enforcing tenancy contracts compared to wage-labour contracts, we may be able to say very little about the sizes of operating units. This provides another illustration of the intimate connection between the markets for land and labour.

· Under more general assumptions about technology, it may not be possible to maximize the combined output either by a pure tenancy arrangement or by a pure wage-labour contract: a mixed contract may be necessary. A simple example would be where the production functions were identical and homogeneous but exhibited increasing returns to scale over the relevant range. In this case there would be only two un-dominated contracts of the sort under consideration: one where A rents all the land of B and hires all the labour of B and one where B rents all the land of A and hires all the labour of A. An alternative arrangement could be the formation of a co-operative or partnership.

More than two landowners

Consider briefly the case of three landowners, whose rectangular ownership units are shown in Figure 9.1(b). Suppose again that the corn production functions are identical, strictly quasi-concave and linear homogeneous, and that all three families have given labour endowments. If the labour–land endowment ratios differ and if tenancy contracts are costless, there will be a basis for mutual gains through trade. Suppose that the set of tenancy contracts which would equalize labour/land ratios on operating units would involve B leasing some land to A and B also leasing some land to C. This simple case illustrates an extremely impor-tant point. There is no reason why the corn-rent per acre A pays should necessarily equal the corn-rent per acre C pays.[7] There is no mechanism which ensures this. The rents are the result of a bargaining process. This simple case highlights a flaw in the conventional analysis: it *assumes* that land of the same quality will necessarily command the same rent per acre.

Now it might be objected that this example endows B with some sort of 'monopoly' power and that therefore it is not appropriate to use it to criticize an approach which after all purports to deal with the case of very many participants. But the point is precisely that once one truly acknowledges the spatial dimension of land, the agricultural land market is riddled with 'monopoly'. However many participants we introduce, there will not be a mechanism which will guarantee, even in the absence of transaction costs and given perfect information on the part of participants, that the set of final contracts will involve the same rent per acre for land of the same quality.

Consider now the case of five landowners, as shown in Figure 9.1(c). In this case, the set of tenancy contracts required to adjust the pattern of land use to the given set of labour endowments may require A leasing land to B; B leasing land to C; C leasing land to D; and D leasing land to E. As a result of this process B, C and D may end up farming operating units equal in acreage to their ownership units. Thus a complex set of contracts might be required in order to engineer what essentially amounts to a net transaction between A and E. If the costs of negotiating and enforcing contracts were zero, this would not really matter. But, in fact, these negotiation and enforcement costs may be significant. The conventional analysis may be able to take some account of transaction costs, as we saw earlier. But it is incapable of handling complex cases of multilateral contracts.

Large landowners

Consider finally the case of a 'large' landowner who has to decide how to subdivide his rectangular ownership unit into rectangular operating units for leasing to tenant farmers. He has to decide on the number of operating units and on their sizes. His decision will depend on whether he exercises monopoly power in relation to prospective tenants or whether he is one of many large landowners. If he is one of many, his decision problem will depend on the relationship between the market rental value of a unit and its size and shape. Suppose that for rectangular units there is a differentiable relationship between market rent and size:

$$R = R(N)$$

Suppose also that there is a fixed cost involved in entering into each tenancy contract. Maximization of his total net rent will require that for the ith and jth operating unit

$$\frac{dR_i}{dN_i} = \frac{dR_j}{dN_j}$$

where R_i is the rental value of the ith unit, N_i is its size and so on. The optimal allocation of the land may well involve all of the operating units being of the same size but this is *not* inevitable.[8,9]

What constitutes the optimal structure from the point of view of the landlord will depend on the nature of the relationship between rental value and size. This is turn will depend on whether the agricultural sector comprises prospective tenants who are primarily peasant families reliant on their own labour and simple techniques or capitalist farmers who hire labour and use modern machinery. This will influence whether it is preferable to have a large number of small operating units or a small number of large units. A further consideration will, of course, be the cost of entering into tenancy contracts: an increase in this cost may reduce the optimal number of units.

A system of large ownership units offers the greatest potential for relatively rapid changes in the operating structure. Where large areas of land are under unified ownership and control, operating units can be more readily amalgamated, fragmented or consolidated in response to changing economic circumstances. If we reinterpret Figure 9.1(c) so that all the land now belongs to one owner with the five sub-divisions now being initial operating units, it will be that much easier for a single landowner to engineer the sort of restructuring we considered earlier. Even more importantly, it will be considerably easier for a single landowner to alter the structure to, say, three larger units. This might be extremely difficult to accomplish if there were five landowners, each wanting to be a farmer rather than a hired worker and each being suspicious of any form of partnership. That a system of large ownership units offers greater potential for structural change than a system of peasant proprietorships is not merely an *a priori* proposition. It is borne out by events in England. The large estates certainly facilitated the transition to large capitalist farms.

The rate of structural change will, of course, depend on the legal and *de facto* security of tenants. Where sitting tenants are on long leases of fixed duration landowners may be obliged to wait for their expiration before changing the structure. Even where tenants do not enjoy legal security, landlords may be reluctant to evict them. Consequently the pace of amalgamation may be set by the rate at which tenancies fall vacant as tenants die, retire or seek other employment.

IV The ownership structure

Neighbouring owners

Much of the analysis of the last section is applicable, with suitable modification, to studying changes in the ownership structure. For example, consider the possibility of the two owners in Figure 9.1(a) entering into a transaction involving the transfer of land ownership. Suppose that the options of leasing and of wage labour are not available for some reason or, if available, are unacceptable to the two owners. Two extremely important points must be emphasized. The first point is that even if there exists the possibility of increasing the combined flow of outputs by the transfer of land from A to B there may still not be the basis for a transaction. The most important reason in the context of our isolated economy is that, if payment by instalments is ruled out, payment will have to be in terms of current corn. The only forms of wealth are land and corn. It is easy to see why there might not be a basis for trade. It is likely that a family would only resort to selling land if obliged to do so to meet current consumption requirements.[10] The second point is that even if there is a basis for trade – in the sense that there is some acreage for which A's reservation price is more than matched by B's limit price – the transfer of ownership may still not take place. Neither family may be aware of the fact that there is the basis for a mutually beneficial transaction. Even daily contact may not lead to the communication of this information. A landowner may well have designs on a neighbour's property but be reluctant to inquire whether he would be prepared to sell.

These two points are not of relevance only to our isolated economy. They are of general relevance. In many predominantly agrarian economies, land is the most important form of wealth. Peasants only sell land if forced to do so or if they intend to use the proceeds to buy land elsewhere. For this reason the most likely cause of land transactions is the differential impact of changes in agricultural prosperity on different landowners. It is easy to see how a self-perpetuating trend towards greater concentration of landownership can arise and how rich landowners can emerge. Contrary to popular belief, the large English estates of the eighteenth and nineteenth centuries had, in fact, been established primarily in this way. The large landowners expanded their estates by acquiring the land of yeomen farmers. The expansion of the great estates was most rapid during the late seventeenth and early eighteenth centuries. The smaller landowners experienced severe hardship as a result of the burden of taxation and of low agricultural prices. Many were obliged or persuaded to sell their land. The owners of the great estates were barely affected by the adverse conditions. Many owners instructed their agents to acquire, irrespective of cost, any available land in the neighbourhood. Other prospective buyers were unable to compete. The motivation for expansion was very seldom to exploit economies of size in *farming*. Occasionally the motivation was to reap economies of size in *landownership*, notably by being able to afford full-time specialists in estate management. But, often enough, expansion had remarkably little to do with economic considerations. The purchasers were mainly concerned with enhancing their social prestige and with furthering their political ambitions.

Inheritance laws and customs

A crucial consideration is the nature of inheritance laws and customs relating to land. A landowner may or may not have the power of devisability, that is, the right to determine to whom ownership of his land passes on his death. The law may itself stipulate this. If the owner does have the power of devisability, the law may stipulate what happens if the owner dies intestate.

In many countries, the laws or customs are such that land is divided on the death of the owner between the members of the family. Deaths of landowners result in fragmentation of ownership units. Where this happens one of the most powerful long-term influences on the ownership structure is the rate of change of population. Increases in population are likely to result in fragmentation. It should not, of course, be thought that the rate of population change is somehow determined exogenously. It has been suggested that where land is fertile, affording its cultivators relatively high living standards, population increases are likely to be relatively high.[11] As a result the fragmentation of units through inheritance may be most rapid on fertile land. Similarly improved farming methods may stimulate population growth, possibly leading to smaller farming units.

Large estates are seldom broken up by subdivision between family members on the deaths of their owners. In England, when the devisability was established, the majority of the larger landowners adopted as customary the previous law of primogeniture, the principle whereby real property descends to the eldest son. The large estates were created by a patient and laborious process. Every effort was made to ensure that they were preserved intact. In addition to adopting the principle of primogeniture, the device of settlements was employed. Settlements not only prevented the current incumbent from selling land. They also denied to the incumbent the power of devisability: the land would pass to his eldest son, whether he himself liked it or not. Cheshire (p. 261) has explained why landowners often sought to render land inalienable for generations:

Old age especially, satisfied with its own achievements and often irritated by the apparent follies of a degenerate time, is inclined to restrain each generation of beneficiaries within close limits, and to provide for a series of interests. A landowner views the free power of alienation with complacency when it resides in his own hand but does not feel the same equanimity with regard to its transfer to others.[12]

The ownership structure and the operating structure

Under a system of universal owner-occupancy the ownership structure and the operating structure necessarily coincide. This carries potential implications for the performance of the agricultural sector. Changes in the operating structure require corresponding changes in the ownership structure. This means that desirable changes in the operating structure may be impeded by the difficulties inherent in transferring ownership. Moreover, changes in the ownership structure imply corresponding changes in the operating structure. This means that undesirable changes in the operating structure may be impelled by factors which pertain more to landownership than to farming. For example, attempts to redistribute wealth through the taxation of wealth passing at death or through a periodic wealth tax *may* lead to fragmentation of ownership units and therefore of farming units.

The possibility of leasing land provides an additional degree of flexibility. In this case the operating structure can be changed without any necessary change in the ownership structure. For example, as we saw earlier, two neighbouring owners may enter into a tenancy contract whereby one rents part of the other's land. Also, as we saw earlier, a large landowner may restructure the farms on his estate. Moreover, changes in the ownership structure can take place without this necessarily implying a change in the operating structure. An important example is the 'sale-and-leaseback' arrangement, whereby a small landowner sells his land to a large landowner and, under the same arrangement, enters into a tenancy arrangement with respect to the same land. Another interesting example is provided by the remarkable activity in the English land market in the third decade of the twentieth century. Prior to then, someone selling a large estate typically found that it did not pay to subdivide the estate into separate lots, for the reasons explained by Thompson in the quote at the beginning of the chapter. But during the 1920s a new factor predominated. A landowner wishing to sell a large estate discovered that, rather than selling the estate in its entirety, it was more lucrative to split the estate and sell farms to sitting tenants. If the owner himself did not recognize this, syndicates of land speculators certainly did. They bought entire estates and re-sold them to tenants. This period witnessed a remarkable fragmentation of large estates with owners being forced to sell their estates to pay past death duties or in anticipation of future death duties and with reluctant tenants being obliged to buy their farms or face the prospect of almost certain eviction. In this way considerable fragmentation of ownership units was accomplished without any inevitable changes in operating units.

With the possibility of leasing, we would expect the operating structure to be more responsive to changing economic circumstances. However, the rate of change in the ownership structure may be more or less rapid as a result of the possibility of leasing. It might be less rapid to the extent that leasing is an alternative to transfers of ownership. Neighbouring owners may elect for a tenancy contract rather than a transfer of ownership. However, it could be more rapid to the extent that it permits the expansion of ownership units to dimensions beyond the sizes which could be justified by farming considerations.

Structural change and labour markets

As we have intimated earlier, there is likely to be a close connection between land markets and labour markets. We have seen that wage-labour contracts may be an alternative to land transactions, in the form of either leaseholds or transfers of ownership. The existence of wage-labour contracts might therefore reduce the extent of structural change. In practice, however, the existence of wage-labour contracts and of labour markets is likely to expedite structural change in response to changing economic circumstances.

The possibility of obtaining employment, as an agricultural worker or in some other occupation, provides an option for a peasant farmer who is struggling to survive through cultivating his land. The prospect of a more or less stable wage-income may be more appealing than the uncertainties involved in farming on his own account. A small owner is much more likely to be persuaded to sell his land if the opportunity for wage labour exists. Structural change is often a symptom of more fundamental changes in the economy, such as a shift to wage-labour. Structural change may proceed most rapidly as a result of industrialization. If there is net migration from rural to urban areas and if this outweighs population increases within the rural sector the scope for increases in farm sizes will be enhanced. If younger people are anxious and able to move to towns and cities, fragmentation through inheritance may be reduced. The limitations on this process of outmigration, as many developing countries have discovered, is the difficulty of providing food for urban workers. As a result of the loss of agricultural labour, output typically falls; at the same time those remaining on the farms may increase their own consumption. If migrants to the urban areas return to the countryside, the trend to larger farms may not be reversed. They may have to return as hired agricultural workers.

The existence of a market for agricultural workers is also necessary for there to be incentives for the expansion of farming units beyond sizes which can be cultivated through family labour. Exploitation of economies of size in farming may effectively require hired workers to provide the necessary labour services. Even if there are no economies of size *per se*, farmers may wish to expand their acreages nevertheless and the possibility of hiring workers may enable them to do so.

V Changes in land use

We will now consider briefly the sorts of factors which cause changes in land use. We are not interested in the shifting use of land between different types of agricultural activities as such. Rather we are concerned with the movements of land between agricultural and non-agricultural uses. There are various forms of non-agricultural use. We will focus, first, on the case where the alternative to agricultural use is to leave land idle and, second, on the case where the relevant alternative is use for urban purposes. The former is the more important phenomenon for a predominantly agrarian economy. The latter is usually more relevant to a developed economy.

Agrarian economy

In a predominantly agrarian economy with 'surplus' land the major determinant of changes in the amount of land under cultivation is likely to be changes in population. The simplest hypothesis is that an increase in population will lead to an increase in the cultivated area, whereas a decrease in population will lead to a reduction in the cultivated area. Certainly this hypothesis is broadly supported by changes in land use in mediaeval England. The overall increase in population was, as one would expect, associated with an expansion in the cultivated area. Moreover, the catastrophic population fall resulting from the Black Death of 1348 led to vast areas of previously cultivated land being left idle.

The proposition that population changes affect the cultivated acreage is, of course, a basic feature of the Ricardian theory of rent. Increased food requirements can be met either by more intensive cultivation of the existing area or by extending the margin of cultivation. The responsiveness of the cultivated area will depend on the extent of differences in the characteristics of land, that is, in the properties of the soil and in climatic

conditions. The greater these differences, the less responsive the cultivated area is likely to be. Where uncultivated areas are considerably 'less
fertile', increased food requirements may be met entirely through intensification of cultivation.

A very important consideration, one which the Physiocrats appreciated, is that the bringing of additional land into cultivation may
involve significant initial investment. In order to prepare land for
cultivation, trees may have to be cut down, boulders and stones may
have to be cleared away, the natural terrain may have to be modified,
means of drainage or of irrigation may have to be provided for. These
high initial costs will have implications for the responsiveness of the
cultivated area to the pressure of food requirements. Even with a fairly
steady upward trend in population, the extension of the margin of
cultivation may be somewhat sporadic. A period of colonization may be
followed by a period wherein increased food needs are met through
intensification. When the pressure on the existing land becomes sufficiently great there may be a further spurt of colonization. These high
initial costs may also result in a form of ratchet effect, in the sense that
whereas population increases may lead to increases in the cultivated
area, albeit sporadically, subsequent declines in the population may lead
not to the abandonment of the colonized land but rather to the less
intensive use of the land. Whereas, *ex ante*, unprepared land may be
much less appealing than land which is already under the plough, once it
has been cleared its 'natural fertility' may be just as high. Indeed, it may
be even higher, so that if there is a reduction in the cultivated area as a
result of a population decline the land which is taken out of production
may well be 'old' land rather than land which has recently been
colonized.

The rate of colonization of new land will typically depend on institutional arrangements. A significant consideration will be who owns
uncultivated land. If all land is under private ownership, the decision to
bring land under the plough will be taken by owners according to
whether it pays them to do so. They may choose not to do so, even
though there are landless peasant families who would like to have the
opportunity to cultivate the land. There may be a land shortage even
with a land surplus. If uncultivated land has not been appropriated into
private ownership, an important consideration will be the ease with
which prospective colonizers can acquire property rights which are
sufficiently extensive to provide adequate incentives. The higher the
initial preparation costs the longer the guaranteed duration of occupancy
will have to be.

Institutional arrangements may also be critical to the extent that the colonization of land may be beyond the capacities of individual families. There may be a significant time-lag before the land is productive. Individual families may be unable to feed themselves during the initial investment period. Moreover, the necessary investment activities themselves may effectively require labour inputs in excess of those which individual families are able to provide. Investment projects are often undertaken on a collective or co-operative basis. The tribe or the village-community undertakes to clear land or provide irrigation, even though the land may subsequently be farmed on an individualistic basis by separate families. An important consideration will be the location of uncultivated land in relation to currently inhabited and cultivated areas. If the land is nearby it will be that much easier to prepare the land for cultivation. It may be possible to use labour during seasons where the labour requirements of cultivation are low, so that land clearance takes place with little disruption of the existing production process. Necessary expenditure on accommodation and on transport facilities may be considerably less.

Changes in land use naturally depend on techniques of production. Even with unchanging techniques, techniques are likely to be important. They determine the extent to which it is possible to intensify cultivation in response to increased food requirements.[13] Changes in land use are frequently associated with changes in techniques of production. Changes in technique are necessarily entailed in the critical transition from shifting cultivation to the sort of settled agriculture we have, in fact, been focusing on in earlier chapters. The most common form of shifting cultivation, still employed by millions of people, is the slash-and-burn technique. Trees and bushes are cut, left to dry and then burned. This clears the land, kills weeds and provides a rudimentary form of fertilizer in the form of ashes. The land is cultivated for one or perhaps two years. The land is then left fallow for a number of years, perhaps twenty or thirty years, and allowed to revert to secondary fallow or bush. This technique requires a low density of population relative to cultivable land. It has been observed that, in fact, many societies have population levels quite significantly less than the levels which could be sustained on the available land using these methods. Consequently certain increases in population may be accommodated without altering farming methods. But there comes a point where increased population pressure requires new farming practices.

Critical developments under settled agriculture are the adoption of methods which permit more than one crop per year and the introduction of rotational methods which preserve the fertility of land. It has been suggested that such changes in the mode of production played a crucial role in the emergence of capitalism in England.

Urban economy

In a developed urban economy the most important phenomenon is the loss of land to urban and industrial activities. Under a system of *laissez-faire*, there are a number of implications for agriculture. One implication is that urban 'needs' for land often take precedence over agricultural considerations. Frequently the land which is taken out of agriculture for urban development is the most fertile agricultural land.[14] Another implication is that agricultural landowners may secure very significant capital gains – or 'unearned increments' – by buying land at its agricultural value and subsequently discovering that they can resell the land at 'inflated' values to developers. This in turn may have a further feedback effect in the market for agricultural land if these sellers then look for alternative land to purchase with their new wealth. But a far more important implication is that the possibility of securing capital gains is an invitation to speculators to enter the agricultural land market. Not interested in agriculture as such nor even in the prospect of medium-term or long-term increases in the *agricultural* value of agricultural land, they may well be interested in the possibility of sizeable relatively short term capital gains.

For these and other reasons, governments in certain countries have chosen to intervene in one way or another.[15] Frequently they have sought to control changes in land use by requiring that plans for changes be submitted to public bodies before permission for their implementation is granted. The market mechanism is largely supplanted by adminis-trative decisions. The control of changes in use does not, of course, eliminate the market entirely nor does it remove the possibility of capital gains. The granting of planning permission typically confers an increase in the market value of the land concerned. Consequently, expectations about the future granting of planning permission are likely to have a significant impact on the current demand for certain types of land, particularly land in the rural–urban fringe. As a result of what is commonly described as 'hope value', the market value of agricultural land may diverge quite considerably from the perceived value of the land as an agricultural input.

We have already referred to the recurrent view that society as a whole should appropriate for itself increases in land values attributable, not to the energies of landowners, but to the progress of society. The notion that society should appropriate unearned increments has not, by any means, been confined to academic scribblings. Certain governments have sought to implement this. There is a particularly evident incentive to do so where the granting of planning permission results in an increase in value. These attempts have not always been successful. A particularly illuminating example is the attempt in the 1947 English Town and Country Planning Act to nationalize all development values by imposing a betterment levy of 100 per cent. The idea was that land would change hands at existing use value. The attempt failed. Landowners were reluctant to sell land to developers. It has been argued that there was some *inherent* flaw in the system, that it removed all incentive for development. This is fallacious. More to the point, landowners expected that the development charge would be repealed by the next Conservative Government. And so it was.

10

Evaluation and comparison of land tenure systems

In addition, we must bear in mind that the assumption of perfect competition and mobility and divisibility of the factors of production only very imperfectly correspond to reality. In small-scale agriculture, for example, the "last" worker employed is, frequently enough, the *only* one – for the simple reason that the area of land is so small that it does not permit the employment of more than one labourer in addition to the owner, and sometimes not even one. Wicksell (p. 120).

I Introduction

We will now consider some implications of the previous chapters. We are interested in evaluating and comparing different institutional arrangements. Systems will be differentiated according to the ownership of land and labour and according to who undertakes the entrepreneurial function. We will focus on four *pure* forms. The first system involves pure peasant proprietorships, whereby peasant households cultivate their own land using their own labour. The remaining systems involve the ownership of land and labour by separate groups. Under the second system, the owners of land hire workers. Under the third system, the workers rent land. Finally we will consider the system whereby some third party undertakes the role of co-ordination and both rents land and hires workers. The last three systems correspond to Wicksell's classification. In each case we will think in terms of well-defined economic classes. But we will not assume that all members of a group are homogeneous, in the sense of owning the same amounts of resources and of having the same preferences.

II Agricultural resource allocation under certainty

Meaning of and requirements for efficiency

Hitherto we have avoided, as far as possible, the use of the term 'efficiency'. We will now consider efficiency in the allocation of resources within agriculture, assuming, initially, no uncertainty with respect to prices or yields. In order to provide a framework for a subsequent

148

consideration of alternative institutional arrangements, we will define efficiency in the context of a very simple case.

Consider a central planner who has perfect information about resource availabilities and about techniques of production. He has complete freedom to decide on the precise allocation of given aggregate amounts of homogeneous agricultural land and homogeneous agricultural labour. He must decide on the number and sizes of operating units and on the allocation of labour between operating units. Suppose initially that these resources are used in the production of a single commodity, corn. In this context, efficiency requires that, given the available resources, the total output of corn must be maximized.

Suppose that the non-stochastic corn production function for an operating unit is given by

$$C = C(L, N)$$

where C represents the (maximum) output of corn at the end of the production period, L represents the amount of labour employed on the operating unit during the production period and N represents the size in acres of the operating unit, the form of the function being the same for each operating unit.[1] We will assume throughout that this production function is homothetic and strictly quasi-concave. A requirement of efficiency is that the marginal rate of substitution between land and labour be the same on each operating unit. Given identical, homothetic, strictly quasi-concave production functions, efficiency requires that the labour–land ratio be the same for each operating unit.

The property of homotheticity is quite a general one. It is implied by homogeneity. But it does not imply homogeneity.[2] We must therefore consider the implications of different assumptions about returns to scale. We will consider two 'extreme' cases. One case is where the micro production function is linear homogeneous. With this technology, scale as such does not matter. From the viewpoint of efficiency, provided that the labour–land ratio is the same on each farm, the precise number and sizes of farms do not matter. The other extreme is the case where the micro production function, though still homothetic and strictly quasi-concave, exhibits a zone of increasing returns followed 'immediately' by a zone of decreasing returns, the precise point of transition involving 'local' constant returns. With this technology, scale does matter. The precise number and sizes of farms do matter. The central planner has considerably fewer degrees of freedom. There is a unique 'efficient' size of a farming unit, this being the size at which there are local constant returns to scale, this in turn being the size at which, in Wicksell's terminology, 'average product' is maximized. The central planner must allocate the available resources in such a way that not only is the labour–land ratio the same on each farm but also each farm is of the efficient size.[3,4] These alternative assumptions about technology will play an important part in our comparison of institutional arrangements.

We do not, in fact, want to conduct our discussion of efficiency on the basis of the assumption that there is only one agricultural product, corn. In order to avoid the complications of investigating the nature of consumer demands and the process of the formation of prices for agricultural products, we will adopt in Sections II to IV Wicksell's assumption that the prices of agricultural products are given to the agricultural sector as a whole. We may suppose that they are governed by world market conditions. In this case the problem of the central planner is to maximize the *exchange value* of aggregate output. This does not complicate matters. Instead of using the corn production function, we will substitute a relationship between the (maximum) value of output of a farm and the levels of labour and land inputs. This is simply the 'revenue function' we have been using throughout earlier chapters.

So far we have supposed that the only inputs are land and labour. Physical capital goods can be incorporated in various ways. The simplest way is to treat durable capital goods and circulating capital goods differently. In the Walrasian manner, we can postulate the existence, at a point in time, of given stocks of durable capital goods of different varieties and different vintages. We can assume that any depreciation in these durable capital goods is independent of whether they are employed productively or not, so that there is no complicating inter-temporal trade-off; that the services of these capital goods have no potential productive use outside the agricultural sector; and that there is no possibility of buying or selling these goods on the world market. As regards circulating capital goods, we can assume that the country concerned imports these at given world market prices, the payments to be made at the end of the production period. Under these assumptions, the objective of the central planner is to maximize the excess of the value of aggregate agricultural output over the cost of importing the circulating capital goods. With this in mind, the central planner will have to decide on the quantities of circulating capital goods to import and on precisely how to deploy these, the durable capital goods, the land and the labour.[5]

Given that the micro 'revenue function' is homothetic and strictly quasi-concave, efficiency requires that the ratio between any two inputs be the same on each production unit. Efficiency also requires, for each circulating capital good, not only that its marginal revenue product be the same on each production unit but also that this common value equal its world price. The inferences we drew in the two-factor case about different technological assumptions still apply. The incorporation of physical capital goods makes no formal difference as regards whether or not the sizes of production units matter as such. However, from a practical point of view, the presence of physical capital goods may render the assumption of linear homogeneity less plausible.

Pure peasant proprietorships

Consider a system whereby peasant households cultivate their own land using their own labour and their own capital. To keep it a *pure* system, we exclude both the hiring of agricultural labour and the leasing of agricultural land. Transfers of landownership are permitted. Moreover, transactions with respect to physical capital goods are permitted. Peasant households may enter into transactions with each other. They may purchase durable capital goods from producers in the industrial sector who, to conform with our discussion of the central planner, have given stocks as a result of past production. They may purchase imported circulating capital goods.

Under a system of pure peasant proprietorships the prospect of efficiency in the allocation of resources within the agricultural sector is remote. Suppose for the moment that the only inputs are land and labour. We have seen that a fairly general assumption about technology requires that the labour–land ratio be the same on each production unit. Suppose that each family has a given amount of labour time, determined by the number of workers, which it intends to devote to cultivation. We will refer to this as its labour endowment. Assuming that there has not recently been some land reform which has allocated, or re-allocated, land between families according to the number of workers, we may suppose that the inherited structure is such that labour–land endowment ratios differ. The question is whether there is any mechanism which will lead to efficiency in the actual utilization of resources.

There is one possibility. Efficiency in the allocation of resources might be attained through transfers of land ownership. The pattern of land ownership and use might adjust to the labour pattern. Families with relatively high labour–land endowments might purchase land from those with relatively low labour–land endowments. But the arguments developed in the previous chapter suggest that little reliance should be placed on this. It is unlikely to happen partly because of transaction costs. Such costs may be considerable: in the light of spatial considerations, a highly complex restructuring may be required to achieve efficiency.[6] More importantly, the general reluctance of peasant households to sell land unless compelled to do so will undermine any such process. This reluctance to part with land may be due to the 'non-economic' considerations referred to by Postan in the quotation at the beginning of Chapter 8. But it may have a solid economic foundation: as we have noted before, land is often the most secure form in which to hold wealth. Given a highly imperfect financial capital market, given the risks entailed in lending money, given the uncertainties attached to the future real value of financial wealth particularly in an economy suffering from inflation, a prudent peasant household will be understandably wary of exchanging land for money.[7]

Even if labour–land ratios do coincide for each family, this may not be sufficient for the attainment of efficiency. It would be sufficient if the micro revenue function exhibits constant returns to scale. But in the case of variable returns to scale there is no reason why the resulting pattern of resource allocation would be efficient. Indeed, the efficient size of productive unit *may* require labour inputs in excess of the labour endowment of even the largest peasant family.[8]

There is another possible case in which efficiency in the allocation of resources may be achieved. Suppose that there are constant returns to scale. Suppose also that each family has a given endowment of labour which it can use in cultivating its own land or devote to part-time off-farm employment. Assuming no institutional rigidities, assuming that all families face the same wage rate for part-time off-farm employment and assuming that all families *do* avail themselves of this opportunity, then the marginal revenue product of farm-labour would be the same for each. In the present context little reliance should be placed on this mechanism for attaining efficiency. Since the system under consideration does not involve hired agricultural labour, the possibility of part-time work for another farmer is *ipso facto* excluded. The possibility of part-time industrial work may also be excluded in practice to the extent that, for certain families anyway, such jobs may only be available at a considerable distance away. This possibility for achieving efficiency would not merit more than a footnote were it not for the prevalence in the literature of the assumption that part-time off-farm employment is available. Many analyses seem to take for granted the existence of all markets, irrespective of the institutional arrangement under consideration.

Granted these inflexibilities with respect to land and labour, there might seem to be some consolation in the prospect of efficiency in the inter-farm allocation of physical capital. But the attainment of efficiency may be impeded for various reasons. The markets for physical capital goods may exhibit various imperfections. In particular, there may be divergencies between acquisition prices and salvage prices. This may result in a close correspondence between the pattern of ownership of these resources and their use, with many households not participating in certain factor markets at all. Furthermore, any imperfections in the financial capital market will be transmitted into other markets. A peasant household whose borrowing is dictated largely by consumption needs may be effectively excluded from acquiring certain inputs at all, particularly durable capital goods. There will be a greater prospect of efficiency if industrial producers of durable goods are prepared to retain ownership and lease their services to farmers or if households purchase durable factors jointly. Moreover, inter-household transactions may take the form of the leasing of the services of durable capital goods rather than of outright transfers of ownership. However, as Wiens has recently argued, if the rental is paid at the end of the production period, a household which leases an asset to another runs the risk of a default in payment. The effect is similar to that of a divergence between acquisition price and salvage price: it may further accentuate the correspondence between ownership and use. This argument applies *a fortiori* to the lending of money.

Land and labour under separate ownership

We will consider now the Wicksellian case where land and labour are owned by distinct groups. We will initially examine two systems: one where the owners of land hire labour and one where the owners of labour rent land.

The system whereby landowners hire workers offers a greater prospect of efficiency in the allocation of resources within agriculture than a system of pure peasant proprietorships for one main reason. There is a greater likelihood of a tolerably efficient pattern óf labour allocation. Under a system of wage-labour, labour is potentially more 'mobile'. Whereas under a system of pure peasant proprietorships the pattern of labour use corresponds to the family pattern, this is no longer necessary with the hiring of labour. If there is a perfect labour market and if wages are paid at the end of the period, an owner-operator who seeks to maximize his terminal financial wealth will wish to equate the marginal revenue product of hired labour to the market wage rate. If wages are advanced, then provided that there is a perfect financial capital market, efficiency in the allocation of labour over farms will still be achieved. Complete efficiency will, of course, not be attained because of imperfections in markets. But even granted these imperfections, there is at least some sort of mechanism in operation.[9]

Where production involves only labour and land, the equalization of the marginal revenue product of labour over production units will imply overall efficiency if the technology is characterized by constant returns to scale. However, if there are variable returns to scale, land transactions may also be required to attain efficiency. Under this system, these can only take the form of outright transfers of ownership. Compared to peasant proprietorships, this system *may* be associated with a greater commercial orientation on the part of landowners. Decisions as to buying and selling land may be based more closely on economic considerations. This may result in greater activity in the market for the ownership of agricultural land. But this possibility should not be exaggerated. The very nature of the system suggests that status depends on landownership.

The system whereby labourers rent land also offers a greater prospect of efficiency in the allocation of resources compared to pure peasant proprietorships. As we emphasized in the last chapter, the leasing of land provides additional flexibility, in that the operating structure need no longer coincide with the ownership structure. Changes in the operating structure do not require transfers of landownership. Under this system a peasant family may rent land from more than one landowner. Moreover, large landowners may restructure operating units in the light of changing economic conditions. The additional flexibility afforded by leasing is also an advantage of this system compared to the system whereby landowners hire workers.

It might seem that this system would suffer in comparison to the wage-labour system as regards the allocation of labour. But this should not be exaggerated. There may be some sort of accommodation between farm sizes and family sizes. This may come about as a result of a large landowner having an incentive to restructure farms as a result of changes in the sizes and compositions of his tenant families. More importantly, it may come about through the operation of competitive forces, since there is a presumption that relatively large units will be leased to families with relatively large numbers of workers.

Capitalist tenant farmers

A system whereby a group of 'specialized' farmers undertakes the role of co-ordination offers the greatest prospect of flexibility and efficiency. This system involves both the leasing of land and the hiring of labour. As such this system enables the breaking down of the correspondence between the ownership and use of both land and labour.

In order to highlight the importance of technological considerations, it is worth considering Wicksell's 'concrete, though somewhat artificial, example'. He assumes an area of 10,000 square miles devoted to agriculture and a working population of 160,000 homogeneous adult men. He further supposes that the territory is sub-divided into 10,000 homogeneous estates, or what we have referred to as ownership units, of one square mile each. We will also assume, although Wicksell does not do so, that there are 160,000 families each comprising one of the adult men and his dependants.

Assuming constant returns to scale, it is necessary and sufficient for an efficient allocation of resources that labour–land ratios on each operating unit be equal, that is, that the labour–land ratio everywhere be sixteen to one. Efficiency can be achieved in two 'interesting' ways. First, each landowner can employ sixteen men. Wicksell, himself, explains how under a system whereby landowners hire labourers, this *will* be the outcome with a perfectly competitive labour market.[10] Second, each landowner may sub-divide his ownership unit into sixteen operating units each of 0.0625 square miles. There would then be 160,000 operating units, each of which would be leased to one of the families.[11] Thus efficiency could be achieved through a system whereby labourers rent land. From the point of view of technological considerations alone, there is no particular rationale for any intermediaries, though efficiency could, of course, be achieved in any number of ways by a system involving capitalist tenants.

Consider now the case of variable returns to scale. Suppose that, by chance, efficiency just happens to dictate that there be 10,000 operating units each of one square mile and that sixteen men be employed on each. There is clearly no problem for the system whereby landowners hire labourers since the efficient operating structure coincides with the owner-ship structure. However, there is a problem for the system whereby labourers rent land. Family sizes are 'too small', in that each comprises only one labourer. Wicksell does refer to the possibility of labourers, either singly or *in combination*, renting land. But this begs many issues. Moreover, the case where families combine into groups of sixteen to rent land may appropriately be regarded as a different institutional arrangement. Suppose that instead, by chance, efficiency just happens to dictate that there should be 160,000 operating units, each of 0.0625 square miles and each with one worker. There is clearly no problem for the system whereby the owners of labour rent land since the efficient 'labour structure' just coincides with the family pattern. However, there is a problem for the system whereby landowners hire workers: ownership units are 'too large'. Barring the fragmentation of ownership units through transfers of land ownership, efficiency cannot be achieved under this system.

If efficiency dictates any other pattern of factor use, *both* systems encounter problems and the system with a third party as co-ordinator comes into its own. Suppose that efficiency dictates that there be 40,000 farms each of 0.25 square miles and each with 4 men. Whereas this pattern could relatively easily be accomplished through a system of capitalist intermediaries, under the other systems there would have to be either the formation of co-operatives of labourers or transfers of landownership amounting to a quadrupling in the number of landowners. Suppose, instead, that efficiency requires that there be 5,000 farms each of two square miles and each with thirty-two men. Whereas this pattern could be accomplished relatively easily through a system of capitalist intermediaries, as regards the other systems both ownership units and families are 'too small'. Under the other systems there would have to be either the formation of co-operatives of workers; or some form of co-operation between neighbouring landowners; or transfers of landownership resulting in a halving of the number of landowners. Clearly technological considerations, taken in conjunction with the pattern of landownership, can imply a rationale for the existence of a third class who undertake the entrepreneurial role.

It is difficult to say anything definite about the technology of agricultural production, certainly in a regime involving only land and labour. Increasing returns, though likely to prevail at very small sizes, may well soon be exhausted. As has often been observed, there are considerably fewer prospective benefits from specialization of labour in agriculture than in industry. Irrespective of whether constant returns to scale is a reasonable approximation where only labour and land are involved, where agricultural production involves the use of physical capital goods, as in practice it does, this assumption becomes less appealing. Wicksell, himself, argued that the assumption of constant returns to scale 'is, of course, very seldom realized as a general principle in a given branch of production; the scale on which an enterprise operates nearly always has some influence on its average product' (p. 129).[12] In contrast, Wicksteed argued that linear homogeneity is more or less self-evident provided that inputs are defined correctly and comprehensively.

Certainly the common argument that the existence of 'decreasing returns to scale' implies that some relevant input has been omitted from the specified production function, so that all inputs are *not* being altered proportionately, is a persuasive one. However, the possibility of a zone of increasing returns to scale is less easily dismissed. The formulation of the production function is critical. If the inputs into the production process were to be specified in terms of, say, the number of shovels or the number of tractors, then since a shovel and a tractor are indivisible, activities employing them could not be perfectly divisible.[13] If, however, the production function is specified in terms of the flows of services provided by shovels or tractors during the production process, as we have for durable capital goods, this source of indivisibility does not arise. The assumption of constant returns to scale may be a reasonable one. However, to argue that constant returns to scale is a logical necessity would be unwise since it is easy to conceive of plots of land sufficiently small that tractor services could not meaningfully be employed on them.

The formulation of the production function in terms of flows of input services is inevitable if one is to allow for institutional arrangements whereby the producers of durable capital goods retain ownership and lease their services to farmers or whereby peasant households purchase durable capital goods jointly. We suggested earlier that such arrangements might promote greater efficiency in the utilization of resource services. Without now wishing to detract from the possible importance of such arrangements, it is worth noting that spatial considerations will typically be important. In particular, time may be lost in moving, say, a tractor from the land of one farmer to the land of another, the time spent depending on the distance involved. A similar complication arises in relation to labour services. If a labourer works for two or more land-owners he will typically have to spend time commuting between their farms. The time spent will depend on which particular landowners he works for. The considerations involved are clearly analogous to the issues raised by the spatial characteristics of operating units.

Institutional arrangements and distribution

An important consideration in the case where land and labour are under separate ownership is whether or not institutional arrangements affect distribution. In general, institutional arrangements will matter unless there are constant returns to scale and unless all relevant markets function perfectly. Assume that there are constant returns to scale. In the case where landowners hire workers the equilibrium market wage rate will equal the common value of the marginal product of labour. By Euler's theorem for a linear homogeneous function, the implicit rent of land will equal the value of the marginal product of land. In the case where workers rent land the equilibrium market rent will equal the common value of the marginal product of land and the implicit wage rate will equal the value of the marginal product of labour. Provided that the relevant markets do function perfectly, the implied distributive returns to individuals and classes will be independent of who assumes the entrepreneurial role. However, as we have seen, if there are variable returns to scale, institutional arrangements will, in general, affect the resulting aggregate value of output. Consequently in this case the distributive returns to individuals and classes will, in general, depend on whether landowners hire workers or whether workers rent land or whether some third party assumes the entrepreneurial role.

III Agricultural resource allocation under uncertainty

Meaning of and requirements for efficiency

Where there is uncertainty regarding prices or yields, the meaning of 'efficiency' in the allocation of resources is no longer clear-cut. In general, the delineation of efficiency in the allocation of resources cannot be separated from which members of society bear the uncertainty and from their attitudes to doing so. An exhaustive consideration of this issue would detract from our main concern. Consequently, following Stiglitz, we will adopt a particularly simple specification of the impact of uncertainty, one which permits a straightforward delineation of productive efficiency.

We will consider the case where a single product, corn, is produced using only land services and labour services. For each operating unit, the output of corn is a stochastic function of land and labour, the common micro-function being

$$C = g(\theta) . F(L, N)$$

where θ represents the 'state of nature', where the expected value of $g(\theta)$ is one and where the variance of $g(\theta)$ is strictly positive. We will assume that the function $F(L, N)$ is strictly quasi-concave and linear homogeneous. The assumption of linear homogeneity enables us to separate the issue of uncertainty from the technological considerations discussed in the previous section.

Consider a central planner with perfect information about the available resource services and about the stochastic micro production function. He does not know at the beginning of the production period what value θ will take. His appropriate course of action is to equate the labour–land ratios on all operating units. *Whatever the value of θ turns out to be,* the aggregate output of corn will be maximized by this strategy. It would make no difference if the central planner did know at the beginning of the period what the value of θ would be.[14] Note that equating the labour–land ratios is also both necessary and sufficient for maximizing the aggregate *value* of corn output at the end of the period. In this context it makes no difference whether the central planner is certain or uncertain what the world price of corn will be at the end of the period. The simplicity of the appropriate strategy is, of course, a consequence of the multiplicative formulation of the effect of nature and of the restrictive assumption that the proportional impact of the state of nature is the same for all operating units, irrespective, for example, of their location.

Alternative institutional arrangements

Consider the situation whereby land and labour are owned by distinct classes. The most interesting institutional arrangement in this context is one whereby landowners and workers enter into share contracts. But before turning to such a system it is worth considering briefly, first, the case where landowners hire workers for fixed wages and, second, the case where workers rent land for fixed payments.[15]

Under a system whereby landowners hire workers for fixed wages, efficiency in the allocation of resources will be attained in a special case. If all landowners are risk neutral, they will seek to maximize expected terminal wealth. Assuming that wages are paid at the end of the period, each landowner will demand that level of labour which would equate the wage rate and the *expected* marginal revenue product of labour. Given a perfectly functioning labour market, efficiency will be attained. The labour–land ratio will be the same on all operating units. The aggregate value of corn output will be maximized whatever the state of nature.[16]

If, however, landowners are averse to risk then, in general, efficiency in the allocation of resources will not be achieved. For a risk averse landowner the expected marginal revenue product of the optimal level of labour is strictly greater than the wage rate. Except by coincidence, expected marginal revenue products of labour will differ between units. They will differ as a result of different degrees of risk aversion and different amounts of owned land.

It is worth noting the distributional consequences of uncertainty in the context of this simple economy. If landowners are risk neutral then the equilibrium wage rate will be the same as it would have been if there had been no uncertainty, that is, if $g(\theta) = 1$ for all θ. The *expected* return to a landowner will equal what his certain return would have been. If, however, landowners are risk averse, the wage rate will be lower than under certainty. The expected return to a particular landowner may be higher, the same or lower than it would have been under certainty. Although it is perhaps likely to be higher, it must be remembered that, to the extent that there is inefficiency in the allocation of resources, the expected aggregate value of output will be lower than the aggregate value of output under certainty.

Consider now the institutional arrangement whereby workers assume the entrepreneurial role, paying landowners contractually stipulated rents which are independent of the actual levels of output. The propositions regarding resource allocation and distribution are analogous to those under the previous system. Thus, if workers are risk-neutral and if the rental market does function perfectly, productive efficiency will be attained and the equilibrium level of rent will be the same as it would have been under certainty. If, however, workers are risk averse productive efficiency will not be achieved, in general.

If both landowners and workers are risk averse, there will be an incentive for some form of risk sharing. Thus landowners may assume the entrepreneurial role, paying workers contractually stipulated shares in output together perhaps with stipulated fixed fees. Alternatively workers may assume the entrepreneurial role, paying landowners stipulated shares in output together perhaps with stipulated fixed rents. Such institutional arrangements will not, in general, result in productive efficiency. According to Stiglitz, productive efficiency will result if both groups can 'mix' contracts, that is, if each individual worker can enter into different contracts with different landowners and each individual landowner can enter into different contracts with different workers.[17] But Stiglitz's *formal* analysis ignores spatial considerations. If a worker were to enter into contracts with many different landowners then, as Stiglitz does acknowledge, he may have to spend time moving between disparate plots of land. Such costs are not simply one reason why such mixing of contracts is unlikely to occur. If the mixing of contracts can and does occur and if the resulting set of contracts implies positive commuting costs, then productive efficiency will not be achieved. Thus although the institution of share tenancy does provide the possibility of risk sharing, it is not generally sufficient to yield efficiency in resource allocation.

At this stage it is worth enlarging on a suggestion, in Chapter 7, that if both landowners and workers are risk averse there may be scope for intermediaries. Suppose that a particular landowner and worker are contemplating a contract which would involve, say, a pure sharing arrangement. If they are both risk averse, the sum of the landowner's certainty equivalent (fixed) rent to be paid at the end of the period and of the worker's certainty equivalent (fixed) wage to be paid at the end of the period must be strictly less than the expected value of the output of the farm. Consider a 'risk neutral' prospective intermediary. There must exist contractually stipulated rent and wage payments which would exceed the respective certainty equivalent levels but which would still leave the intermediary with a strictly positive *expected* profit. This might appear to ensure the existence of a basis for a mutually beneficial tri-partite arrangement, whereby the intermediary bears all the uncertainty. There is, however, an important qualification. As we noted earlier, from the point of view of a factor owner the fact that a contract stipulates a fixed payment does not make the receipt of that payment certain if the payment is to be made at some future date. In the case under consideration the issue is more than whether or not landowner and worker are convinced of the integrity of the intermediary. In the absence of other wealth or income, the intermediary would not be able to guarantee payments which the landowner and worker would prefer to the share tenancy. For at least one state of nature the value of output must be less than the sum of the certainty equivalent rent and the certainty equivalent wage. Thus there may not be the basis for an arrangement whereby the intermediary bears all the uncertainty.[18] Clearly the intervention of a third-party is most likely to occur where he has sufficient initial financial wealth to be able to pay landowner and worker at the outset of the production period.[19] In this case he would bear all the uncertainty.

Considering now the case of many landowners and many workers, if risk neutral intermediaries do assume the entrepreneurial role and if the relevant markets do function perfectly, productive efficiency will be achieved in the context of our economy. However, whereas risk aversion on the part of landowners and workers may be a possible explanation of the emergence of capitalist tenant farmers, the existence of such a group does not, of course, mean that they are risk neutral.

Attitudes to risk and financial capital markets

Most economists who have explicitly considered the attitudes of farmers to uncertainty have suggested that they are averse to risk. It must be emphasized, however, that most analyses have been conducted either in an atemporal framework or in terms of a single-period framework. If a longer-term viewpoint is considered, it is clear that there may well be a connection between 'attitudes to risk' and the nature of the market for financial capital.

Consider a peasant household contemplating a number of alternative courses of action, financial capital not being required for production itself. Corresponding to each course of action is a subjective probability density function for financial wealth at the end of the production period under consideration. If we consider the household as having preferences as between these subjective probability density functions, such preferences may depend critically on whether or not there are opportunities for borrowing or lending. Whereas, in the absence of any opportunities for borrowing, a particular level of terminal financial wealth might be 'disastrous' from the point of view of consumption possibilities for the next period, much less 'weight' may be attached to that outcome where borrowing is possible.

One possible connection between risk attitudes and financial capital markets has been identified by Masson. He has demonstrated that risk averse behaviour may result not from a psychological aversion to risk but from imperfections in financial capital markets. Specifically, an individual who is risk neutral in an intertemporal sense may behave as if he were risk averse in relation to a single time period if, say, the rate of interest at which he can borrow money exceeds the rate of interest at which he can lend money. It does not, of course, follow from this that all instances of risk averse behaviour must be attributable to such imperfections. It does not follow that if there is a perfect financial capital market then the appropriate assumption for a peasant household is one of risk neutrality. Fama has demonstrated that if an individual is risk averse, in the sense that his utility function for *lifetime* consumption is strictly concave, and if markets are perfect, then his behaviour in any period will be indistinguishable from a risk averse expected utility maximizer with a one-period horizon. Thus, while the assumption of risk aversion certainly may be more compelling in the absence of a financial capital market or in the case of an imperfect financial capital market, risk aversion is still a plausible working hypothesis even with a perfect financial capital market. It must also be remembered that farmers, even in developed countries, frequently display an aversion to borrowing money *per se*.

IV Labour–leisure choices and incentives

In the previous two sections we assumed 'inelastic' labour supplies. The introduction of labour–leisure choices complicates matters somewhat, even under certainty. Efficiency still requires productive efficiency in the sense that the aggregate value of output be maximized given the amounts of resource services actually employed. This requires, in particular, that the marginal revenue product of labour be the same on all operating units. But, in addition, Paretian efficiency requires that each household's marginal rate of substitution between terminal financial wealth and leisure equal this common marginal revenue product of labour.

The introduction of a labour–leisure choice clearly does not reinstate the system of pure peasant proprietorships as efficient. It is true that each utility maximizing household will equate the marginal rate of substitution between terminal financial wealth and leisure to the marginal revenue product of its own labour. But in the absence of transfers of landownership and of opportunities for part-time off-farm employment, there is no mechanism to equalize the marginal revenue products of labour between households.

Although the system of pure peasant proprietorships is not reinstated as efficient, it is worth noting that with respect to the labour–leisure choice this system may possess an advantage compared to a system involving wage-labour, namely, that whereas a peasant household farming its own land is free to determine its labour input, one which sells labour services for wages may not be. A common feature of actual labour markets is the existence of standard working times, or at least of minimum working times. Such rigidities in labour markets may result not only in differences in the marginal revenue products of labour between employers but also, as Sen has observed, in 'inefficient' levels of labour supplied by households.

One of the undoubted attractions of the system of peasant proprietorships is that, in the absence of distortionary taxes, each peasant household reaps the full benefits and bears the full costs of its own activities.[20] This applies to 'farming' and 'investment' activities, both of which are under unified control.[21] In contrast, a hired agricultural worker on a fixed wage does not have a direct economic interest in the fruits of his own labour. The issue is more than simply whether the hired worker actually spends the contractually agreed number of hours working on the farm. It may be relatively easy for the employer to ensure this. The real issue is the *quality* of the labour input, that is, the energy, care and initiative displayed by the worker.[22] These attributes are particularly crucial in the context of agriculture. A characteristic feature of agriculture is that plans have often to be re-evaluated more or less continuously in response to changing circumstances, the precise timing of activities being of particular importance. Decisions often have to be taken 'on the spot'. Thus an employer who is not actually working alongside his hired labourers will normally need to give them some scope for discretion. A worker who does fall short of his employer's expectations may be fired. But the potency of this 'incentive' for the worker should not be exaggerated. Where a system of hired labour at fixed wages prevails, it may be that most workers display an aversion to hard work. An individual worker may know that his employer has little prospect of finding a replacement whom he knows to be more industrious.

In contrast to the hired worker, a tenant does have a direct interest in the fruits of his own labour. The extent to which the benefits and costs of the tenant's activities are internalized will, of course, depend on the precise nature of the tenancy contract, that is, on the duration and security of his tenure, on the nature of his rental payments and on whether there are provisions for compensatory payments at the termination of tenancies.

One of the most common criticisms of tenancy is that it involves a lack of 'synchronization' between the activities of landowner and tenant. It is suggested that each party takes his decisions about input acquisition and utilization assuming that the other party's behaviour is given. But this supposition is akin to the naive assumption of zero conjectural variations in duopoly. As we have seen, landlord and tenant may discuss in detail their respective activities *ex ante* and, indeed, stipulate them in the contract of tenancy. Even after the leasehold commences, they may continue to consider their activities jointly. We would not argue that there is no foundation whatsoever for this particular line of argument, particularly because of the need for frequent re-evaluations of plans. But its significance has often been exaggerated.[23] An inefficient lack of co-ordination is not *inherent* in a tenancy system. The purpose of a tenancy system is precisely to co-ordinate the use of resources which are under separate ownership. For the reasons explained in Chapter 5, a particular tenancy arrangement may be more or less successful in this.

As important as the formal (or informal) provisions of tenancy arrangements is the extent to which landowners display a genuine interest in agriculture and in their estates. As Adam Smith observed, those who inherit large estates frequently possess neither the requisite inclinations or abilities. Where they can and do spend money on their estates, it may well be on their own residences, to the neglect of the agricultural characteristics of their estates. Moreover, as various Classical economists stressed, notably McCulloch, the under-renting of land may be just as harmful to the performance of agriculture as over-renting. If a landowner does not adopt a commercial attitude to his tenantry and charges rents which are well below what the land is worth, tenants may not exert themselves. Given that landowners may be more interested in social status, in furthering their political ambitions or in hunting, to analyse the operation of a system on the assumption that landowners are always motivated by wealth maximization may convey a deceptive impression of the functioning of the system.

V Institutional arrangements and economic development

Efficiency in the allocation of resources within agriculture, important though it may be, is not the only criterion for evaluating the performance of alternative institutional arrangements, even leaving aside distributional considerations. Indeed, the pursuit of efficiency, so defined, may be regarded as a means to attaining a wider objective, namely the overall development of the economy.

A comprehensive analysis of the role of the agricultural sector in the process of development is, of course, beyond the confines of the present study.[24] Our purpose is simply to indicate that institutional arrangements in the agricultural sector may well influence its contribution to economic development. Even to do this we must be somewhat broader in our outlook than in earlier chapters and be more specific about the linkages between the agricultural sector and the industrial sector. Considering an economy in the early stages of development, we can identify three major contributions. First, the agricultural sector will typically have to release human resources for use in the industrial sector. Second, agriculture will have to increase the amount of food delivered to the industrial sector in order to feed the expanding industrial population. Finally, to the extent that industrialization requires increased domestic savings, agriculture will typically have to bear a significant part of the burden. In considering the relationship between these various contributions and institutional forms, we assume no government intervention.

For our purpose it is sufficient to contrast a system of pure peasant proprietorships with the tri-partite system involving landowners, capitalist tenants and hired workers. Confining the comparison to these two systems enables us to bring out the sorts of issues involved with a minimum of repetition.

Pure peasant proprietorships

A system of pure peasant proprietorships in agriculture may impede rather than facilitate industrialization. One of the main reasons is that it is likely to be relatively difficult for the industrial sector to attract labour out of agriculture. There are various reasons for this: the attachment of the peasant to his land and to farming, a preference for working for himself rather than for another, the risks involved in moving to the industrial sector typically with no guarantee of obtaining employment at all, let alone at a wage which would be preferable to farming his own land.

Furthermore, if people are attracted out of agriculture there is then the problem of feeding them. The impact on the marketed surplus of food of an out-migration of labour will depend on the effects, first, on agricultural production and, second, on the consumption of food by the agricultural sector. The likely impact of an out-migration of labour on agricultural output is a controversial issue. Some development economists have asserted that there is frequently surplus labour in agriculture in the sense that people can be withdrawn from agriculture without this involving a reduction in agricultural output. The naive form of this argument supposes that the marginal product of labour is zero. A more sophisticated form of this argument differentiates between the agricultural labour force and the amount of labour-time devoted to agricultural production. This argument supposes that, although the marginal product of labour-time is not zero, part of the labour force can still be withdrawn without this leading to a reduction in agricultural production since the lost labour time can be made up by those who remain working harder. But the relevant question is whether those who remain will do so.[25]

Under a system of pure peasant proprietorships those who remain may well work *less* hard. To the extent that those who remain are better off, they may choose to take part of their increased real income in the form of greater leisure. Moreover, even if agricultural production does not fall, those who remain may consume more food. Consequently, the marketed surplus of food may not rise sufficiently to feed adequately an expanding industrial population. This might be mitigated by a shift in the terms of trade in favour of agricultural goods compared to industrial goods. But a 'perverse' response to an improvement in the terms of trade is possible under this system. Moreover, particularly in the early stages of development, there may be few industries producing consumption goods for sale to peasants.

Tri-partite system

Compared to a system of peasant proprietorships, the tri-partite system is more likely to facilitate the process of development. An important consideration is that, where the agrarian system involves hired agricultural labour, it is likely to be much easier for the industrial sector to expand its labour force. The existence of a class of landless labourers provides a pool from which the industrial sector can draw. A landless agricultural worker is much more likely to be willing than a peasant proprietor to move to industrial areas. He is likely to be less attached to agriculture. He is already accustomed to working for someone else. In addition, he may be 'pushed' into such a step by being fired by his agricultural employer.[26] A further advantage of this system is that the intermediary class may constitute a pool of entrepreneurial talent on which the industrial sector can draw.

Under the tri-partite system, the problem of feeding the expanding industrial population may be less acute. This system necessarily involves some degree of commercial orientation on the part of farmers. *Ceteris paribus*, farmers will wish to expand their production in response to a rise in the prices of agricultural goods. But other things may not be equal. The key to the likely course of events under this system lies in the agricultural labour market. As a result of the reduction in the agricultural work force, there may be an increase in the agricultural wage rate. An important consideration is how the remaining agricultural workers respond to a wage increase. At a higher wage rate they may wish to work longer hours. But even if labourers would like to work fewer hours, the institutional rigidities characteristic of labour markets may prevent them from doing so. This contrasts with peasant farmers who are free to decide how much labour time to devote to cultivation. Thus a wage-labour system may be less likely to result in increased leisure.

The contribution of the agricultural sector to development will depend crucially on what landowners do with their rents, that is, on whether they re-invest them in agriculture or invest them in the industrial sector or spend them on imported luxury goods. Similarly much will depend on what tenant farmers do with their profits. It is quite likely that capitalist tenant farmers will use their profits productively. How landowners will use their rents is more debatable. The inequality in wealth and income which is likely to accompany this system may offer the prospect of much more rapid development than a system of peasant proprietorships, but whether this is realized will depend very much on attitudes and inclinations.

VI Some concluding comments

It was suggested in Chapter 1 that assertions that alternative institutional arrangements are 'equivalent' in terms of resource allocation should be treated with suspicion. We have argued in this chapter that institutional arrangements will, in practice, influence both the allocation of resources and distribution. It may be objected that we have 'prejudiced' the case by contrasting *pure* forms. But this is how Wicksell compared alternative arrangements. Moreover, if the 'equivalence' proposition is to be meaningful, it must apply to pure systems.

It is difficult to pin down precisely what certain economists, such as Cheung, are actually arguing. On the one hand, they seem to be advancing a form of 'equivalence' argument.[27,28] On the other hand, they seek to 'explain' why in some particular context one arrangement is chosen rather than another. There is a danger of inconsistency, unless it is clearly specified that a subset of the assumptions upon which the equivalence argument is based no longer holds when explanations are provided of why certain institutional arrangements are chosen. Consider the explanation based on different transaction costs. If there are different transactions costs then the implied resource allocation will not be the same under different institutional arrangements. Transaction costs are not 'transfer payments'; they imply a use of resources for effecting transactions.

It was also suggested in Chapter 1 that dogmatic rankings of alternative land tenure arrangements should be regarded with suspicion. If this chapter has extolled the virtues, from an efficiency point of view, of a tri-partite system, the primary reason for this was to counter-balance the widespread view that the 'best' system is necessarily one involving peasant proprietorships. Our analysis suggests that there may well be a conflict between the desire for tolerable efficiency in the allocation of resources and the desire to prohibit the leasing of land and the hiring of labour on ideological grounds.

A fundamental problem with the often recommended 'land-to-the-tiller' strategy concerns its effects on the structure of resource use and allocation. If concomitant measures are taken to prohibit wage labour and inter-peasant transactions with respect to agricultural land, the system is unlikely to be efficient in terms of resource allocation. If both leasing and transfers of ownership through sale are prohibited (and if these measures are actually successful), both the ownership and operating structures will be 'frozen'.[29] Even if the initial distribution of land is based on family sizes and does achieve a tolerably efficient pattern of labour–land endowment ratios in the short-run, the relative sizes and compositions of families will alter over time.[30] Inefficiencies in resource allocation are almost bound to arise.[31]

If, instead, only the leasing of land is prohibited and transfers of ownership through sale are permitted, efficiency might be achieved through transactions in the ownership market. But we have already argued that little reliance should be placed on this. Indeed, we have suggested that, if anything, transfers of ownership would be more likely to result in further divergencies between labour–land ratios. The answer would seem to be to permit both transfers of ownership and the leasing of land. Certainly this would be more conducive to achieving a tolerably efficient allocation of resources. But it must be clearly understood that if a reform does permit inter-peasant transactions of any form, it is not altering fundamentally the original system of property rights, only the specific pattern of resource ownership. Over time class differentiation within the peasantry is likely to emerge.[32]

Notes

Notes for Chapter 1

1   In England it is strictly incorrect to refer to the 'ownership of land'. An individual cannot own land itself, but only an 'estate' in land. In law, all land is held directly or indirectly from the Crown. This notion dates from the feudal system, established after the Norman Conquest.

The essence of the feudal system was that the King granted land to 'tenants-in-chief' in return for agreed services. These tenants-in-chief, in turn, granted part of their land to 'mesne' tenants in return for stipulated services. A mesne tenant might further subinfeudate land to another tenant and so on. Feudalism was a system of government based on landholding and on personal ties between lord and tenant. The obligations of landholding were just as real and tangible as the rights.

Over the succeeding centuries, the obligations of landownership paled into insignificance. All the emphasis was placed on rights. By the eighteenth century, the 'sacredness' of private property in land was firmly established. The only significant restrictions on private property rights involved respecting the private property rights of others.

Since the latter part of the nineteenth century, there has been yet another fundamental transformation in the conception of property rights in land. The view expressed by John Stuart Mill, in the quote at the beginning of the chapter, has substantially been adopted. Statutory intervention has restricted freedom of contract; it has led to a remarkable proliferation of controls over land use; it has permitted a notable increase in the compulsory acquisition of land by public bodies. According to Lord Justice Denning (p. 71): 'The significance of the social revolution of today is that whereas in the past the balance was much too heavily in favour of the rights of property and the freedom of contract, Parliament has repeatedly intervened so as to give the public good its proper place.'

2   As Mishan (p. 123) has observed, in a somewhat different context but in reference to the same sorts of pronouncements, certain economists seem to come perilously close to asserting that 'what is, is best'. This is an illustration of the superficiality alluded to earlier.

3   This is not meant to suggest that Neo-classical economics is useful, whereas Classical economics is not. It is rather to suggest that theorizing can be useful. As both Marx and Mill observed, those who criticize 'theory' *per se* seem to be unaware that they themselves are 'theorizing' constantly, albeit in a less explicit manner.

169

4   We will not refer to econometric work in this book. To do so *satisfactorily* would considerably expand the scope of the book.

Notes for Chapter 2

1   Cited in Routh (p. 38).
2   Le Trosne, cited in Gide & Rist (p. 34).
3   Cited in Gide & Rist (p. 32).
4   As Napoleoni (p. 14) has observed, Quesnay and Mirabeau recognized that the capitalist tenant farmers might *temporarily* share in the net product. Farmers who, by improved techniques, reduced their costs below prevailing levels might benefit, at least until their leaseholds were renewed.
5   Quesnay's *Maximes générales du gouvernement économique d'un royaume agricole* of November 1767, reprinted in Napoleoni.
6   Cited in Gide & Rist (p. 42).
7   The essence of this argument was that the imposition of a tax on rent would lead to a fall in the market value of land. Present owners would suffer. However, a new purchaser of land would be unaffected. The price he paid for the land would be correspondingly lower by virtue of the tax on rent. He would get the same return on his investment. See Walras (Lesson 42).
8   See Tuma.
9   J. S. Mill (p. 57).
10 The loss of the distinction between capital investments embodied in the land – such as buildings, fences, drainage – and durable capital not attached to land – such as livestock and implements – was unfortunate.
11 Sometimes the actual payment from tenant to landowner might diverge from the natural rent, leaving the tenant with correspondingly more or less than the normal profit. According to Smith, such discrepancies were typically attributable to the ignorance of tenant or landowner.
12 Indeed, many of the building-blocks had been provided in the *seventeenth* century by Sir William Petty.
13 Unless it is explicitly stated that quotations from Ricardo are from his *Essay*, they are taken from his *Principles*.
14 Malthus recognized, and indeed emphasized, the importance of *both* of these considerations.
15 In treating the Ricardian theory of rent, we are supposing that the economy consists of one sector, agriculture. A complication which arises when a manufacturing sector is introduced is whether or not the rate of profit is determined within agriculture. In the 1815 *Essay*, referred to earlier, Ricardo did envisage rates of profit elsewhere as being determined in the agricultural sector. According to Sraffa, in his Introduction to Ricardo's *Works*, although Ricardo never stated this explicitly, the basis for this view was that 'in agriculture the same commodity, namely corn, forms both the capital (conceived as composed of the subsistence necessary for workers) and the product; so that the determination of profit by the difference between total product and capital advanced, and also the determination of the ratio of this profit to the capital, is done directly between quantities of corn without any question of valuation. It is obvious that only one trade can be in the special

position of not employing the products of other trades while all the others must employ *its* product as capital. It follows that if there is to be a uniform rate of profit in all trades it is the exchangeable values of the products of *other* trades relatively to their own capitals (i.e. relatively to corn) that must be adjusted so as to yield the same rate of profit as has been established in the growing of corn; since in the latter no value changes can alter the ratio of product to capital, both consisting of the same commodity' (p. xxxi). He abandoned this theory in the *Principles*, where wage goods comprised manufactures as well as food. Nevertheless the agricultural sector retained a crucial role in determining the course of the rate of profit over time.

It is worth noting that Malthus had disputed Ricardo's initial theory, contending that the agricultural rate of profit no more regulates the rates of profit elsewhere, than the rates of profit in other trades regulate the rate of profit in agriculture. (See Sraffa's Introduction to Ricardo's *Works*, p. xxxi.)

16 See O'Brien.

17 This particular criticism of Jones is an example of the tendency to suppose that Ricardo's theory depended on the existence of differential fertility. As we have seen, Ricardo was prepared to accept the possibility of 'absolute rent'.

18 Section IV of this chapter draws quite heavily on Skouras, from whom the quotations from Scitovsky's *Welfare and Competition* are taken.

Notes for Chapter 3

1 Wicksell in effect employs what we have described as the 'conventional approach' when, for example, considering the institutional arrangement whereby workers rent land. Walras, himself, in Lesson 18 of his *Elements of Pure Economics* treats the services of land in terms of his auctioneer. A more recent example of the 'conventional approach' is provided by the analysis of Bardhan & Srinivasan.

It should be emphasized that our criticism cannot be levelled at the Arrow–Debreu economy wherein 'goods' at different locations are regarded as different 'commodities' (or different 'economic objects'). But if each plot of land is to be treated as a different commodity the basic assumption of the Arrow–Debreu economy that all economic agents are price-takers for all commodities cannot be justified.

Notes for Chapter 4

1 For simplicity, we are assuming that there are no autonomous payments or receipts. For example, the farmer does not have to meet land taxes or mortgage repayments; nor does he have any source of income other than farming.

2 Profit, as defined, may be interpreted as including an implicit rental for the land the farmer owns. In order to bring it into line with the Classical definition of profit, we could assume that this implicit rent is zero.

3 We are assuming in this section that there is no uncertainty with respect to yields or prices. The implications of uncertainty will be considered later.

4   This is *not* to say that a *marginal* change in $\bar{K}_t$ will necessarily affect his production decision. For example, in the case of no possibility of lending, if the financial capital constraint is not binding, a marginal increase in $\bar{K}_t$ would be added to savings, leaving the level of capital advances unaffected.

5   The dependency of the average rate of interest on how much he wishes to borrow and/or on his wealthiness may well be attributable to uncertainty on the part of prospective lenders. This does not imply a logical contradiction with our assumption of perfect certainty on the part of the farmer. He might be perfectly certain about the relationship between total revenue and the level of capital advances, whereas prospective lenders might well not be.

6   Such a utility function is similar to one employed by Flemming.

7   See, for example, Sandmo; Baron; Batra & Ullah; and Hawanini. In treating uncertainty, we will employ the approach of expected utility maximization rather than the more general but less familiar state preference analysis.

8   We have considered the case of a perfect financial capital market. Note that if there was no opportunity to borrow or lend, the farmer's utility function might well be different. The possible relationship between attitudes to risk in a single period context and the nature of the financial capital market will be enlarged upon in Chapter 10.

9   The valuations placed on the terminal state of the land, V_{t+1}, could be derived by the method of 'backward induction', a technique widely employed in dynamic programming and increasingly employed in economic theory. [See Hey (pp. 79–80).] Thus we could, in principle, derive from an explicit multi-period model 'the prospective profitability from farming the land in subsequent periods' as a function of the characteristics of the land at the end of the period under consideration. Note that V_{t+1} would, in general, depend on opportunities to borrow or lend in succeeding periods.

It is, however, not necessary to suppose that the farmer works through such a formal calculation. V_{t+1} represents his valuation whatever way he arrives at it.

Note finally that the analysis could be modified to incorporate the acquisition of durable capital goods and to allow for various forms of uncertainty.

10   The analysis follows closely that of Nakajima.

11   See both Sen and Nakajima.

12   We could have specified that consumption expenditure be at least as great as some subsistence level and perhaps even that terminal financial wealth be at least as great as some required level. But this would complicate the analysis unnecessarily.

13   For these and other comparative static propositions, see Nakajima.

14   See Nakajima.

Notes for Chapter 5

1   Under the English feudal system, there were two types of peasants who laboured on the lord's land: the 'free' socage tenants and the 'unfree' villeins. Socage was an integral part of the feudal structure, whereas villeinage was strictly not a feudal tenure in the pure sense of feudalism, but rather

originated before the Norman Conquest and was absorbed into the feudal system. It is often thought that the crucial distinction between socage tenants and villeins was that the former were protected against their lords by the royal courts whereas the latter were regarded as tenants at the will of their lords and were only protected by the customs of the manorial courts. Although this was obviously important, the really crucial distinction was that whereas the duties of socage tenants were fixed and certain, the villeins did not know from day to day what kind of work would be assigned them. Pollock & Maitland (p. 371) have described the status of villeins: 'When they go to bed on Sunday night they do not know what Monday's work will be: it may be threshing, ditching, carrying, they cannot tell ... The tenure is unfree, not because the tenant holds at the will of the lord, in the sense of being removable at a moment's notice, but because his services, though in many respects minutely defined by custom, cannot be altogether defined without frequent reference to the lord's will.'

2 We will not attempt a formal analysis of labour services. At one level the analysis would seem to be simple: in terms of the analysis of the peasant household in the previous chapter we could deduct the labour time which must be devoted to the lord's land from the total labour endowment to obtain an endowment which is available for use on the farm and suitably modify the utility function. But this simplicity may be deceptive. A crucial consideration will be the particular times which the peasant has to work on the lord's land during the production period. He may well be obliged to provide labour services at the most critical points in the agricultural season, notably sowing and harvest times. This will have implications for the relationship between the level of the peasant's labour devoted to his own land and maximum total revenue from his produce. In other words, maximum revenue does not simply depend on the amount of labour used over the production period but also on the precise timing of its application.

3 This may, in fact, be regarded as a special case of a more general case whereby money rents are linked by some formula to product price.

4 This list of possibilities is not meant to be exhaustive. Note, in particular, that some form of mixed arrangement is possible.

5 Moreover, once one admits uncertainty surrounding the profit outcomes of production decisions, it is no longer generally true that the levels of fixed costs do not affect production decisions. See Sandmo.

6 Cited in Taylor (p. 381).

7 The history of settlements is extremely complicated and involved a protracted struggle between landowners and the courts. What emerged from this conflict was the so-called 'strict settlement', whereby *A*, the owner of a fee simple estate, would grant to himself a life tenancy with the provision that on his death his son *B* would have a life tenancy, the land thereafter passing to *B*'s eldest son *C*. The first person to have the full power to alienate the land would be *C*. But, on reaching his majority and before coming into possession, *C* would be persuaded by his father *B* to draw up a new settlement which gave *C* a life tenancy with a life tenancy to *C*'s eldest son *D*, the land thereafter passing to *D*'s eldest son *E*. *C* would be persuaded to do this by the need for an income until the death of his father. This

system has been described by Sir Frederick Pollock: 'The lord of the mansion is named by all men its owner; it is said to belong to him; the park, the demesne, the farms are called his. But we shall be almost safe in assuming that he is not the full and free owner of any part of it. He is a 'limited owner', having an interest only for his own life. He might have become the full owner ... if he had possessed the means of waiting, the independence of thought and will to break with the tradition of his order and the bias of his education, and the energy to persevere in his dissent against the counsels and feelings of his family. But he had every inducement to let things go their accustomed way. Those whom he has always trusted told him, and probably with sincere belief, that the accustomed way was the best for the family, for the land, for the tenants and for the country. And there can be no doubt that it was at the time the most agreeable to himself' (p. 9).

8   The tenant cannot claim twice for any improvement: in assessing the amount of compensation for high farming, appropriate allowance must be made for any compensation for unexhausted improvements.

Notes for Chapter 6

1   Cited in Tawney (p. 154).
2   The assumption of an invariant operating structure implies that a unit cannot be leased to someone who farms other land. Thus one person cannot enter into a leasehold contract for more than one unit, unless they would be operated separately through farm managers. Similarly someone who owns a unit can only become a tenant on some other unit if he leases out his own unit. Where one individual owns several operating units the assumption of an invariant operating structure requires that if he decides not to lease more than one of the units those which are not leased must be farmed separately through farm managers.
3   The analysis is a relatively informal adaptation of the very formal application of the theory of co-operative games with transferable utility to simple trading situations. Such applications of the theory are to be found in Von Neumann & Morgenstern; Telser; and Bacharach.
4   The term 'prospective tenant farmers' includes both those who were tenant farmers in the previous period and are contemplating continuing in farming and those who were engaged in other occupations and are considering entering farming.
5   If he could undertake part-time off-farm employment if he became a tenant, this would be relevant to the determination of his limit rent.
6   Strictly his reservation rent will be lower assuming that his utility of wealth function exhibits decreasing absolute risk aversion. This property is due to Pratt and Arrow. They defined absolute risk aversion as

$$R_A = -\frac{U''(W)}{U'(W)}$$

Decreasing absolute risk aversion implies

$$\frac{dR_A}{dW} < 0$$

For a discussion of this property, see Hey.

7 This is a two-person co-operative game. We could obtain a determinate solution by applying, for example, the approach of Nash. However, this approach involves very restrictive assumptions and is not worth pursuing for our purposes.

8 See, for example, Whetham (p. 435) and Colin Clark (p. 3).

9 The impact of a tax on rent may extend to other groups as well. Thus the resulting increase in rents might lead tenant farmers to work harder and produce greater outputs which might drive down the prices of agricultural products. In this event consumers of farm products would benefit whereas those owners who would farm their units themselves irrespective of the tax would be adversely affected.

10 The simplest case would be where AB was linear with a slope of 45°, implying a constant 'differential'. This would follow from the traditional analysis based on profit maximization. However, where utility depends on leisure or where there is uncertainty there is no reason why AB should take this form.

11 Note that there would be no problem of instability: an increase in the market rent of one type of unit will lead to an increase in excess demand for the other type of unit. The two types of units are 'gross substitutes'.

12 Sraffa [Ch. XI] noted briefly that the order of fertility may vary with variations in the rate of profit and wages. This observation has recently been amplified by Montani.

13 Af Heurlin's proposition has been explained by Turvey.

14 Strictly we should say that 'the prospective tenants' limit rents would be at least as high and possibly strictly greater where this compensation provision does not apply'. We are implicitly assuming that revenue maximization would lead to a deterioration in property values. A similar *caveat* applies to the following paragraph in the text.

15 We are *not* claiming that, where contracts incorporate compensatory provisions both for damage and for unexhausted improvements, market rents would be higher than if there were no compensatory provisions at all. This is perhaps likely, but not inevitable.

16 For a formal analysis of the case of 'multiunit trade', see Telser.

Notes for Chapter 7

1 In this chapter we will dispense with cumbersome time subscripts.

2 The assumption that the behaviour of a tenant will not be affected by the rental share may be 'justified' by supposing that he has a certain endowment of labour, that there is no possibility for part-time off-farm employment and that his preferences are lexicographic. Provided that the marginal revenue product of labour is everywhere positive and that the rental share is less than one, he will use his entire labour endowment.

3 Alternatively such dependency could arise from tenant maximization of

utility defined over terminal wealth and labour input, with no opportunity for part-time off-farm employment. This would be more complex than the case considered in the text, since, as we have seen in Chapter 5, a tenant might respond to an increase in rental share by working more or less time on the farm.

4   It is easily demonstrated that if the revenue–labour function takes on the simple form $Z = AL^a$, where $0 < \alpha < 1$, the landlord would set a rental share equal to $(1 - \alpha)$. Thus the tenant's share would equal the elasticity of revenue with respect to his labour input.

5   Given the assumptions we have been employing, the notion of a limit rental share is not useful. Even if he agreed to a rental share of one, the prospective tenant would be no worse off since he could devote all his time to off-farm employment. This is, of course, an extreme example of why it does not pay the landowner to extract as high a rental share as possible.

6   We can illustrate this in the simplest special case. Suppose that $Z = A . L$ where $A > 0$. Suppose that the tenant's utility function takes on the simple form

$$U = (1 - r) . Z - b . L^2 \qquad b > 0$$

implying quadratic disutility of effort. Maximization of utility by the tenant implies

$$Z = (1 - r)K$$

where $K = A^2/2b$. The optimal rental share for the landlord – that is, the rental share which maximizes $r . Z(r)$ – is easily shown to be 0.5. Thus if the landowner knows the general forms of the revenue–labour function and of the tenant's utility function, he does not need to know the specific values of A and b. Irrespective of their values, a rental share of 0.5 will maximize his rent. It should be emphasized that Hurwicz & Shapiro demonstrate that such a rental share is optimal for the landlord in a much broader class of cases.

7   A possible explanation of the observed frequency of the 50:50 division has also been advanced by Bell & Zusman. Their analysis applies Nash's bargaining theory to negotiations between a landowner and a tenant under certainty. They claim that for plausible values for production elasticities the division between landlord and tenant will be close to 50:50. They conclude [p. 587]: 'In practice, of course, the bargains which are struck need not conform exactly to those predicted by Nash's solution. But if Nash's solution is empirically valid, and given that the bargaining process is repeated year after year in circumstances of unchanging technology and social institutions, then there will be a long-term tendency for contracts to center on some average value. Moreover, if in most situations the solution is not very different from one-half, agents will save themselves the bother of detailed arithmetic and settle for the magic number which has also the advantage of sounding equitable. Thus that particular rental share is elevated to the status of a social norm.'

8   Let r_1 be the new share which would leave the landlord unaffected; that is,

$$r_1[Z(L^*) - w.L^*] = \hat{r}.Z(\hat{L})$$

so that

$$r_1 = \frac{\hat{r}.Z(\hat{L})}{[Z(L^*) - w.L^*]}$$

At any rental share above r_1, the landlord would be better off.

Let r_2 be the new share which would leave the tenant unaffected; that is,

$$(1 - r_2)[Z(L^*) - w.L^*] = (1 - \hat{r})Z(\hat{L}) - w.\hat{L}$$

Rearranging gives

$$r_2 = \frac{\hat{r}.Z(\hat{L})}{[Z(L^*) - w.L^*]} + \frac{[Z(L^*) - w.L^*] - [Z(\hat{L}) - w.\hat{L}]}{[Z(L^*) - w.L^*]}$$

At any rental share below r_2, the tenant would be better off.

Since

$$[Z(L^*) - w.L^*] > [Z(\hat{L}) - w.\hat{L}]$$

it follows from the expressions for r_1 and r_2 that

$$r_2 > r_1$$

Thus there exists a set of rental shares which would yield mutual gains. Specifically both would gain provided that

$$r_1 < r^* < r_2.$$

9   Let r_1 be the new share which would leave the landlord unaffected; that is,

$$r_1.Z(L^*) = \hat{r}.Z(\hat{L})$$

so that

$$r_1 = \frac{\hat{r}.Z(\hat{L})}{Z(L^*)}$$

At any rental share above r_1, the landlord would be better off.

Let r_2 be the new share which would leave the tenant unaffected; that is,

$$(1 - r_2).Z(L^*) - w.L^* = (1 - \hat{r}).Z(\hat{L}) - w.\hat{L}$$

Rearranging gives

$$r_2 = \frac{\hat{r}.Z(\hat{L})}{Z(L^*)} + \frac{[Z(L^*) - w.L^*] - [Z(\hat{L}) - w.\hat{L}]}{Z(L^*)}$$

Since

$$[Z(L^*) - w.L^*] > [Z(\hat{L}) - w.\hat{L}]$$

it follows from the expressions for r_1 and r_2 that

$$r_2 > r_1$$

Thus there exists a set of rental shares which would yield mutual gains. Specifically both would gain provided that

$$r_1 < r^* < r_2.$$

10 The landowner will choose L and r so as to

maximize $r.Z(L)$

subject to $(1-r).Z(L) = w.L.$

Let

$$\theta = r.Z(L) - \lambda[w.L - (1-r)Z(L)]$$

where λ is a Lagrange multiplier. The necessary first order conditions are

$$\frac{\partial \theta}{\partial r} = Z(L) - \lambda.Z(L) = 0 \tag{1}$$

$$\frac{\partial \theta}{\partial L} = r.\frac{dZ}{dL} - \lambda.w + \lambda(1-r)\frac{dZ}{dL} = 0 \tag{2}$$

$$\frac{\partial \theta}{\partial \lambda} = w.L - (1-r).Z(L) = 0 \tag{3}$$

From (1), $\lambda = 1$. Therefore, from (2)

$$\frac{dZ}{dL} = w \tag{4}$$

From (3) and (4)

$$(1-r) = \frac{dZ/dL}{Z/L}$$

11 Formally, the tenant would maximize $[(1-r).Z(L) - w.L]$ subject to $r.Z(L) = \bar{R}$, where $\bar{R}$ is the landowner's reservation rent.

12 We are *not* claiming that the levels of tenant inputs would necessarily be increased by switching from a simple share rental arrangement to, say, a fixed rent. For example, as we have seen in Chapter 5, a peasant for whom the alternative to farm work is leisure might work fewer hours as a result of the recontract. What we *are* asserting is that there would exist a fixed rental agreement which would dominate the share rental agreement, in the sense that both parties would benefit.

13 An exception to the foregoing propositions is the case where the tenant has a set of inputs which he would employ on the farm irrespective of the terms of the tenancy. In this case *all* of the tenancy forms would be equivalent. The simple share-tenancy arrangement would no longer be dominated.

14 *Ex post* the landlord may be better off, worse off or unaffected by the switch, depending on what revenue actually turns out to be.

15 We have shown that the switch would benefit the tenant without affecting the landlord. The rental share which would leave the tenant's *ex ante* welfare

unchanged would be strictly greater than $\bar{r}$. A switch to any share between these two extremes would benefit *both* parties.

16 In the case of a risk neutral tenant and a risk averse landowner, we could, of course, show that the fixed-rental format would dominate the share-rental format. In this case there is no incentive for risk sharing.

17 We are *not* suggesting that a recontract would or should make this particular stipulation. The parties might be able to do better still by some other stipulation regarding the levels of inputs and the manner of their use. We are simply indicating that there must exist scope for mutual gains.

18 A large landowner with many tenants might employ an agent to act as rent collector. He is then liable to be defrauded by the rent collector! In time, landowner and agent might come to a new agreement whereby the agent agrees to pay a fixed sum to the landowner. The agent would thereby assume the uncertainty as well as the task of enforcing contracts. Indeed, in time the agent might persuade the peasant farmers to become his hired workers, so that he becomes the new tenant of the landowner. This simple story is by no means implausible. It is quite likely that substantial capitalist tenant farmers emerged in this manner.

19 As Ip & Stahl have observed, increasing marginal costs of enforcement will mean that landowners will stop short of enforcing precisely the stipulated levels of inputs.

20 We must be careful not to take a single period out of context. As Cheung has observed, a tenant's incentive to violate the terms of a contract will be correspondingly less to the extent that he wishes to renew the contract at the expiration of the current lease.

21 We have not attempted an exhaustive review of the literature on share tenancy in this chapter. In addition to the cited contributions, the interested reader is referred to the article by Gale Johnson, who was the first to raise doubts about the 'inefficiency' proposition, and to the contributions by Reid.

Hallagan has recently suggested that a system of fixed wage contracts, share contracts and fixed rent contracts 'solves' the problem confronting landowners of 'selecting' workers where they have incomplete information about workers' abilities *ex ante* and where they will be unable to monitor the input of 'entrepreneurial' abilities by workers. The workers, who do know their own abilities, will segregate *themselves* according to their respective abilities. Those with the lowest entrepreneurial ability will sign wage contracts; those with the highest entrepreneurial ability will sign fixed rent contracts; those with entrepreneurial ability falling within some intermediary range will sign share contracts.

Hallagan goes on to suggest that a system of fixed wage, share and fixed rent contracts can also serve to 'match' different types of landowners with different types of workers. Thus landowners with high entrepreneurial ability will offer wage contracts; those with low entrepreneurial ability will offer fixed rent contracts; those with entrepreneurial ability falling within some intermediary range will offer share contracts. Thus landowners with relatively high entrepreneurial ability will team up with workers with relatively low entrepreneurial ability. Although Hallagan is not explicit on this point, the 'matching' rationale does not depend on landowners having imperfect information about the entrepreneurial abilities of workers. The coexistence of different contract forms can be explained by heterogeneity of workers together with, say, costs in monitoring the actual entrepreneurial inputs by workers. Although in this and the previous chapter, we have drawn attention to the possible significance of imperfect information on the part of landowners as to the abilities and preferences of prospective workers, Hallagan seems to exaggerate its importance. The 'matching' rationale seems to be more compelling than the 'screening' argument as an explanation of the observation, cited by Hallagan, that fixed rent tenants typically have higher incomes than sharecroppers and that sharecroppers typically have higher incomes than wage labourers. It was on account of likely heterogeneities that, in the last chapter, we treated farm workers and prospective tenants as potentially different, if not exactly 'non-competing', groups.

Finally it is worth drawing the reader's attention to the article by Roumasset, which was published after this book was written.

Notes for Chapter 9

1 There is the possibility of equilibrium with a negative excess demand. In this case rent per acre must be zero.
2 See Batra & Ullah.
3 If we had not assumed that all land has the same characteristics, it would not necessarily be true that an operating unit should ideally be connected. An ideal unit might comprise both land in a valley and land on the mountains. The reason that connectedness is, in general, a desirable feature is that it saves commuting costs of various types. One of the disadvantages of the manorial open-field system was that each family cultivated disparate plots.
4 Maximization of combined output requires that the marginal rate of substitution between land and labour be the same on each unit. For a homogeneous function the marginal rate of substitution depends only on the input ratio. Moreover, for a strictly quasi-concave homogeneous function, a given marginal rate of substitution is associated with a unique input ratio. Therefore, given identical production functions, for the marginal rates of substitution to be the same on both units the input ratios must be the same.
5 Since the production functions are *linearly* homogeneous, for any $0 \leq \lambda \leq 1$ and $0 \leq \mu \leq 1$

$$C_A(\lambda\bar{L},\ \lambda\bar{N}) + C_B((1-\lambda)\bar{L},\ (1-\lambda)\bar{N}) = C_A(\mu\bar{L},\ \mu\bar{N}) + C_B((1-\mu)\bar{L},\ (1-\mu)\bar{N})$$

where λ and μ are the proportions of the total resources devoted to the Ath operating unit under two alternative allocations.
6 L''_A, L''_B, C''_A and C''_B have not been shown in Figure 9.2 in order to avoid complicating the diagram.
7 The objection that if the contracts involve a higher corn-rent per acre for A than for C then there would be an incentive for B to lease a little less to C and a little more to A is fallacious.
8 The optimal allocation of the land would involve all of the operating units

being of the same size if $R(N)$ was assumed to take on one of certain simple forms. But the relationship between rental value and size may be a complex one. For example, the relationship between rent per acre and farm size for a sample of farms in England and Wales in 1974 is given by the following table:

Farm size (acres)	15 to 29	30 to 49	50 to 99	100 to 149	150 to 299	300 to 499	500 to 699	700 to 999	1,000 and over
Rent per acre (£s)	8.76	9.09	8.17	7.67	7.99	8.67	9.02	8.26	6.55

Source: *The Farmland Market*, No. 5, January 1976

Rent levels for 1973 differed in absolute levels but exhibited a remarkably similar pattern. For our purposes, Cheung's analysis of the decision of a landlord as to how many (share) tenancies to subdivide his land into is not appropriate since he *assumes* that the farms will necessarily be of the same size. In addition, he treats the number of farms (or farmers) as a continuous variable when it can only take on integer values.

9 If the relationship between rental value and farm size was such that dR/dN diminished throughout there might be the possibility that the optimal structure involved an infinite number of infinitesimally small units. We are saved from this uncomfortable possibility by assuming that the fixed cost of concluding a tenancy contract is strictly positive. Moreover, in practice, the market value of a unit is likely to be zero if it is below some minimum size.

10 In view of this, if a land transaction were to take place, it seems more probable that it would involve family B being obliged to sell land to A, thus leading to a greater disparity between labour–land ratios. At least this would seem more probable if the ratio of 'workers' to 'dependants' is the same for both families. With more mouths to feed and less land, family B is more likely to find itself with a corn harvest insufficient to provide for its consumption needs during the subsequent production period.

11 See Sen.

12 Cheshire (p. 261) has also explained why these attempts led to protracted conflict between landowners and the courts: 'The law is moved, and from the earliest times always has been moved, by a deep seated antipathy to this human love of power. It is one thing to permit the free power of alienation, another to allow it to be exercised to its own destruction.'

13 To take the extreme case, if production involved fixed proportions, output could only be increased by bringing additional land into cultivation.

14 There are often high initial costs associated with changes in use. These costs are likely to be asymmetric. Thus the cost of changing land from agricultural to urban use is likely to be much lower than the cost of changing from urban to agricultural use. This might not seem to be of much consequence in so far as the long-term trend typically involves an increase in land used for urban areas. But often industrial activities are relocated leaving derelict land, possibly what was once good agricultural land but which, following its industrial use, could only be reclaimed at very high cost.

15 The abatement of negative externalities is often cited as a rationale for public intervention in land use, particularly for zoning. In the present context, controls on land use conversion are advocated in order to reduce 'urban sprawl' with attendant benefits of lower costs of publically provided services and lower commuting and transportation costs.

Notes for Chapter 10

1 The analysis is very similar to that of neighbouring farmers in the last chapter, except that we were not concerned there with efficiency as such. In that chapter, we emphasized the importance of the shape as well as the size of an operating unit. This is no less important in the present context. However, to avoid being tedious, we will not continually refer to this. We will assume that the aggregate area of agricultural land is rectangular and that, if efficiency requires that the constituent operating units be rectangular, the central planner will ensure this.

2 Specifically, a homothetic function is a monotonically increasing transformation of a homogeneous function.

3 There is a complication: the efficient number of farms may take on a non-integer value. But, following Georgescu-Roegen (p. 16), this complication can be regarded as very minor, assuming that the efficient size is very small relative to the available aggregate amounts of land and labour. It may be recalled that we were not prepared to assume this problem away in the context of a landowner deciding how many farms to create on his ownership unit. To do so would involve assuming a very large landowner indeed.

4 It is worth noting that, even if the micro production function exhibits increasing and then decreasing returns, the macro production function for the agricultural sector as a whole may reasonably be assumed to exhibit constant returns to scale. See Georgescu-Roegen (p. 16).

5 Too much should not be read into this differential treatment of durable and circulating capital. We simply wish to avoid having to introduce the terminal value of the stocks of capital goods into the central planner's calculations. In this context we should also make explicit that we are assuming that agricultural activities have no effects on the properties of agricultural land. There is, in fact, an analogous implicit assumption with respect to labour.

6 In the light of spatial considerations, the attainment of efficiency may require a complex re-structuring even if labour–land ratios *are* the same. Each ownership unit might comprise disparate plots.

7 These imperfections and uncertainties explain why one particular line of argument merits no more than an endnote. This argument supposes that prospective purchasers and current owners always decide how much land to buy or sell in terms of present value calculations, the present marginal valuation of land being equal to the sum of the discounted marginal revenue products. The argument continues that, in the absence of transaction costs, transactions will result in an equilibrium state where all landowners have the same present marginal valuations and, given certain further assumptions, the same current marginal revenue products. This argument is typically couched

in terms of a land market in which each participant responds to a given market price per acre, land being perfectly divisible and homogeneous. We will not repeat our criticisms of this approach.

8 In this context, Georgescu-Roegen's rejection of Kautsky's argument for the superiority of large-scale production over peasant farming is, to say the least, odd. Georgescu-Roegen asserts that where all available resources must be used in production as long as they increase output, 'the superiority of the large-scale production is poor economics'. But this is a *non-sequitur.*

9 Suppose that there is a tendency for landowners to hire entire families, say, because employers provide housing. Even though the pattern of labour use corresponds to the family pattern, there may still be some sort of meshing of farm sizes and family sizes. Thus landowners with relatively large farms are likely to hire families with relatively high numbers of workers.

10 According to Wicksell: 'This distribution of labour, however obvious from the data, comes about in reality as the result of competition on two sides ... So long as wages are materially *lower* than the marginal product of the sixteenth labourer, it will be to the advantage of every landowner to employ more than sixteen labourers. But all the landowners cannot simultaneously succeed in this object, and consequently their endeavour must result in a rise of wages. Again, if wages are *higher* than the marginal product, each of the landowners will content himself with less than sixteen workers which will result in unemployment and a fall in wages through the competition of the unemployed. The final wage, equal for all the labourers, must therefore lie somewhere between the marginal product of the sixteenth and that of an imaginary seventeenth labourer on any one of the estates in question' (p. 114).

11 Wicksell himself does not consider the system whereby labourers rent land in the context of this specific example, but he does subsequently consider this system in general terms. He does so in terms of the conventional approach. Each labourer in deciding how much land to demand equates the marginal revenue product of land to market rent. 'If all the land is not at once taken into cultivation, or if, conversely, the demand of all the groups of labour for land is not satisfied, then it is clear that competition, in the former case between landowners and in the latter between labourers, would cause a fall, or a rise, in rent until competitive equilibrium was restored. In a word, rent is here determined by the marginal productivity of land, and conversely wages are determined by the surplus divided among all the labourers in the group – the labourer becoming the residual claimant' (p. 125). It is not necessary to resort to this story. We can explain this outcome (more plausibly) in terms of a process of contracting and recontracting. Assume that for a labourer the relationship between his offer rent and acreage (for a rectangular operating unit) is strictly concave, reflecting a diminishing marginal revenue product of land. Note, first, that, since the labourers are identical, if a landowner enters into contracts with n tenants it will always pay him to create n (rectangular) units of *equal* size. Note, second, that any set of provisional contracts which involves landowners leasing to different numbers of tenants will be blocked by a recontract between landowners with relatively small numbers of provisional tenants and labourers with relatively

small provisional acreages. Any set of provisional contracts which involves some of the labourers not renting land at all will, of course, also be blocked. It follows that the set of final contracts will involve 160,000 operating units of equal size. The set of final contracts will also involve the same rent for each unit and therefore the same rent per acre. But this is an *implication* of the analysis and depends on Wicksell's particular assumption about the form of the ownership structure.

12   It is worth noting that Wicksell, when seeking to demonstrate the 'equivalence' of the three institutional arrangements, initially assumes constant returns to scale. He does not acknowledge the possibility of variable returns until he considers the third system involving intermediaries. He then presents the rightly celebrated argument that competition will result in 'local' constant returns to scale on each unit (with the return to each factor equalling the value of its marginal product and entrepreneurial profit being zero.) But he does not reconsider the other institutional arrangements under this technology.

As the quotation at the beginning of this chapter illustrates, Wicksell is, in other respects, explicit about the restrictive assumptions in his analysis; certainly he is more circumspect than many others who cite the proposition that the institutional arrangement 'does not matter'. With regard to the particular reference to the indivisibility of labour, we would not expect any of the institutional arrangements under consideration to achieve efficiency precisely, if this requires non-integer amounts of labour on each unit.

13   See Arrow and Hahn (p. 60).

14   To avoid any misunderstanding, it is perhaps appropriate at this stage to emphasize that our use of a central planner in this and the previous section should *not* be taken as implying that a system of centralized planning would, in practice, lead to efficiency.

15   We are continuing to assume perfectly inelastic supplies of land and labour.

16   This proposition depends on the particular way in which uncertainty is incorporated, one which does not allow for different expectations on the part of landowners. All landowners are assumed to know the form of $g(\theta)$.

17   Stiglitz also demonstrates that productive efficiency will be achieved if landowners (but not workers) can mix contracts and if there is a 'stock market' in farms, enabling landowners to buy shares in other farms.

18   This complication is not confined to the case where some third party assumes the entrepreneurial role. It may arise whenever one party contracts to pay another party a fixed fee at some future date. Thus, although he does not appear to acknowledge this complication, it can arise in the cases considered by Stiglitz.

19   The landowner's certainty equivalent rent at the *beginning* of the period will, of course, not necessarily equal his certainty equivalent rent for the end of the period: indeed, it is likely to be lower. The same applies to the worker.

20   We are ignoring the possibility of technological external effects between neighbouring farmers.

21   It is worth pointing out that a peasant owner may not have complete control over his activities. Credit agencies often restrict the ways in which a borrower can use funds. This may result in a misallocation of funds. It has

been suggested that this typically results in a bias towards investment in permanent improvements, since this better protects the interests of the lender.

22 See Stiglitz.

23 In an evaluation of alternative tenure systems, Schickele has advanced this 'division of control' argument. With regard to cash rent tenancies, he states: 'The landlord controls the rate of input of durable factors, the tenant that of non-durable factors. How does this separation of control over two classes of factors affect the efficiency conditions of the farm enterprise?

The first condition of maximum farming efficiency is that the intensity of the production organization is pushed to the point where marginal cost equals marginal returns for the enterprise as a whole. The landlord, however, under a cash rent tenancy will push the input of durable factors only to the point where their marginal cost equals the marginal increment in rent the tenant is willing to pay. Since the landlord has no control over the rate of non-durable factors, he tends to assume the present level of non-durable factors as given which results in rapidly diminishing marginal returns of durable factors (according to the law of proportionality of factors). An increase in the intensity of durable factor inputs involves an increase in the intensity of non-durable factors if optimum combination and maximum efficiency is to be achieved' (p. 190). This argument seems to beg a number of issues. The argument presumes a sitting tenant. If the tenancy contract is of long duration at a fixed rent, the landlord will have to bargain with the tenant *ex ante* in order to secure an increase in rent. If such a negotiation does take place, the level of durable inputs which Schickele supposes will result would, in fact, be dominated by an agreement which would result in 'optimum combination and maximum efficiency'. During the negotiation the tenant certainly would take into account how he himself would respond. The tenant might have an incentive to understate the advantage to him of any improvement, in the hope of negotiating a lower rent level. But there would be no incentive for him to keep to himself the levels of durable factors which would result in 'maximum efficiency'.

If the tenancy contract is one of short duration and the landowner is relying on negotiating a higher rent on the renewal of the contract, it is not clear why the landowner would 'tend' to ignore the fact that it would pay the tenant to alter the levels of non-durable inputs. The fact that the landlord cannot control these levels is no reason for him to assume that they will not be altered. The 'marginal increment in rent the tenant is willing to pay', to which the landlord is supposed to equate the marginal cost of durable factors, will take into account the appropriate response of the tenant. To be *correct*, Schickele should have asserted that 'the landowner will equate the marginal cost of durable factors to what he *thinks* would be the marginal increment in rent the tenant would be prepared to pay, this being lower than what he would, in fact, be prepared to pay'. To be *convincing*, he would have to provide a much better reason why this discrepancy would arise.

This criticism should not detract from the fact that Schickele's article is a useful one.

24 For references to the extensive literature, and in particular to the work of Lewis, see *The Manchester School*, September 1979, Vol. XLVII, No. 3.

25 Sen's article is particularly illuminating on this point and, indeed, on many other issues considered in this chapter. It is also worth noting that Sen considers a dualistic system.

26 It must be acknowledged that in some developing countries labour seems to have moved too rapidly from rural to urban areas, resulting in urban unemployment. It might be argued that, where this has happened, it will be easier for workers to move back to agriculture given the existence of an agricultural labour market. But this is perhaps debatable.

27 Cheung does *not* contrast pure systems. Rather he develops his equivalence argument in a framework where property rights are well-defined and freely transferable. Thus his analysis assumes that economic agents are free to enter into whatever forms of transactions they wish. Without objecting to the usefulness of this analysis, it would seem preferable to regard this as a *particular type of system.*

28 The more careful proponents of the 'equivalence' proposition (of whatever form) would presumably not deny that 'wealth effects' may result in a different pattern of resource allocation. However, Higgs appears to do so. He has criticized a proposition by Sau that, *ceteris paribus*, an owner operator will work less hard and therefore produce a smaller output than a fixed rent tenant. Higgs argues that this is only valid if the owner operator has no alternative to remaining an owner operator. He claims that if there are transferable property rights in land then 'the owner cultivator pays a real rent by sacrificing either the annuity equivalent of the sale value of his land or the rental return he might obtain by leasing rather than cultivating his land' (p. 430). But it does *not* follow from this that the owner operator will necessarily work the same amount of labour time as the tenant even if they have the same utility function. (In terms of the analysis of Chapters 4 and 5, the relationship between terminal financial wealth and own labour will differ for the two farmers.) The reference to a 'real rent' confuses the issue by conveying the misleading impression that the situations of the owner operator and tenant are equivalent. It obscures the importance of distributional considerations. This is an example of the quite frequent misuse of the notion of opportunity cost.

29 The structures may, of course, alter as a result of the subdivision of land between family members or as a result of marriage.

30 A conflict between efficiency and notions of 'equity' may arise in relation to the determination of the appropriate allocation of land between peasant families. For example, in the simplest case where the amount of labour-time of each worker is the same, efficiency would dictate that the land allocation between households be based on the number of workers. But this may result in widely different standards of living to the extent that worker–dependant ratios vary. This may not be regarded as 'equitable'. (The situation will, of course, be more complex to the extent that in the case of, say, a one-worker household the amount of time he will work will typically depend on the number of mouths he has to feed.)

31 Unless, that is, one believes that population changes will systematically work

towards equalization of labour–land ratios on the grounds that households with relatively high endowments of land per head will tend to have relatively high birth rates. But this would surely be an unreliable mechanism. A more significant possibility is that out-migration of family members to urban areas may be higher for families with relatively little land.

32   The argument that a system of pure peasant proprietorships is likely to be inefficient as a result of inflexibilities is *not* dependent on supposing that there are significant economies of size in farming, that is, on the so-called 'superiority of large-scale production'. If there are such economies, then the case for a land-to-the-tiller policy may be further weakened. If there are substantial economies of size, a policy of promoting voluntary co-operation between peasant households would have much to commend it. Indeed, such a policy might promote greater efficiency in the utilization of resources even in the case of constant returns to scale. Thus suppose that there are two groups of 50 peasant households, where members of each group have the same labour endowments and the same acreages but where the labour–land endowment ratios differ between the two groups. Disregarding spatial considerations, an increase in the aggregate value of output would occur if 50 co-operatives were established where each co-operative comprised one member from each group. The case for promoting co-operation is not dependent on the existence of economies of size.

Bibliography

Anderson, J. *Observations on the Means of Exciting a Spirit of National Industry*, London, 1777.

Arrow, K. J. and Hahn, F. H. *General Competitive Analysis*, San Francisco and Edinburgh, 1971.

Ashley, W. *The Economic Organisation of England*, London, 1923.

Bacharach, M. *Economics and the Theory of Games*, London, 1976.

Bardhan, P. K. 'Agricultural Development and Land Tenancy in a Peasant Economy: A Theoretical and Empirical Analysis', *American Journal of Agricultural Economics*, Feb. 1979, **61**(1), pp. 48–57.

Bardhan, P. K. and Srinivasan, T. N. 'Cropsharing Tenancy in Agriculture: A Theoretical and Empirical Analysis', *American Economic Review*, March 1971, **61**(1), pp. 48–64.

Baron, D. P. 'Price Uncertainty, Utility and Industry Equilibrium in Pure Competition', *International Economic Review*, Oct. 1970, **11**(3), pp. 463–80.

Batra, R. N., and Ullah, A. 'Competitive Firm and Theory of Input Demand Under Uncertainty', *Journal of Political Economy*, May/June 1974, **82**(3), pp. 537–48.

Bell, C. and Zusman, P. 'A Bargaining Theoretic Approach to Cropsharing Contracts', *American Economic Review*, Sept. 1976, **66**(4), pp. 578–88.

Blaug, M. *Economic Theory in Retrospect*, second edition, London, 1968.

Buchanan, D. H. 'The Historical Approach to Rent and Price Theory', *Economica*, 1929, **9**, pp. 123–55.

Carey, H. C. *Principles of Social Science*, 3 vols., Philadelphia, 1858–59.

Carlson, S. *A Study on the Pure Theory of Production*, London, 1939.

Chayanov, A. V. *The Theory of Peasant Economy*, edited by D. Thorner, B. Kerblay and R. E. F. Smith, Homewood, Illinois, 1966.

Cheshire, G. C. *Cheshire's Modern Law of Real Property*, eleventh edn, London, 1972.

Cheung, S. N. S. *The Theory of Share Tenancy*, Chicago, 1969.

Clark, C. *The Value of Agricultural Land*, Oxford, 1973.

Clark, J. B. *The Distribution of Wealth*, New York, 1899.

Debreu, G. *The Theory of Value*, New York, 1959.

Denning, A. T. *Freedom Under the Law*, London, 1949.

Dobb, M. *Theories of Value and Distribution since Adam Smith*, Cambridge, 1973.

Edgeworth, F. Y. *Mathematical Psychics*, London, 1881.

Fama, E. F. 'Multiperiod Consumption–Investment Decisions', *American Economic Review*, March 1970, **60**(1), pp. 163–74.

Fawcett, H. *Manual of Political Economy*, London, 1863.

Flemming, J. S. 'The Consumption Function when Capital Markets are Imperfect: The Permanent Income Hypothesis Reconsidered', *Oxford Economic Papers*, N. S., July 1973, **25**(2), pp. 160–72.

George, H. *Progress and Poverty*, 4th edn, London, 1882.

Georgescu-Roegen, N. 'Economic Theory and Agrarian Reforms', *Oxford Economic Papers*, Feb. 1960, **12**(1), pp. 1–40.

Gide, C. and Rist, C. *A History of Economic Doctrines*, London, 1945.

Hallagan, W. 'Self-selection by Contractual Choice and the Theory of Sharecropping', *Bell Journal of Economics*, Autumn 1978, **9**(2), pp. 344–54.

Hallett, G. *The Economics of Agricultural Land Tenure*, London, 1960.

Hawanini, G. A. 'A Mean–Standard Deviation Exposition of the Theory of the Firm under Uncertainty: A Pedagogical Note', *American Economic Review*, March 1978, **68**(1), pp. 194–202.

Hey, J. D. *Uncertainty in Microeconomics*, Oxford, 1979.

Higgs, R. 'Property Rights and Resource Allocation under Alternative Land Tenure Forms: A Comment', *Oxford Economic Papers*, N.S., Nov. 1972, **24**(3), pp. 428–31.

Hsiao, J. C. 'The Theory of Share Tenancy Revisited', *Journal of Political Economy*, Oct. 1975, **83**(5), pp. 1023–32.

Hurwicz, L. and Shapiro, L. 'Incentive Structures Maximizing Residual Gain Under Incomplete Information', *Bell Journal of Economics*, Spring 1978, **9**(1), pp. 180–91.

Ip, P. C. and Stahl, C. W. 'Systems of Land Tenure, Allocative Efficiency and Economic Development', *American Journal of Agricultural Economics*, Feb. 1978, **60**(1), pp. 19–28.

Jevons, W. S. *The Theory of Political Economy*, Harmondsworth, 1970.

Johnson, D. Gale. 'Resource Allocation under Share Contracts', *Journal of Political Economy*, April 1950, **58**, pp. 111–23.

Jones, R. *An Essay on the Distribution of Wealth and the Sources of Taxation*, London, 1831.

Kautsky, K. *The Economic Doctrines of Karl Marx*, New York, 1936.

Kelso, M. M. 'Needed Research in Farm Tenancy', *Journal of Farm Economics*, Feb. 1941, **23**(1), pp. 291–304.

Lefèvre, G. S. *Agrarian Tenures*, London, 1893.

Low, D. *Landed Property and the Economy of Estates*, London, 1844.

McCulloch, J. R. *Treatises and Essays on Subjects Connected with Economical Policy*, Edinburgh, 1853.

Malthus, T. R. *Principles of Political Economy*, 2nd edn, London, 1836.

Marshall, A. *Principles of Economics*, eighth edn, London, 1969.

Masson, R. T. 'The Creation of Risk Aversion by Imperfect Capital Markets', *American Economic Review*, March 1972, **62**(1), pp. 77–86.

Meek, R. L. 'Physiocracy and Classicism in Britain', *Economic Journal*, March 1951, **61**, pp. 26–47.

Mill, James. *Elements of Political Economy* in *James Mill: Selected Economic Writings*, edited by D. Winch, Edinburgh, 1966.

Mill, John Stuart. *Principles of Political Economy*, London, 1886.

Mingay, G. E. *English Landed Society in the Eighteenth Century*, London, 1963.

Mishan, E. J. *Cost–Benefit Analysis*, London, 1972.

Montani, G. 'Scarce Natural Resources and Income Distribution', *Metroeconomica*, 1975, **27**, pp. 68–101.

Nakajima, C. 'Subsistence and Commercial Family Farms: Some Theoretical Models of Subjective Equilibrium' in C. R. Wharton Jr (ed.), *Subsistence Agriculture and Economic Development*, London, 1970.

Napoleoni, C. *Smith, Ricardo, Marx*, Oxford, 1975.

Nash, J. 'Two Person Co-operative Games', *Econometrica*, Jan. 1953, **21**, pp. 128–40.

O'Brien, D. P. *The Classical Economists*, Oxford, 1975.

Petty, W. *The Economic Writings of Sir William Petty*, edited by C. H. Hull, 2 vols., Cambridge, 1899.

Pigou, A. C. *The Economics of Welfare*, 4th edn, Edinburgh, 1938.

Pollock, F. *The Land Laws*, 3rd edn, New York, 1896.

Pollock F. and Maitland F. W. *The History of English Law before the time of Edward I*, 1898, revised 2nd edn, 2 vols., Cambridge, 1968.

Postan, M. M. *The Medieval Economy and Society*, Harmondsworth, 1975.

Rao, C. H. H. 'Uncertainty, Entrepreneurship and Sharecropping in India', *Journal of Political Economy*, May/June 1971, **79**(3), pp. 578–95.

Reid, J. D. Jr. 'Sharecropping as an Understandable Market Response: The Post-Bellum South', *Journal of Economic History*, March 1973, **33**, pp. 106–30.

Reid, J. D. Jr. 'The Theory of Share Tenancy Revisited – Again', *Journal of Political Economy*, April 1977, **85**(2), pp. 403–7.

Ricardo, D. *An Essay on the Influence of a Low Price of Corn on the Profits of Stock*, reprinted in Vol. IV of *The Works and Correspondence of David Ricardo* edited by P. Sraffa and M. H. Dobb, Cambridge, 1966.

Ricardo, D. *Principles of Political Economy and Taxation*, in Vol. I of *The Works and Correspondence of David Ricardo*, edited by P. Sraffa and M. Dobb, Cambridge, 1951.

Robinson, J. [a] *Economic Philosophy*, Harmondsworth, 1964. [b] *Economic Heresies: Some Old Fashioned Questions in Economic Theory*, London, 1971.

Roumasset, J. 'Sharecropping, Production Externalities and the Theory of Contracts', *American Journal of Agricultural Economics*, Nov. 1979, **61**(4), pp. 640–7.

Routh, G. *The Origin of Economic Ideas*, London, 1975.

Sandmo, A. 'On the Theory of the Competitive Firm Under Price Uncertainty', *American Economic Review*, March 1971, **61**(1), pp. 65–73.

Sau, R. K. 'Land Tenancy, Rent and the Optimal Terms of Trade between Industry and Agriculture', *Oxford Economic Papers*, Nov. 1971, **23**(3), pp. 437–44.

Schickele, R. 'Effects of Tenure Systems on Agricultural Efficiency', *Journal of Farm Economics*, Feb. 1941, **23**(1), pp. 185–207.

Scitovsky, T. 'A Note on Profit Maximization and its Implications', *Review of Economic Studies*, 1943, **11**, pp. 57–60.

Scitovsky, T. *Welfare and Competition*, London, 1952.

Sen, A. K. 'Peasants and Dualism with or without Surplus Labour', *Journal of Political Economy*, Oct. 1966, **74**(5), pp. 425–50.

Skouras, A. *Land and its Taxation in Recent Economic Theory*, Athens, 1977.

Smith, A. *The Wealth of Nations*, Harmondsworth, 1970.

Sraffa, P. *Production of Commodities by Means of Commodities*, Cambridge, 1960.

Stiglitz, J. E. 'Incentives and Risk Sharing in Sharecropping', *Review of Economic Studies*, April 1974, **41**, pp. 219–55.

Sutherland, D. *The Landowners*, London, 1968.

Tawney, R. H. *Religion and the Rise of Capitalism*, Harmondsworth, 1961.

Taylor, H. C. *Outlines of Agricultural Economics*, New York, 1935.

Telser, L. *Competition, Collusion and Game Theory*, London, 1972.

Thompson, F. M. L. *English Landed Society in the Nineteenth Century*, London, 1971.

Torrens, R. *An Essay on the External Corn Trade*, London, 1815.

Tuma, E. H. *Twenty-six Centuries of Agrarian Reform*, Berkeley, 1965.

Turvey, R. 'A Finnish Contribution to Rent Theory', *Economic Journal*, June 1955, **65**, pp. 346–8.

von Neumann, J. and Morgenstern, O. *The Theory of Games and Economic Behaviour*, Princeton, 1944.

Walras, L. *Elements of Pure Economics*, London, 1954.

Ward, J. T. *Farm Rents and Tenure*, London, 1959.

West, E. *Essay on the Application of Capital to Land*, London, 1815.

Whetham, E. H. 'The Theory of Rent in Practice', *Farm Economist*, 1954, 7 (11–12), pp. 434–5.

Whewell, W. *A Mathematical Exposition of some Doctrines of Political Economy*, New York, 1971.

Wicksell, K. *Lectures on Political Economy*, Vol. I, New Jersey, 1977.

Wicksteed, P. H. *The Common Sense of Political Economy*, 2 vols., London, 1933.

Wiens, T. B. 'Uncertainty and Factor Allocation in a Peasant Economy', *Oxford Economic Papers*, March 1977, **29**(1), pp. 48–60.

Young, Arthur, *Travels in France* 1787, 1788 *and* 1789, ed. by C. Maxwell, Cambridge, 1970.

Index